Yesterday, Tomorrow

Literature, Culture and Identity

Series Editor: Bruce King

This series is concerned with the ways in which literature and cultures are influenced by the complexities and complications of identity. Looking at the ways in which identities are explored, mapped, defined and challenged in the arts, where boundaries are often overlapping, contested and re-mapped, it considers how differences, conflicts and change are felt and expressed. It investigates how such categories as race, class, gender, sexuality, ethnicity, nation, exile, diaspora and multiculturalism have come about. It discusses how these categories co-exist and their relationship to the individual, particular situations, the artist and the arts.

In this series:

Mineke Schipper, *Imaging Insiders: Africa and the Question of Belonging*

Gillian Whitlock, *The Intimate Empire: Reading Women's Autobiography*

Yesterday, Tomorrow

Voices from the Somali Diaspora

Nuruddin Farah

CASSELL
London and New York

Cassell
Wellington House, 125 Strand, London WC2R 0BB
370 Lexington Avenue, New York, NY 10017-6550

First published 2000

British Library Cataloguing in Publication Data
A catalogue record for this book is available from the British Library.

ISBN 0-304-70701-5 (hardback)
       0-304-70702-3 (paperback)

Library of Congress Cataloging-in-Publication Data
A catalogue record is available from the Library of Congress

Typeset by BookEns Ltd, Royston, Herts.
Printed and bound in Great Britain by Creative Print and Design (Wales)

Preface

As a Somali, I was swept into the vortex of our nation's political crisis in early 1991 soon after the collapse of Mogadiscio.* I was living close by, in Kampala, Uganda, where I was a professor of literature at Makerere University. I remember flying into Nairobi when I received an urgent phone call from my immediate family and thinking that I would sort out what I took to be a pushover problem, in a matter of weeks. I was then of the optimistic belief that reason would reign, and that full-scale strife would be averted. Even though it didn't occur to me at the time that there was much to my immediate family's sense of dislocation, I remained on guard. In spite of this I couldn't help remarking on a feeling of elation and one of frenzied agitation on the faces of the men and women I met in Nairobi: elation, because they had survived; frenzied agitation, because many of them were preparing for war, ostensibly to retake their looted properties in Mogadiscio by invading the city. Nairobi was astir with ill-starred, ill-founded rumours of certain clan families being rounded up in Mogadiscio and massacred. I was ill with grief, not knowing what to believe, and unsure of how to react. I felt as though I had been invited to a funeral wake at which the very person whose death was being mourned was not only alive, but bizarrely having a wild time.

Much of what I was told by those who had fled to Nairobi did not make sense, and I said so to anyone who cared to listen. None the less I was surprised at their bitterness, shocked at the claims and counterclaims being made by one or the other of the clan families. I had never encountered so much hate, which was freely and wilfully expressed. If I disregarded their messages of doom, it was because I did not credit the pronouncements of the new arrivals from Mogadiscio with being unbiased. I perceived them to be party to

---

* This is the Italian name of the capital of Somalia, more familiar to English readers in the spelling Mogadishu.

the ruin of our country, members of a privileged class more likely to look after its own interests than those of the nation. I also felt that, to inveigle me into becoming more sympathetic to them, some invoked the sentiments of the clan. Untrusting and cynical of their motives, I refused to be implicated in their self-serving machinations. What's more, I took a marked distance from their position, reminding them that it would be to everyone's advantage to give peace a chance. I advised that we should all accept and bear our share of the blame for the collective failure.

I spent most evenings with Somalis, counselling peace, and my daytime hours with Kenyan government ministers, in the naive hope that we might be able to set in place the mechanism by which a cessation of hostilities between the regime and the militia groupings might be made effective. I had tried to intervene before, in Kampala, through the good offices of Museveni, and failed. By nature I am a pessimist, but in those days I was an inveterate optimist.

One thing became evident as I flew back and forth between Mombasa and Nairobi, now trying to set into motion a peace machine and failing, now working at finding a college for my son, who had recently arrived in a boat. Kenyans from all walks of life were caught in the turmoil that was Somalia. Some were clearly nonplussed at the sight of Nairobi being taken over by affluent Somalis, apparently on a spending spree, ostentatiously expending their plunder.

In Mombasa, however, to which coastal city the poorer category had fled, a fund of popular kindness was in abundance, generosities extended to the destitute Somalis arriving in dhows. Being Muslims, the locals welcomed their co-religionist Somalis with open arms. Other Kenyans, notably the police and immigration officials at entry points, were having a field day extorting cash, and making a mint out of the Somali presence. I was struck by the difference between the Somalis who made it to Nairobi and those who fled to Mombasa.

Nairobi, on the other hand, attracted former army officers or politicians, apostates with no orthodoxy to their belief systems other than their fickle-minded self-preservation. They were yesterday's people, decided on buying their way out of a political morass of their own making. They were clearly bent on paying their way into a tomorrow, destination Europe or North America. Full of themselves and unperturbed, they argued that Kenya was up for grabs, from the highest official in the country to the lowest-paid peon. It would dawn on me only later that it was not Kenya that was under the hammer but Somalia: whose assets were going dirt cheap, given away in exchange for a mere entry visa, a stay permit of a longer duration; whose state structures were being dismantled, and sold in bits to the meanest bidder; whose gold statues had been melted in Abu Dhabi; whose factories had been taken apart and sold as scrap metal. It was staggering to witness an entire country being auctioned off. I kept reminding myself that, for what the country had been worth, Somalia had formed part of a Cold War grand design, and that one knew that, sooner or later, it would be pawned off by local criminals in cahoots with others of a wickedly calculated mindset. So it didn't matter who was buying what, or to whom things were being sold. Nor did it matter who was putting up the bread, and who might end up winning the jackpot!

In Mombasa, the refugees dwelt on spectral memories, of grenades falling, and of uncollected corpses rotting at the city's roundabouts. Distraught, I understood the deeper meaning of a Somali wisdom in which a high value is placed on owning one's own home, as this affords a greater sense of privacy, of self-honour and of dignity. My father, my son, one of my younger sisters and a nephew, who were among the first to arrive in the coastal city, shared rooms with people whom they had not known before. I remember my sister alluding to 'one's home being one's protector, a custodian to one's secrets, a sentry at the gate to one's sense of self-pride. Having no home of one's own and no country enjoying the luxury of peace: then perhaps one is a refugee.'

Thanks to her first-hand knowledge of refugees, for she had worked as a nutritionist with the UNHCR before the collapse, my sister knew what she was on about. My father, for his part, was familiar with the idea of displacement, as he had lived through several wars, some native to the Horn of Africa, others external to it. My exile got me acquainted with living in the peripheries of societies of which I've not been a full-fledged member. Not comfortable with the miserable conditions of the camp, I applied to rent a house in the city for my immediate family, and I was denied permission. A fat-bellied, bad-toothed, ill-mannered police officer in charge of district security turned down my request, saying, 'In Kenya a Somali is either a *shifta*-bandit, or a refugee. There is no running away from this historical fact.'

Maybe here lies the genesis of the book, in the words of a man who worked out for himself who we were when we hadn't. All the same, I didn't start thinking of writing this book until 1993, after a close friend, Arne Ruth, then Chief Editor of Sweden's most influential paper, *Dagens Neheter*, asked that my wife and I interview the Africans in Sweden. Our visit to Stockholm coincided with two related gruesome incidents. The first of these was the apprehension, by the police, of a Swede otherwise known as 'the Laserman', a serial murderer, with a South African past, determined to cleanse the country of its dark-skinned immigrants. The second was the arrest of a Somali refugee youth, who had killed, in self-defence, one of three racists who cornered him in the butcher's section of a supermarket. With nowhere to run, the youth turned on his pursuers, stabbing one of them to death. It hasn't been an easy book to write, not least because the very crisis which prompted the Somalis to seek refuge elsewhere continues unabated. For several years now, Somalis have had no choice but to become refugees, to count themselves among a growing community of the country's internally displaced who are in some way worse off than the refugees, or to ally themselves with one or other of the armed militia groupings. As a people, we've been at the mercy of the traffickers in human misery, cowboy politicians who have cut up our country into fiefdoms run by a cabal of criminals who claim to have the mandate of the clan as their constituency. I have been plagued by doubts, and the Lord knows I've thought of abandoning the book project more than once, dismayed by the sorrow which has been of a piece with being a Somali. If I haven't let go of it, it is because I wish somehow to impose a certain order on Somalia's anarchy, in syncopated assumption of the wisdom that the person whose story has been told does not die. So here are the voices of the refugees, the exiles and the internally displaced: I serve them to you with humility, I serve them raw, tearful, pained. Here is a nation of narratives held to ransom. Here is an ocean of stories narrated by Somalis in a halfway house.

It has been a difficult book to write for another reason: because, as a novelist, I am used to depending on my own resources, not on the kindness of a motley of virtual strangers, nor on the collaborative support of so many friends. Here are my thanks to a legion of persons who've been of help. To do the research for this book, however, I've had to raise funds: in Sweden, I was on the payroll of the newspaper *Dagens Neheter*; in Switzerland, Caritas offered a one-off grant with conditions that I gave readings and lectures at the same time as I interviewed the Somali refugees in that country; in Italy, I undertook a lecture tour for a pittance in order to visit many cities where the Somalis were concentrated; in England, I had a more relaxed time, being attached to the School of English at the University of Kent; a year later I did a less successful stint at St Antony's College, Oxford. A special tribute is owed to the Somalis who were generous with their time, and who divulged their life histories to me. I hope I have been fair in my renderings of what they told me. I've tried my utmost to be equal to their trust in me.

While I cannot mention all the reports, pamphlets and books which I have read and consulted, and from which I have greatly benefited, it is my pleasure to mention a few: *The Somali Challenge: From Catastrophe to Renewal*, edited by Ahmed I. Samater (Lynne Reiner Publishers, 1994); *The Somali Community in Cardiff*, published by Save the Children Fund (UK) as a report in July 1994; *Refugees: The Trauma of Exile*, based on a Red Cross Workshop held at Vitznau, Switzerland, and edited by Diana Miserez (Martinus Nijhoff, 1988); *An Anthology of Somali Poetry*, translated by B. W. Andrzejewski with Sheila

Andrzejewski (Indiana University Press, 1993); *Frontiers: The Book of the TV Series* (BBC, 1990); and finally *Documenta X: The Book* (Cantz Verlag [Kassel, Germany], 1997).

Portions of this book appeared in *Transition, London Review of Books* and *The Observer*.

To be more specific, I am thankful: in Sweden, to Arne Ruth, the late Lena Persson, and Ingemar Karlsson, who looked after us handsomely; to Per Wastberg and Anita Theorell, who lent us their apartment; to Lilijana and Coni Dufgaran; to Gabi Gleichman; to Anders Paulrud; to Sigrid Segerstedt-Wiberg for her generosity of spirit; and finally to Thandika Mkandawire for sharing with us the insights deriving from his own lengthy exile. In Switzerland: my gratitude to the director of Caritas, to the staff, in particular Harry Sivic who looked after me, and to the head of the seminary in Lucerne where I lived for the duration of my stay; to Zakaria and Maryam Farah; to Othmar Dubler and Maria Maier. In Italy: to Itala Vivan and Erico Dodi; to Edo, Daniela and Anna-Chiara Lugarini; to Sandro Triulzi and Paola Splendore; to Anna Pulglielli; to Khadija Ali Mahmoud; to Suldaan Gaarane; to Faduma Max'ud Derie and Abdullahi Cayrow. In Britain: to Patricia Haward; to Abdulrazak Gurnah; to Lyn Innes; to Alistair Niven; to Jeremy Harding; to Nasir Warfa; and of course to my series editor at Cassell/Continuum, Bruce King; to the editorial director, Janet Joyce; to Sandra Margolies, the senior house editor, who got the best out of me; and to my agent Deborah Rogers, who stayed by me, helpful as ever. I am also grateful for their generosity of spirit, to Dr Mohammed Chambas; Yusuf Hassan; Mandla Langa; Allan Taylor; Kwame Karikari; Willie Kgositsile; Karin Sfreddo and her brother Sandro.

Foremost among my debts, however, is the one I owe to Amina Mama, my partner in life, who in the initial stages assisted me with some of the research by conducting the interviews with me. She has been an inspiration to me, a model of scholarly rigour, and it gives me great pleasure to acknowledge my intellectual indebtedness to her.

On more than one occasion I've had to make judicious decisions to alter the names of the Somalis I interviewed for considerations of safety. I have, however, used a person's true name when the permission has been granted. Needless to say, I remain solely responsible for inaccuracies, or infelicitous gaffes.

Cape Town
November 1999

To
Somalis,
whoever and wherever they are,
and in loving memory of a very dear friend,
Jacqueline Bardolph

PART I

Chapter One

I remember the renegade tears coursing down the refugees' cheeks. My younger sister had been among the first boatloads of fleeing Somalis to arrive in Mombasa. She spoke of what happened, grieving.

'We just escaped,' she said when I met her in Mombasa's Utange refugee camp, 'leaving our beds unmade, the chairs in our dining rooms upturned, our kitchens unswept, our dishes in the sinks, our future undone. We ran as fast as we could, not bothering where we might end up, in the country and among the displaced, or out of it and among the stateless refugees fleeing. We fled, locking up our family house as though we were going away for a weekend trip into the country. Afraid of what might occur to us if we stayed on, we didn't question the wisdom of our decision to leave.'

Dejected in spirit, emaciated of body after an arduous sea journey in an overcrowded dhow, emptied of wise thoughts by the perils of first joining the displaced, then leaving Somalia and going into exile, she and my father told me what I understood then to be upmarket tales of horror. Most of these sounded incredible, a great many boasting of apocryphal qualities, spoken meanly, I thought, in order to dishonour the good name of the *other* clan. I asked my father, then in his eighties, why he fled, and he responded, 'We fled on the say-so of our clanspeople.'

'Why didn't you inquire into the matter before upping and leaving?' I wondered. 'You might have found your Kenyan papers if you had the calm to look for them. You wouldn't be a refugee then, would you? Were you not at one time entitled to hold Kenyan nationality?'

He spoke as though he hadn't heard me, for he said, 'We were like a horde of ants, blind with fear, and fleeing ahead of a hurricane.' Then, after a pause, 'Alas, we had no idea we were fleeing in the direction of the storm, not away from it. You see, every one of our clanspeople caught the virus, whereas those of the clans who remained probably contracted the contagion of staying.'

I was reminded of a formidable riddle often put to children, maybe to ascertain how alert they are. Children are asked: If a hunter comes upon twenty deer, aims and shoots, killing none, how many deer remain? You seldom encounter a child who gets it right first time.

I looked at my father, whom I was meeting for the first time in about seventeen years. He was in a hospital in Mombasa, recovering from an injury to his spine. Not that our not-meeting face to face had brought us any closer, because he and I continued our habit of disagreeing on every topic. Whereas my sister, in her effort to keep the peace, changed the course of our conversation at every available opportunity. And so when I asked my father, perhaps rather aggressively, why he thought he would be killed if he stayed on, simply because he was from another clan, it was she who replied. She said, 'It wasn't who one was, or what clan one was born in that mattered, it was the nadir of helplessness. That made us up and go.'

'You're saying everyone has fled?'

'I know many of the *other* clans who fled,' she said, 'even though they may have escaped in different directions, and not necessarily first to Kismayo, and then to Mombasa.'

I could see that my father was displeased with my sister's intervention. Angrier with those who had made him flee than he was with either of us, he said, 'I am old enough to care less about what you think, so let me tell you that we fled because we met the beasts in us, face to face.'

I pointed out to him, and not in the kindest language, that people made up stories, and that they were fed on facts bleached of the hue of truth, facts stuffed with a salvo of falsehoods, one family against another, for political gains.

Despite her attempt, my sister did not succeed in changing the subject of our conversation. For my father was now in rage. He was half-shouting: 'Mogadiscio* has fallen into the clutch of thugs, no better than hyenas, who have no idea what honour is, what trust is, what political responsibility means.'

My sister attempted to change the topic of our talk.

My father went on, venomously, 'Would you ask a hyena to watch over your beef stew? Because you would be a fool if you trusted a hyena, wouldn't you?'

I said, 'Somalia's clan spectrum has more colours in the rainbow of its affiliations than an anthropologist might suggest. And for all we know, the warring clans may be fewer in number than the peace-loving ones, the Somalis who pursue sedentary vocations. It is those of the nomadic stock who are more vocal, and who claim to be the prototype Somali. These are the bellicose beasts, forever at each other's throat, beasts who remain mistrustful of one another's intentions. What is more, we are unscientific about a number of things, including how many of us there are.'

My sister remarked, 'To flee is not an admission of guilt on our part. As for your question, why run? What would you want us to do, buy guns instead of running?'

I thought about what she had just said. That people might flee in the same way that, on seeing other deer run, a frightened deer may run too.

'We heard fear in the footsteps of those running,' my father continued, 'and sensed fright in the faster pace of our hearts. I reckon it is wiser to join the masses of people fleeing, and then ask why they were escaping, than to wait, and then be robbed, raped, or left dead by the wayside, unburied. What's the point of remaining in a Mogadiscio emptied of all one's people?'

I reiterated how I didn't see what was happening as a war between clans, and hoped that history would prove me right. Then I described what was afoot as a battle between men so charged with power-greed that the friction between them would light a great fire which, if driven by ill winds, might engulf us all.

And then they gave me an up-to-date account of what they planned to do about our property if they could get a word through to a niece of mine in whose care our houses, cars, assortment of white goods, and items of houseware and of a personal nature were left. I was facetious, retorting that any property lost to Mogadiscio's lumpen might be considered as due payment for unpaid debts owed to the country's disenfranchised.

Taking me seriously, my father said, 'A lot of things meant a great deal when the country functioned. Property meant something, being "educated", being neighbourly, being responsible to the community, all these meant something. But with rank anarchy prevailing, no significance may be attached to property, to human rapport, in short to the nature of things. Because life has no more the same meaning as it did before the civil war.'

In the silence which followed this, my attention was drawn to a group of women and children in near tatters, most likely visiting an ailing relation, recuperating. My sister explained who they were: the sort born into poverty and who would die poor, without a decent pair of shoes to their name. I asked myself if there was any point in their fleeing. I wondered what their old selves would say to their new selves when the two met up not in a slum in Mogadiscio, but in a refugee camp in Mombasa. Then my sister and I got down to the business of how soon she might take up the UN job that had been offered to her. But she insisted she would rather she didn't, until we organized somebody to look after the old man. I doubted if my brothers or I would be as committed to taking care of our aged parents as my sisters had been, first our mother, who was bedridden for nearly four years before dying, and then our father, a cantankerous man lately cursed with poor health, and needing help round the clock. Part of me was relieved that the generous-spiritedness of our womenfolk never failed to allay our worse fears, the women mending the broken, healing the wounded, taking care of the elderly and the sick, martyrly women, forever prepared to sacrifice their lives for the general good of the entire community. Another part of me was in a murderous mood as I thought about the disastrous consequences of the civil war, without a doubt the work of men, as all civil strifes have been throughout the history of humankind. I asked myself: what would become of us without the mitigation, the kindly interventions of our women?

Other than my own immediate family, I ran into other Somalis in Mombasa's refugee camp, escapees who had brought along with them damaged memories.

Time and time again they spoke of the terror which they had lived through, their demeanour undignified, their eyes mournful, their temperament as runny as the lachrymal catarrh affecting an uncared-for orphan. They put me in mind of the earth just dug up and piled by a tomb as yet unfilled: I sensed that, buried among the ashen memories which they had brought along, there were incommunicable worries. There were areas of their lives that I had no access to, because I was not there when the horror came to visit their homes. They were part of a 'we', sharing the communal nightmare. That I was not included in the 'we' was made clear to me. But then I was not assumed to be part of the 'they' either.

I was nonplussed by the tempestuous outpouring of strong sentiments and emotions expressed in intense clan terms. There was such venom in their recollection that I was taken aback, maybe because I had been unprepared for it. Shocked, perhaps not so much by what any of my interlocutors said, as by the severity and the depth of the hurt, which now ran in their blood.

'We know who *we* are,' several of them repeated again and again, their voices as bitter as the bolus of poison. 'What has occurred in Mogadiscio has taught us who we are.' What did they mean by '*us*'? This was not some sort of double-talk, saying one thing and meaning something totally other: they were wholeheartedly committed to a new form of Somali-speak, in which '*us*' refers to a post-colonial realpolitik governed by the anachronistic sentiments of clannism. I found myself needing to make it clear to every single one of them that I belonged neither to '*us*' nor to '*them*'.

I derived no pleasure from being alone either. I was just as sad, remembering things, my remembrances on a leash, as eager as a bitch on heat.

And before I was conscious of it I was playing host to a memory, that of my last day in Somalia in the month of August 1974. As part of a *safar-salaamo* farewell, all the members of my immediate family, young and old, had come to the international airport to see me off.

I had little desire to publicize my departure, for fear that my trip might be cancelled. But not so my family, who threw a sort of *despedida* (send off), Latin American style. In the family home, prayers were said to bless my departure with verses of the Koran. My sisters gave a party of eats, to which a few of our intimates and a couple of my in-laws were invited. Later, with everyone in their smartest get-up, we took photographs. They were pleased that I was leaving for Europe, because they believed not only that better opportunities were in wait for a young writer, but that I would be out of the reach of Siyad Barre's Security. I wasn't happy to leave, because I had the premonition that I might not return.

I remember standing with several of them, posing for a group photograph, then sharing an aside with an elder brother, who gave me advice; I recall my mother warning me of the perils of alien lands, 'You came back with a foreign wife before, I suggest you return alone this time!'; I remember a sister requesting that I write newsy letters more often; I recall my son, wholly enthralled and enjoying the *despedida*, asking that I send him clothes, bicycles and things from England so he could show off to his mates. (Neither my son nor I was blessed with the foresight that thirteen long years would pass before we would meet again.) I remember my father, on one of his high horses, appearing enraged about a promise I had allegedly forgotten to honour, but refusing to tell me what it was, no matter how many times I begged him. Later, taking me aside as the final call for our flight was made, he said, 'You are not a blessing, but a curse. May ill-luck be your companion in this and the next life too.'

The years have borne testimony to the condition of my exile, a darkness with enough light to enable me to make sense of my comings and goings, never for once bothering if I were blessed or cursed. Years later, in Berlin, I was to learn of my beloved mother's death in April 1990, after a long illness. I was devastated not to have seen her again. Looking back on it now, I am all too relieved that she did not live to experience the civil strife which brought about the fragmentation of the land she so much loved.

Not long after I met my father as a refugee in a camp in Mombasa, he too encountered his death in a land marked by uncertainty. He died a quiet death, on Friday 12 July 1993, two days before he was due to join my sister, who had by then migrated to the USA. Until his death he remained undecided if he should stay on in Kenya, as a well-looked-after octogenarian refugee, return to Mogadiscio or follow my sister to the USA, where she had established a base for any member of our family to join her. As for my oldest son, he had truanted from his school in Montreal, going back to Mogadiscio against my counsel. Because he had fled, leaving his papers behind, he too ended up in the same refugee camp in Mombasa, and later at a college in Nairobi, before finally joining my sister in Detroit.

The sad encounters I have since shaken hands with are more numerous than I can list here. My scattered family includes a sister stranded in Holland, stateless, another sister with asylum papers in Canada, a brother with eleven children, two other sisters, my son in the USA, two other brothers, one in Dire Dawa awaiting the outcome of his sponsorship to North America, the other holding a high government post in the Ogaden, Ethiopia, where he has moved to from Mombasa: all of them migrants riding the wind of their fortune or misfortune. During the *despedida* at Mogadiscio's airport I could not have foreseen how my leaving, when I did, would be followed by deaths in my immediate family, and eventually, and most importantly, the painful death of my country itself. What catastrophes!

Because my fate and those of my fellow-nationals are tied to our country's destiny, any talk about Somalia brings me sad associations. And I wonder if my years of exile have been futile, now that there is no 'country' to return to. But then there are essential differences between those committed to going back to the land of our neurosis and inspiration and those admitting to never wanting to return.

Another major difference is that whereas a *despedida* was thrown to honour my departure, they had no such gathering to see them off, or to wish them well. They fled!

I spent almost four weeks in Kenya, travelling between the coastal city of Mombasa and Nairobi, where I was onerously engaged in the task of talking to senior Foreign Ministry officials known to be close to the country's President, Daniel arap Moi.

The city of Mombasa boasted a large presence of Mogadiscians for the first time in its history, its streets full to bursting with Somalis loudly communicating with one another in the guttural sadness of their tongue. Clothed in the tawdriness of their sorrow, almost all of them would explain that they had come on dhows from the southern coastal city of Kismayo, although some may have started their sea journey from somewhere else, or travelled overland from the hinterland to the west or north of the metropolis.

On arrival they were kept in quarantine for a few days before being taken in convoys to the Utange refugee camp, located a few miles outside the city centre. The camp security fell to the Kenya police, whereas feeding and registering its inmates were UNHCR responsibilities. Uniformed guards manned the exits and entrances of the camps. I felt repulsed by what I saw or heard daily: stateless and not-yet-refugee Somalis being harassed by the Kenya police, UNHCR officials displaying a racist arrogance.

Two days after my arrival I was introduced to the head of the unit, a Kenyan who commended my sister for being ever so helpful as his interpreter whenever he talked to some of the Somali women. 'For somebody in a refugee camp,' he said, 'your sister is highly impressive.'

I asked, 'How so?'

'She's highly educated and respectable,' he said.

For a brief moment I was in two minds whether to remind him that, among the inmates of the camp, there were more than a dozen professors of Somalia's National University, several former ministers of government, and at least one famous film-maker; in short, men and women who, if the circumstances had permitted it, might have been welcomed by Kenya's highest civil authority.

He ventured, 'But you don't look like a refugee yourself.'

I asked, 'How do refugees look?'

Smiling wisely, he said, 'They don't look like you.'

I told him that I might have been a refugee if I had come from Mogadiscio, on a dhow, which docked in Mombasa's harbour. Like my sister, my father or my son. 'But tell me, how are they defined, the Somalis?' I asked. 'Refugees, asylum-seekers, visitors?'

'They are defined as a people of a halfway house,' he said.

'How do you mean?'

'Whether defined as such or not, they are in a refugee camp,' he answered. 'And being Somali and our neighbours, perhaps we need not bother to define them. Even so, some may seek asylum, some may apply for a visitor's visa to be stamped in their Somali passports. But then they themselves consider Kenya as a halfway house, a place from where they would launch themselves further afield, into Europe, the USA or Canada.'

When I made to speak, he raised his hand, indicating that he was no longer interested in what I had to say. He said, 'Anyway your sister has our permission to come and go. My men have instructions not to bother her.'

'What about the others?' I asked.

'We have a problem with many of them.'

He wasn't specific as to what the problems might be, or if a little greasing of a palm might make it vanish, like the tally of a magician replacing a handkerchief with a pigeon.

'Given how things are in Kenya, did it ever occur to you', I asked, 'that your country might blow up, and that you might seek refuge in Somalia?'

'I consider that possibility,' he admitted. 'Daily.'

'I bet you do not like the thought,' I ventured.

The white of his pale palm facing me in the gesture of a man surrendering, he took a theatrical pause, and looked around before saying, 'Now please!' Meaning, Please go!

As I did his bidding, I thought that in the throes of dying, the body-politic that *was* Somalia displaced a leviathan. The leviathan in turn begat a monster with unsavoury character traits, and the monster begat numerous unsightly gnomic figures with a gangster's mindset, a gangster carrying out miscarriages of justice. In the evil creatures begotten in this manner, wickedness began to find cause to celebrate, reproducing itself in worrying numbers, multiplying as fungi. The contagion spread, corrupting civil society, which in turn caused the death of the body-politic. A virus begotten out of violence infected the land with a madness.

Such was the mayhem in Mogadiscio, in the initial stages, that there was no knowing where politically motivated necroses ended and where other kinds of gangrene began. However, before long, you couldn't tell the undefined violences apart; they merged, becoming one for all intents and purposes, in the end bringing about the collapse of Somalia's civil society and, along and down with it unto death, the entirety of the country's state structures.

I did not need to be reminded that very few people anywhere in the world are perhaps aware that one time Somalia played host to one of the largest refugee influxes in the continent, with the 'guests' from Ethiopia accounting for more than a quarter of the nation's population.

This was a point alluded to by several of those with whom I had spoken, one of them the former director of a refugee camp in Somalia for close to eight years, from 1981 to 1989. He quit six months before fleeing the carnage in Mogadiscio, and then became a refugee himself, for all intents and purposes, even though, in Kenya, he could not be granted the status officially.

'Such a precarious existence, the African's!' he said.

There was a truth in what he said, but I asked him to please elaborate. He struck me as a man standing in the midst of debris. He wasn't the type who would easily abandon himself to a feeling of despair.

'Love, personal dignity, wealth and power are short-lived in Africa,' he said. 'More than anybody else, perhaps because I worked with refugees, I appreciated what it meant to live in peace long before our land was visited by its own plague. I am overwhelmed with pain as I think of the wars erupting all over the continent, and of state structures collapsing, cities being ravaged. And I am reminded of an elderly Oromo refugee who was in the camp I ran and who once spoke of peace and war as small cuts of cheap metal set in silver. I had not understood what he meant until I got here, a refugee.'

'Do you know where he might be, that elderly Oromo?'

'He fled more or less the same time I did: he may be here for all I know, although I have not seen him. If not, then he fled back to where he came from, and perhaps has ended up in a camp for the displaced, somewhere in Ethiopia, trying to adjust to his new circumstances,' he said.

'What do you reckon is his status now?'

'No longer designated as a refugee, because he is back in his country, I suspect he will be at the tail end among the displaced, travelling round the vicious circle of his ill luck. For a start, he was born poor, and remained disadvantaged, politically disenfranchised, and then became a refugee, and is currently displaced.'

A silence, as vast as the sorrow with which he was surrounded, engulfed us all. I asked, 'How are you coping?'

'I sleep less,' he said, 'and I question myself often, wondering if I have been sufficiently humane to the refugees of the camp I ran for years. My mind goes repeatedly over the tiniest details. Although I did better than most, I often conclude regretfully that I had failed in my duty to the refugees, who were, more often than not, mere numbers in columns, now in the in-tray, now the out-tray, a seven a.m. to three p.m. job, best forgotten before our siesta.'

'Your future prospects as a refugee?' I wondered.

'It is as though the night has descended early in my life, the darkness total, a darkness with no tone to it at all, none whatsoever.'

I asked, 'What prospects are there for a refugee?'

'None,' he said.

Later the same day, in Mombasa.

I was early for the appointment with my interviewee, whom I came upon entertaining other Somalis living in the same refugee camp. Once introduced, I was warmly welcomed and asked to join them, and I did. Served highly sugared tea, I was also offered the only decent chair by one of the guests, who sat on a mat on the floor with the others. We sipped tea, and sat in the open dusty courtyard, amiably talking politics. I sensed that they had all been humbled by their recent experiences, and that they were different from the men they were, in Mogadiscio, in December 1990.

They exchanged tales manufactured in the rumour mills set up in exile. Taking turns, they repeated the tall tales they had heard. Patient with one another, they heard each other out as each produced counter-versions, made additions or incorporated his own deletions. I had been familiar with some of the tales. Even so, I felt no nearer to knowing which part of it had its origin in the apocryphal imagining of rumour-mongers, and which part in the mansion of truth.

Some of the stories were colourful, some purposeful, with a moral to them. In some, the names of highly placed Kenyans were mentioned as accomplices in the plundering of Mogadiscio's wealth. In one, X was reported as having been escorted, sirens and all, to a plane on the runway of the international airport, a plane allegedly full of army officers who, having looted the safes of the foreign exchange reserves of the Somali Central Bank, shared their booty with him, in exchange for travel documents. Another story pulled us in a different direction, deeper into the whirlpool of controversy: in this, a Sudanese peace delegation flew into Mogadiscio as it burnt, and departed with the looted properties of the foreign embassies given to them by one of the warlords, in exchange for a supply of arms.

Even if they didn't make into the world's newspaper headlines, because they could not stand up in court, and even if they were without base, the fact remained that they provided Somalis with a sense of vindication, incriminating *others* as accomplices in the ruin of the country, as culpable. Some of these made it into the world press: the Sayyid's statue, entirely of gold, dismantled by marauders, who sold it dirt cheap to a merchant in Abu Dhabi.

Then our conversation touched on Mogadiscio's latest mayhem, as picked up on the grapevine. The tension grew palpable, prickly as three-day-old stubble. The other guests left. I stayed.

Although looking younger than his years, Ciroole was in his late fifties, wise in his silences, discreet in his comments, but very outspoken in his assessment, pronouncing a most severe indictment of the Somali character.

Ciroole was an assumed name for a man nicknamed 'Grey-haired', who had fewer white hairs than I. He didn't want to volunteer his true name or preferred one with a pseudonymous ring to it, apparently because he had taken an assumed name in advance of his departure for Canada, someone explained. Another version had it that he had adopted a new identity once he got to Mombasa so he would distance his old self from the memories associated with it, and from what had happened to his female folk, all raped, including his four-year-old granddaughter. Shocked, I had asked why anyone would rape a small child, and was told that it was the done thing, the rapists feeling safer and believing they would not contract AIDS from the rape victim.

Ciroole had the calm to describe Ali Mahdi Mohamed as 'a political cowboy, with a hat on, happy and prepared to kill for it.' At my prompting he referred to the cowboy film culture on which many Mogadiscians had been raised, in which the *capo ladare* (the leader of the bandits) was seen as a cunning specimen, fascinatingly manipulating the odds to his advantage until near the end of the film, when luck would change sides. It was commonplace to watch sadness spreading on the faces of the audience as the leader of the bandits met death at the hands of his victims.

It was in passing, perhaps on his way to develop an idea to do with cowboys and bandits, that Ciroole told me, as though in an aside, that the marauders had surprised him and his female folk in their Medina hideout. If Western films are the epitome of justice ultimately winning, they also stipulate that those who are to bring about the triumph of the moral good must fight, or that someone else or the larger community must pick up the gauntlet. Ciroole fought not to absolve his honour nor to punish the culprits, who did terrible things to his female folk, but to preserve his sense of being, his closeness to his family. He fought against fear itself.

'In humans,' he went on, 'fear is an emotion going hand in hand with reasoning. As the marauders did their horrid stuff to us, I relegated myself in my rage to the status of an unfearing animal, wild in my wish to avenge a greater loss, my humanness. A part of me saw the nation raped. Another part assumed a humbled status, pillaged by those attaching no high value to nationhood.'

Silent, I waited for him to continue.

'Somehow,' he said, 'humbled further by physical torture, I ceased thinking about my pedestrian worries, and concentrated my mind on the tragic events in the land. I didn't hurt when they tormented me, not as much as when they raped my womenfolk; or when I heard about the deadly shoot-out at the Afgoi checkpoint between the United Somali Congress [USC] and the Somali Patriotic Movement [SPM].'

I asked, 'How did you hear about the first shot which allegedly started the civil war?'

He said, 'I was told of the shoot-out by a torturer doing his morning shift, my hands and feet alternately tied to one another, my body cast into the posture of a contortionist in sadistic pain. It took some time before the news reached my conscious mind.'

And then?

'I recall being amused at discovering that the flip-flop-wearing marauders, whom I never believed to be true members of any genuine political movement, were more keen on dispossessing me of my pair of shoes than they were on torturing me because I belonged to another clan. Nor were they in the least bothered about the tragic consequences of the shoot-out. They were dust-laden bandits, happy to discard their sarong in exchange for an imported pair of jeans.'

'What did they suggest? Beasts?'

'Upon calm reflection, with the pain gone, I spotted elusive power in their strides, and located in their eyes. Studying them with my half-ruined sight, I discerned their nervous demeanour and saw that they had probably set aside the grand moral ideals of the USC if they adhered to them. Maybe in the mayhem following Siyad's evacuation of his citadel, maybe they too were consumed with greed as much as the rest of the country was.'

Was there anything else worth remembering about them?

'They had badly trimmed toenails with jagged ends,' he said.

I said, 'How come you noticed that?'

'Because of the upside-down position I was held in.'

'What else did you notice?'

'I didn't like what they did with their fingers when they were not torturing me. They picked their noses, or in an absentminded way continued touching their balls. I also hated listening to their voices, or the way one of them yawned, his ugly mouth opening wider and wider, as if having his tonsils examined.'

I can still hear Ciroole's voice in my recall, his lips astir with torrents of studied contempt pouring out of him. He might have been a river in the rainy season bursting at the banks, no matter what anyone did. 'What did you do for a living?'

He ran a computer business for his bread and butter. But he was a full-time lecturer in the Faculty of Sciences at the National University, He went on, 'Here in Mombasa, so as not to "become" a refugee, I have chosen the vocation of a researcher, and I am busy writing about the refugees. To this end, I have drawn up a questionnaire and I go round daily filling them myself with orally supplied answers, because my informants are illiterate. Then I transcribe them in long-hand.'

He went inside, returning with a sample of his questionnaire.

'As an afterthought, I have included a general knowledge section, perhaps for a dare,' he said. 'If only to ascertain how little we know about our country's history or geography. It strikes me as if modern knowledge is a plot hatched primarily to dissuade the Somali laity from running their affairs on a scientific principle.'

'You are writing things down so as to understand things?'

Ciroole replied, 'Writing things down imposes a sense of self-moderation.

Composing poetry in the oral form, on the other hand, poses no restrictive aesthetics on its practitioner with regard to its truth content, only form.'

I asked, 'Do you think that we are half-beasts frenziedly caught in history's full beam?'

'As in cowboy films,' he said, and trailed off.

'How do you mean?'

Ciroole said, 'Living on an *ad hoc* basis makes a country vulnerable to lawlessness. One is often preoccupied with the daily chores, the worry of surviving in a land where everything "good" is in short supply.'

I noted that not once did he mention the names of the clans that are supposed to be engaged in warfare.

'Western films aside,' he said, 'a large number of the residents of Mogadiscio went to sleep late at night after working a whole day without achieving anything of much consequence; an equal number woke up at dawn to anxieties that could not be wished away. With no luxury to think wise thoughts, no time in which to engage in calm reflections, and no morally sound mechanisms with which to redeem themselves, many attached no meaning to their own inaction. They were hardly in a position to anticipate, much less expect, that a tragedy for which they are wholly or in part responsible has befallen their nation.'

We talked in general terms about how many of our people link the events which led to the civil war to the Somalis' ill-founded loyalty to the clan, a wraparound concept, perhaps one of the most abused tropes in our vocabulary. The clan is seen as both the evil common denominator and an explicator of all actions, good or bad, as well as an indispensable form of social organization.

Then he talked about how the acronyms of the armed political factions are viewed as being synonymous with the families which founded them, clans whose youth gangs work as freelance looters because of their special nature, even though they organize themselves around the idea of a clan in whose name they fight. He said, 'But what a tragic mess!'

I excused myself before taking leave of him; and said it was high time for me to return to the area of the camp where my father, my sister, my son and my nephew were staying in an attempt perhaps 'to sort out their lives which were one hell of a mess!' He shook his head despondently, and I added after an appropriate pause, 'Their mess, your mess, my misery!'

I doubt that I knew what I was saying. So I left.

Chapter Two

Mohamed Sheikh Abdulle, one of Mombasa's newly arrived Somalis, told me how he prayed as he fled, a no man's land separating him from becoming a refugee. 'But now that I am here and a refugee, I realize what a great distance the four days' sea journey from the Somali coast to Mombasa has proved to be!' he said.

'But why are they fleeing, in waves?' I asked.

'They continue to arrive in outward-bound waves of heart-wrenching groans,' he replied. 'As we fled, I felt as though the whole place was drenched with the residual flow of afterbirth, that the long shorelines of the peninsula were bursting with the flotsam of fear, of men, women and children jamming the littoral and land borders with the jetsam of the ejected.'

'But why?'

'Escaping, we fell victim to the pervasive violence,' he said, 'our progress now intercepted, now frustrated. And at the newly mounted checkpoint manned by the ragtag militia, we were made to identify our clan, to help them decide if you are their possible quarry, or victim of vengeance. To flee or not to flee were not viewed as choices, they were seen as a condemnation.'

I thought of the Algerian *pieds noirs* (Algerians of French descent), and of their *cercueil ou valise* choices. Most Somalis chose neither the coffin nor the suitcase, for coffins were of no use in a Mogadiscio in which the dead were left to rot in the open heat; and unlike the fleeing *pieds noirs*, many of our people never owned enough things to fill a suitcase.

I asked, 'What are the alternatives open to those not wishing to escape and not wishing to stay on in Mogadiscio? How can they avoid the threat of violence?'

Apparently many of these ended up in another city, town or village where they felt safe. 'I saw so many men and women terrified and feeling helpless in their friendlessness. I thought ahead of the cul-de-sac of displacement lying as if this were in wait for them to swell the number of the disenfranchised. By crossing the border, we became a UNHCR statistic, to wit asylum-seekers, refugees.' We fled because of the banditry.'

As Somalis, I argued, many of us ought to have experienced *burcad*-banditry in our respective home areas, all through our lives. Why was this very different?

He explained that the incidents of banditry were few and far between; and that the number of persons involved was no more than a handful. 'Nowadays,' he went on, 'with the city of Mogadiscio turned into a gangland, you found your brother, son, husband or relative among the brigands, in a city shared out by gangs and militia vigilantes, each with their own fiefdom. No one enjoys immunity from the crime of thuggery, and nobody is innocent either. Nor is one shocked to hear apocryphal tales of horror, of a body torn limb from limb, pieces deliberately scattered in the room where it has been decapitated. A miasma of sorrow hovers over the whole land as each group disavows itself of what the destroyers have done to our civil society, ruining it beyond recognition.'

The city is turned into an abattoir; Mogadiscio's residents flee, afraid of being set upon by either the vigilantes of the United Somali Congress militiamen or the reckless bombing by Siyad's men. The middle classes flee, hardly stopping until they park their vehicles in the manner of weekenders on a picnic at one or other of the satellite towns and villages around the city. They pause, awaiting news. When a less affluent ragtag of escaping humanity looking the worse for wear joins them in their places of refuge, the middle classes flee further afield in a southerly, westerly or northerly direction, intent on finding somewhere safe for their own kind.

A few days into the mayhem, an invisible line was drawn between those who flee and those who do not, one's choice depending, in the end, which side of the drawn line you stood on. It depended on whether you were a member of a generic clan whose people felt safe only if they escaped, or of another generic clan, which stayed. Mohamed Sheikh Abdulle said, 'Many of those who first fled to Kismayo and then Mombasa are allegedly of one generic clan.'

'But you chose not to flee with your clanspeople?' I said.

'I did not escape, no.'

'Why?'

He replied, 'Because I had hoped things would be worked out.'

As Mogadiscio emptied of half its long-term residents, the character of the city altered, in a matter of days, from one with cosmopolitan leanings to a ghost town in the clutch of insanity. It ceased being an all-inclusive city with an ancient history, and became one betrothed to fear, a city run by gunmen, a place ruled by murder, mayhem, a madness unleashed. Wedded to total despair, even the city noises and the silences were interpreted differently. In place of the muezzin's call to the faithful, in place of the ubiquitous music blaring out of tea houses, you heard the sound of gunfire, or were dreadfully conscious of the silences. Mohamed Sheikh Abdulle concluded, 'Our city was turned into a place with death sitting in the centre of its eye.'

Everybody was subjected to one kind of violence. Mohamed Sheikh Abdulle divided the forms of violence, which differed in substance and quality, into phases: *before* and *after* Siyad's fall from authority. Then he further contrasted these forms of violence to those which were unleashed *before* and *after* the split within the United Somali Congress into two camps, one under Ali Mahdi, the other Aideed's.

After the split, violence assumed a ruthlessness, with ugly features never known before, something akin to violence-as-a-spectacle, violence to one's faculties, to one's intelligence, to one's sense of smell, what with the unburied corpses, hundreds of them, rotting in the city's streets. 'Being vectors of a virus we had no idea existed,' Mohamed Sheikh Abdulle said, 'it was violence as a substitute for elusive power, violence with both its beginning and end in power-greed, pure and simple.'

I said, 'And then you left?'

Drenched with the wetness of tears flowing into his throat, he could not bring himself to speak. He choked. His eyes blinked from moisture, his cheeks were wet with sorrow.

He said, 'Pain everywhere!'

Mohamed Sheikh Abdulle was referring to the pain associated with hurried departures, the pain of being separated from one's loved ones, presumed dead, loved ones obstinate enough not to heed one's counsel, when it was suggested they leave. He went on, 'I think of the fools who, in their effort to hold on to their meagre possessions, lost everything they held dear, their wives', their children's and their own lives.'

He spoke the last few words with sad emotion, but the wells of his eyes remained dry as he told me how his own family and his brother's family were sent a couple of biers wrapped in shrouds, each with notes anonymously written, informing them in the clearest language that they had better vacate their houses for *wadani* indigenes. Otherwise they would all be killed.

'And then you quit?'

'But my brother didn't.'

'Saying?'

' "Over my dead body!" '

'What made you leave?'

Mohamed Sheikh Abdulle said, 'I took the two coded messages for what they were, quotations from the Koran, Verse 57, Surah xx, copied in full. And below the messages someone using an alias had signed "Wadani". Whereas my brother, foolhardy in his depiction of all "the fleers" as cowards, said he was not ready to cower, that he would rather die. He didn't fancy hiding under his bed, or running at the invocation of a coded Koranic message. There was no dignity in that, he argued.'

I asked, 'Did you suspect who might have sent you the bier, the shrouds and the coded messages, someone you knew, someone coveting what you had?'

He had his suspicions. I wondered, 'Who?'

'It was a former colleague of mine at the university.'

'And he wanted to move into your property?'

'In fact he moved in soon after we fled.'

'What became of your brother and his family?'

'They were murdered in their sleep,' he said.

I kept silent.

He said, 'Their bodies were wrapped in those very shrouds and were carried out of their houses feet first. Only an eight-year-old girl survived the massacre, and she is with us here.'

'I am sorry,' was all that I could say.

Nodding his head, he said, 'Moreover, the imam officiating at my brother's funeral rites recited the very Koranic passage quoted in the anonymous message, Verse 57, Surah xx. I doubt that this was a coincidence.'

The pain of fresh memory presently lodged itself in his throat, making him unable to speak. Instead, his whole body began to tremble, I thought, not so much with weeping as with rage, an anger fiercer than open admission of pain. After a while, he reached inside himself for a trace of calm, and found it when least expected. He said, 'It's the pain of thinking what might have been that is killing me, so much damage caused by our bankrupt political class.'

'And the way forward, out of the morass?'

He might not have heard what I had said. He started speaking: 'We dwell on past horrors in our remembering and concentrate our minds on the future's uncertainties, because we are afraid to face up to our sad fate. Meanwhile our inner fear reproduces all manner of phobias, and these visit us with abject vengeance. Some of my childhood fears, like terror of the dark, of new places, these, for example, have lately been resurrected, and they call on my active recall, making nonsense of my grown-up rationalization. A child crying because its mother is away has no trust in the words spoken to comfort it, for words have no meaning. Such are the terrors calling on my conscious and my unconscious I feel as though I have gone back, in memory, to my childhood days.'

'Tell me, how do you cope with all these pains?'

'On occasion I am able to negotiate with the overwhelming worries, by disorienting them,' he said. 'Mostly and sadly though, the accumulated fears suddenly descend on me, to dominate my nights and days, without allowing for worthy interrogations. To gain a moderate hold on my life I think ahead of the day when I shall interrogate the present from a position of strength, the past from a position of philosophical certainty.'

Then after a long silence, he spoke at his niece's prompting, if only to explain to the eight-year-old girl – a rape victim, and one who witnessed her parents killed right in front of her – why she should not mention the name of her playmate and close friend in pre-civil war Somalia.

The girl's speech was limited to a vocabulary of adverbial pronouns: what, when and why, on occasion in the interrogative forms, but not always. Today she looked terribly distraught, her countenance suggestive of a child suffering from Down's syndrome. She had the habit, at times, of repeating some words her uncle had spoken, in the way a child of two who is learning a language says a word over and over. But she did not say anything to me. On the day I visited the family she was taunting everyone with 'When!'

For Mohamed Sheikh Abdulle, time was in the accusative: as in the victims of rape, of other forms of molestation, thuggery or buggery, violences reducing one to somebody to whom things are done! His concluding remarks were incisive: 'You die more than once when your intelligence, the senses of your smell, and your integrity are violated. I might as well be counted among the dead.'

No sooner had I made some soothing remarks, something like, 'You will see, everything will be all right,' than I regretted saying anything.

He fell ominously silent, the kind of silence that predicts a storm in its wake. A dam had broken, a well of tears spilling over the walls of his self-control. Such was the transport of the sorrow he communicated that I hadn't the courage to say anything, not even the sort of words you speak to a child, crying.

But he resumed speaking, and his voice had changed, his demeanour too. He rose from his chair, the better to gather his strength; he said, 'I hope for your own sake, for mine and for Somalia, that you find a source better informed than I from where or from whom you will receive in an unbiased way all you need to know about the violence we were subjected to in Mogadiscio.'

And without much ado, he left me to see myself out.

To date the best documentation about the mindless violence in Mogadiscio in the early days of the civil war is an account published in the form of an eighty-page memoir. Written in Italian by Hassan Osman Ahmed, who lived through it all, the memoir is entitled *Morire a Mogadiscio*.

So stifling was the fear, according to the author, and so generalized the violence that people did not know what to do. They worried about the basics, about water to drink, food to eat, they worried about the safety of their family, and what to do if they were taken ill, because the hospital ceased functioning. If they had food in the house, they worried about the day when they might run out of it, they worried about their friends and family and whether these had any, or how they might get some to them if they did not. For it was foolhardy to remain indoors, and it was unwise to venture outside one's residence with a view to providing for more of one's needs. Worry, in tandem with fear, reduced everyone to the status of an animal, foraging for the basics. People were aware that their houses or cars were theirs until a gang of youths put their mind to shooting their way in, rogues who then raped their womenfolk, robbed; thugs exacting revenge for one of their dead. People were unable to decide what safety measures to take, whether it was wiser to split, the children and women to be sent ahead, out of harm's way, the men to join later, or to remain together, holding out in a bunker, ensconced in a basement, hidden from the curious eyes of your unneighbourly neighbours.

Morire a Mogadiscio is an admixture of personal reminiscences, and it offers us an astute portrait of Mogadiscio under siege. It is an honest description of the languor which comes as a result of fear and worry, as it is experienced by a potential recipient of it, not a perpetrator of violence. It gives an entrée into the mind of a violated society, and reaches into areas that are otherwise inaccessible to foreign and local journalists, because of their biased position. It is the first-hand account of an educated middle-class Somali who did not flee with the first exodus, but who lost heart and then left, because of the violence.

There is pathos in the story. Two of the author's nephews join the youth gangs. We suffer with him and feel his pain, as we suffer with the city's innocent, the unlucky ones who agonize over what they ought to do. Hassan Osman Ahmed wrestles courageously with personal truths at a decisive time in his and the country's life, watching others measure their swords with the inevitability of death. A witness, he has the courage to give a daily account of the deterioration of the condition of life in Mogadiscio, the total degradation of society's values, the destruction of the city's cosmopolitanism. Together, these eventually lead to the collapse of the state.

We overhear his inner thoughts as he sees the burning of Mogadiscio's cathedral, 'un pezzo della nostra storia, e mio in particulare'. One of the book's most touching moments occurs when the author owns up to having been baptized as a Catholic. It requires such courage to admit to having received his confirmation, like his father before him, at a service held by a Franciscan, Monsignor Filippini, in the very cathedral which is now on fire. Reminiscing with nostalgia, he calls on his childhood, remembering how he used to say his vespers and matins prayers in the 'House of God', now falling in on itself, burning. That he had been a closet Christian in a predominantly Muslim country for the early part of his life lends poignancy to the truth coming out about Somalia.

We are disarmed by his forthrightness, guided by his honest gaze, hearing what he has to say and seeing what he sees; he grows in stature. Thanks to him, we know now what it had been like to have lived through decades of tyranny. And in the end we agree with him that violence is the one medium the displaced, the marginalized and the alienated employ to talk to each other, the one and only idiom comprehensible to each of them.

He is our eyes as we spy on frightened women being sneaked into the mosques after dark in order to allay the family's fear of their being raped at home. He is our ears and the gatherer of the rumours as the news is spread about the districts of Mogadiscio which fall victim to the looters, youth gangs believed to be high on drugs.

Caught between several sets of guns, ordinary folks feel helpless in their fright, and do not know any better than the faction leaders, who are billeted in one or other of the forts built around the idea of the clan. At one point, even the author is seduced by the idea of identifying with his own clan, perhaps in the hope of surviving a season of contradictory conflicts. Somalia is an upmarket whorehouse, where you pay in cash for what you receive in kind.

After several attempts and failures to make headway with the warlords, he leaves on a Yemeni passport. Peace is his elixir, the beacon beckoning to him. He goes to Italy to write up his memoir.

The civil war violence has thrown up a set of acronyms by which the militia groupings are known, not to mention terms of derision used for the gangs of youths, who work in tandem with the vigilantes.

Quite often you will hear a term of derision like *Muuryaan* (also spelt as *Mooryaan*), which has its regional variations. Not being familiar with the etymology of the word, some have traced its root to marijuana, a substance of which the youth gangs are said to be fond, given that they are drug-crazed.

Historian Sheikh Jama Hersi takes us back to the origin of these terms in a book in which he also quotes several recently composed poems about the civil war in Somalia. According to him, the word *Muuryaan* used to refer to a clutch of hunger-driven men, with no honour and no dignity, who would eat or do anything. There are regional variations, some using other contemptuous terms to describe the same phenomenon. *Muuryaan* is widely used in Mogadiscio.

In the North East, around Basaaso, *Jirri* is commonly employed, this being the name of a small bird with a pointed red beak, a bird surviving on ticks, which it picks from cattle. The people in the Shabelle regions use the term *Alalax*, known to refer to an ailing, hungry and thirsty person, presumably because of drugs taken in excess. *Alalax* is their name for the armed thugs. In the North West, however, *Dayday* is the term. This traditionally described someone with no home and no means of livelihood.

The armed rogues operated along with the *Faqash*, a term which aptly describes bent army officers out to loot, mercenaries killing for their own selfish ends. You think about any of these gangs and you think of *Bililiqo*, a compound word consisting of *balaayo* and *liqo*, the former meaning 'damnations', the latter 'swallowing up', each half alluding to the wholesale hogging of authority *à la* gangster.

Every civil conflict brings into being utter destroyers, small-time winners who consist of deviants, hoggers of the sovereignty of other citizens. These are intimidators of ordinary folk, warlords waiting in the wings of opportunism, accomplices to the rapists, arsonists and murderers. Mogadiscio has had its fair share of this lot, a motley of thugs wise in the ways of the streets, who cut deals with other gangs with unsavoury aliases.

One of the most famous groupings of youth gangs is known as *Ciyaal Faay Ali*, the Youths of Faduma Ali. These reigned in the District of Medina. Another, *Ciyaal Sikiin*, the Youths of Razor Blade (not to be confused with a gang of Israeli youths of Moroccan origin, after whom they may have been named), ran the District of Ceel Gaab. *Ciyaal Colla*, the Sniffers of Glue, operated freely anywhere in the city. The most feared gang, the Sniffers of Glue engaged in all-night orgies, sniffing heroin. As freelancers, they were commissioned to execute violence, their services available for hire to anybody willing to pay them in American dollars.

Different youth gangs operated in different regions of the land, but almost always with the approval of the armed political faction nominally in control of the area. The Mogadiscio gangs, at least in the initial stages of the civil war, operated freely and with impunity against the unarmed civilians from *the other* clans, courtesy of the United Somali Congress, the faction which chased Siyad out of Mogadiscio. Known by its acronym USC, the movement was lovingly referred to as the *Jabhadda*, an Arabic loan term meaning 'the Front'. As a political front, it propagated a radical politics in which the interests of the nation were safeguarded. The USC, given that it has never distanced itself from the doings of the youth gangs, is popularly accused of being an accomplice in the murder and looting of innocent Mogadiscians.

Its adherents speak with a forked tongue, decrying the wisdom of retribution, violence meted out to the innocent so as to punish the guilty. Every militia grouping fielded evil forces of mean-spirited thugs, gangs outwitting one another, while at the same time targeting those of other clans, in the hope of introducing a political angle to the violence. The warlords-in-waiting worked in tandem with the gangsters, creating more mayhem. Alas, the country was undone.

As luck had it I met a *Muuryaan* who had fled Mogadiscio across the border to Kenya, and who would eventually end up in Italy and then Zurich, Switzerland, where I would run into him again. However, I did not believe everything he told me; tall tales he made taller by a touch of inventiveness, I thought. A supporter of Aideed and a fighter, the youth assured me that drink, dope, *qaat*, (a mild stimulant which is chewed), women and all other earthly comforts, including accommodation in their favourite areas of the city, were several of the luxury items that were made available to him as a member of the Irregulars. And he confirmed that the *Muuryaans* were often high on an odd mixture of drinks and dope. If one was to believe him, he and his co-fighters were regularly served a mind-bending mix of several substances forbidden to a Muslim.

Insisting that I did not tape our conversation or take notes and that I held my hands on the table between us, where he could see them, he told me how he did what his peers did to dominate his fear. The first principle was to disregard everything society had taught him formally or informally. Only then, he went on, could he enter into the spirit of things, a fighter able to accomplish far in excess of what he might have achieved had he been afraid, or in contact with his moral self.

He explained that a fighter was suspect if he were sober when his mates were drunk or high on a mix of dope and drink. He would be reprimanded if he were caught asking moral questions. There was the day, for instance, when he didn't feel like raping an old woman in her mid-seventies. Penalized by the head of his cell, he was offered a young girl of five.

And when he could not bear the terrible thought of hurting the girl child, he was subject to severe beatings, the head even threatening him with rape. The only way he could bring himself to rape the girl child was to force-feed himself on a high dose of dope and alcohol. He didn't want to end up chained in a dark room for almost a week, a punishment meted out to a cousin of his, a cousin who would eventually quit the country, when the two of them fled it. I asked how he managed to escape.

He answered, 'We robbed selectively, my cousin and I, until we had enough money in hard currency, with which we bought forged documents good enough for us to use to come to Europe.'

'What are your feelings now about your *Muuryaan* days?'

'We used to say that life is a bore when you are cold sober, a monotony when not high on drugs,' he said. 'You can't tell who is good, who is bad when you are sober. You ask yourself too many moral questions and there is never an end to that.'

He went on that being sober made one doubt the rightness or wrongness of one's actions, and the self-questioning ultimately weakens one's resolve. 'You see, when I am not high on something, I wonder if I did the right thing, fleeing.' I asked, how come? He answered: 'Becoming a refugee sobers you up. And I hate this state of refugee helplessness.'

His eyes glittery with the memory of his own mischief, he now said, 'When you are high on a mix of booze and dope and you chew *qaat* for a long time and are entertained by a woman who does what you ask of her, you don't know what fear is, your thoughts are emptied of self-doubt.'

But how did they fight against better-trained armies from America or Pakistan, armies with far more sophisticated weapons, and with more facilities, more experience than they?

He replied, 'We didn't know what fear was.'

'How come?'

'We received no salary,' he said, 'we had no future, and we did what we pleased, robots robbing, and knowing no fear. We were not human. We got given more, the better we performed, and we received nothing but punishments if we did not.'

Although barely twenty-three, he understood many things clearly. He said, 'We were dissuaded from behaving in a disciplined way, and were encouraged to do crazy things now and then, maybe to underline the fact that we were different from the trained armies who, to a degree, were disciplined.'

He cursed every time he uttered the Italian word *disciplina*, as though discipline were the death of all militiamen. He went on, 'We received rewards for coming up with the most absurd ways of exploiting enemy weaknesses, so long as we executed them profitably.'

I asked what he would do if he ran into his parents.

Not flinching, he explained that he had never bothered to find out if they were dead or living and didn't care either way. If sober he wouldn't wish to see them; if high on dope, he wouldn't care! For the first time his voice shook, as if the tremor of remorse had got into it. He said, 'I have killed when I shouldn't, mutilated men and women, humiliated minors when I shouldn't. I have done them all, no regrets.'

I thought of asking him whom or what he fought for, but could not bring myself to do so. After all, I had no way of knowing how he would react if I questioned him about his loyalties. Did he owe his allegiance to the clan, a movement or a warlord?

'Will you buy me another drink?' he pleaded.

I plucked up enough courage to ask him my rehearsed questions.

Cursing, he said, 'You're a spoilsport.' He rose and left.

Then I met Zahra Omar at a friend's house. She was related on her mother's side to Aideed, a fact she stressed by repeating it. I might not have asked her what she thought of Aideed and Ali Mahdi if she had not mentioned that she knew a brother of mine, her colleague. Like him, she had worked in the Ministry of Agriculture, her office two doors away from his.

We talked a little about my younger brother, the last member of our family to quit Mogadiscio. In the course of our talk, I learnt that she would be leaving for Canada to join her man in Vancouver. I asked where she was when Mogadiscio was severed into spheres coming under the warlords' tutelage.

She said, 'We woke up to a ruthless bombardment, and before we knew it, the fate of the city had been decided. It was divided unequally between themselves.'

I asked, 'Which do you root for, Aideed or Ali Mahdi?'

'For neither.'

'Why not?'

She sought refuge in a Solomonic story about two women claiming to be the mother of the same baby. The judge, cunningly perceptive, makes what appears to be a straightforward judgement: that the baby be cut in half and each mother given one half. One of the women is horrified at the outrageous idea, the other looks set to accept her half, and raises no objections. The true mother says to the judge, 'Instead of cutting him into two dead halves, I would rather you gave him to her.' And the judge rules in her favour.

I asked, 'What are you saying in plain language?'

She replied, 'The warlords remind me of the false mother.'

I said, 'Why do they do what they do?'

This time she quoted a proverb in which it is said that a bee may get stuck in the nectar which it has come to suck, until death pays it a visit.

And what's happening to Mogadiscio?

She replied, 'A bleating city, slaughtered like a goat.'

I asked, 'What do you think about them?'

'I think of them what I think of their henchmen,' Zahra said, 'marauders who mark their territory in a manner reminiscent of dogs raising their legs and aiming their pee at a tree in the grounds which they patrol. Like the plunderers with their custom-made signatures, some defecating in the living room after taking out the looted property, others staining the walls of the houses they had disinterred with blood markings, the warlords have their symbols too.'

I said, 'Tell me something about the marauders?'

'You can't talk about the marauders,' she responded, 'without speaking at length about our recent past and our immediate present, our upstarts, middle classes and lumpen.'

All of a sudden she fell silent, in the attitude of somebody who had come on to a precarious drawbridge with no space to turn. I encouraged her forward.

Zahra Omar said, 'Nationalism with its middle-class bias is deemed to be anachronistic to the Mogadiscio lumpen and to the class from which the vigilantes are recruited. They are like untrained dogs of whom their owner has not even nominal control, mad dogs on the rampage, biting, tearing the flesh of their victims and leaving them to die. The corpses rot in the streets, but no one does anything.'

There was a long silence.

She went on without my prompting her: 'Myself, I associate the warlords with a wayward cunningness, more like that of the *ciyaal-dambiilay*, Mogadiscio's urchins. We all know the *ciyaal-dambiilay* "basket boys" and their mentality, the urchins who used to operate in the city centre as city urchins do, survival the be-all, the end-all. Numbering thousands, the urchins were in the habit of staying in the vicinity of Mogadiscio's central market, carrying a rush basket balanced on their heads. They would offer porter services to the buyers, some of whom they knew by sight, by name or reputation. Imagine the urchins taking control of the city!'

'The vigilantes are of "urchin" progeny?'

'Most of those who terrorized the residents were,' she said. 'Later, however, after the collapse of the state following Siyad's flight, the warlords imported herdsmen who were their clansmen to help them gain military supremacy, a proletariat of clan militias.'

'And everything was for grabs?' I helped her on.

Zahra Omar said, 'All civilized behaviour was outlawed, the city looted, mayhem the rule, the law. Foreign embassies were broken into, their computers falling into the hands of illiterates who had no idea what to do with them. You had a world run by "urchins".'

I asked, 'Do you think the warlords, when all is said and done, might be catalysts for Somalia, precursors of the spirit of democracy, to be enshrined in our lives once the civil strife peters out?'

Zahra Omar said, 'If you mean that no one will ever remember the warlords for any good they have done or for what they have constructed, only for what they have destroyed, yes. They are precursors of the spirits of democracy.'

'And yet they don't fight,' I said. 'Others die for them.'

She reacted thus: 'Warlords, *sui generis*, do not fight, I agree with you, they call on their henchmen to do their dirty deeds for them, or youths in their prime and who are high on drugs, who mark their entrances and exits with the wantonness of their violence. My cousin who fights for Aideed told me that he had never had it so good. When I asked what he meant he replied that it was the first time he had known Mogadiscio to open its thighs in gaping preparedness for him to penetrate.'

'What do the youths or the clan henchmen want?' I asked.

'They want what their warlords want.'

I said, 'And what do the warlords want?'

'To get the power they are after,' she said, 'the warlords draw battle lines on the shifting sands of clan self-definition. They want to rule.'

I must have looked dissatisfied, because she interrupted me, saying, 'The warlords remind me of my Mogadiscian tailor, a trickster. He had the habit of cutting up the lengths of material you brought him, and of not bothering to keep to his promises. Every time you called on him he would swear that he was planning to sew your dress. But you could never take the material away from him, knowing that no other tailor would volunteer to complete a tailoring shabbily abandoned by another. Since no two tailors cut in the same way, I had often to leave the material with him, or if I took it in anger, to return to him.'

'What are you saying?' I asked.

'I am saying that the warlords have cut up our country into segments with rough edges', she said, 'in ways that render it impossible for us to put it together again. I suppose we should ask to sew it together again. A Somali proverb says that a headache is cured by the "thing" which brought it on.'

PART II

There is a folktale about a farmer who calls on his neighbour's house to borrow a bull for his cart. Apologetic, his neighbour tells him that he cannot oblige him, because the bull is out at a friend's farm, pulling a cart. No sooner have the two men got on to another subject of mutual concern than the sound of a bull bellowing in their immediate vicinity is heard, the bellowing coming, most probably, from the bull owner's backyard.

Then the man who has come to borrow the bull asks if by any chance that is not his, the neighbour's, bull bellowing. To which the unobliging bull owner replies, either because he means to exonerate himself, or maybe because he is being mean, 'Whom do you have trust in, Sir, the bull, or its master, me?'

Chapter Three

There is a certain urgency to the lives of refugees in the first few days after they flee, as the vastness of what has been lost makes itself known to them in unprepared-for ways.

The terror of survival is all they think of, at first. They sit in groups, forming themselves into circles, with members amenable to one another; they congregate in the shade of a tree or around the brightness of a lamppost, the new totem pole of their togetherness. The refugees celebrate their sadnesses, reminiscing. They engage a million man-hours of refugee time in introspection and self-analysis; consequently they feel more depressed at the end of the day than they were when they woke up. To be a refugee is to be suicidal. Is this why a vast number of them become religiously reflective, pondering on the curse which has paid them and their country a visitation?

Much later, in the small hours of the night, in the privacy of the sleepless dark, with insomnia as their only audience, many of them divulge their secret worries only to their inner selves. This way, they take in what they have done as if unwittingly: coming round ultimately to the fact that they left Kismayo, the southern coastal city, as Somalis, and arrived in Mombasa as 'refugees'. Only four days' sea journey separates them physically from Somalia, but the distance is greater when they go over it in their memories. Perhaps by leaving Kismayo when they did and by coming, stateless, into Kenya, it is as if they have blown up the bridges linking them to their country.

The near-total absence of UNHCR staff from the Mombasa camp, especially international staff, was a topic to which many kept alluding in their deliberations with me. It was an open secret that these staff flew in from Nairobi, making their trip coincide with their weekending plans. They put up in sumptuous beach hotels, enjoying the swimming and night-clubbing facilities that were on offer. This, the refugees felt, was not only cruel, but very unprofessional. I met a Ghanaian, the head of the mission, and his Danish deputy. They both wore a 'don't harangue me' expression on their faces, discouraging the refugees from approaching them.

There were other complications. Having entered as Somalis in broad daylight and been designated as 'refugees' without the privileges attached to this definition, the Somalis could get out of Kenya only with difficulty. For they were fettered by the restrictive laws forbidding them to leave without exit permits. To get these, they would have had to visit lots of offices, grease a great number of corrupt palms. Some, I knew, contemplated leaving in the safety of darkness. These plotted their departures to the minutest details, fearful of the dire consequences if they were apprehended. For they would end up in detention.

Their movements circumscribed within the narrow perimeters of their alienness, the refugees reminded themselves often how fear, in effect, liberated them from a sense of belonging. By braving the unknown, which is the first in a series of fixed steps beginning with the idea of home and ending at the threshold of the refugee's state of mind, the Somalis made a commitment to saving their lives rather than waiting for possible death — an act that required the affirmation of self-regard, and trust in one's inviolable rights to life. To this end they came to Kenya purposefully, to live!

In Kenya, Somalis are described by government officials and in the lingo of ordinary folks as *shifta*-bandits, as poachers, a people engaged in fraudulence. I heard maladroit comments about them everywhere I went, in whatever context the name of our country was mentioned, and whenever they were sighted, standing in groups and chatting in front of a hotel, queuing up at the bureau of the Telecommunications Division from where they made international phone calls.

There was a Kenyan woman I had known for almost fifteen years, she and I having first met when she was a graduate student in hotel administration in the USA. Jeane Mugo was now the deputy manager of a four-star hotel where Somalis stayed. I looked her up when I was in Nairobi, and she and I went for a meal. In the course of our conversation, she told me of her Kenyan receptionist colleagues' friendly disposition towards me. They described me to her as 'un-Somali', which was meant to be a compliment.

'How are they seen, the Somalis?' I said.

She replied, 'They are much of a muchness, which perhaps explains why my colleagues at the reception think of you as "un-Somali". Generally speaking, they are thought to be spendthrifts both of talk and of money, wasteful, loud-mouthed and uncouth. The impression is that they have an uninterrupted supply of money in hard currency, thanks to their families' remittances from their bases in Europe or North America. Implicit in our criticism is this: Do they behave in the way someone applying for refugee status behaves?'

'And they don't?'

'We think not!'

'And they pay for everything in cash?'

'Never by cheque,' she said, 'always cash.'

I said, 'Understandably, because they haven't been here long enough to open accounts in Kenyan shillings, nor are they sure if they wish to be here a day longer than necessary.'

'It's shocking to our system though,' she said, 'that they spend their money as if there is no day after tomorrow. Some don't even bother to go over their bills; you tell them, they pay, no questions asked.'

'Maybe they are an oral people,' I commented.

'I plucked up the courage one day, and asked one of them', she said, 'how come they were all rich, while Somalia, a great deal poorer than Kenya, is collapsing. They fall into two types, the Somalis, he explained. A great number of the spendthrifts putting up in Nairobi hotels are robbers. The source of the income of this group came from the coffers of the Somali state, before Mogadiscio collapsed. Whereas those whose sources of income come from the freemasonry offerings of relatives in Europe or North America are not as wasteful. In fact, many of them are in Mombasa and other refugee camps.'

She said, 'They are so crass, almost all the Somalis.'

'In what way?'

'Their attitude towards us, as Kenyans.'

'How's that?'

'They treat us as though we were no better than the floor mat in front of their rooms,' she said. 'They are uppish. At times they look not at you but through you, with their twitchy noses astir as if disturbed by a rank odour. So!' And she demonstrated what she meant.

I kept silent.

'We can't reconcile what we know about them with what we see,' she said. 'And no matter what I say, I am highly unnerved at their behaviour, as they extend their hand to receive their keys without bothering to look you in the eyes, or to thank you when they have collected it. The wisdom circulated amongst ourselves is that your people have an attitude problem, towards other Africans.'

'Is that the general consensus?' I asked.

'If I were sure this would not strain our friendship, yours and mine, I might have said certain things,' she replied. 'Or am I to be careful lest my indictment of your people should strain our friendship?'

I assured her that nothing she said would hurt me.

She said, 'You don't require a prodigious imagination to know that they are unruly gadabouts of mean income, crass in their talk, brash in their behaviour, arrogant in their dealings with other Africans. The airs they give themselves, as they celebrate their racial identity with such loud aplomb, blazoning their looks with aristocratic attributes. You scratch deeper, and their self-complacency seldom withstands the heat of analysis, temperamental like mercury.'

'What do you mean, temperamental?'

'Envious of Kenya one instant,' she said, 'repeating time and time again how much they are enjoying the tranquillity here, and disparaging of us in the very next moment.'

I suggested that no person is more envious of those enjoying the fruits of peace than those coming from a country where there is a civil war.

'We pity the Somalis, my colleagues and I,' she said. 'But we cannot help our feeling that for a people who have brought a curse on their heads, they do not appear to have been humbled by the experience in any way.'

I was overwhelmed by the feeling that she spoke the generic name 'Somalis' as though it was descriptive of a derangement. This took me back in memory to my own youth, and to tidings pouring out of my father's eager lips as he told us tales about his own childhood in Nairobi, where he grew up, and where he might have stayed on if it had not been for a love gone to seed.

I said, 'The impression you and your colleagues have of them suggests that we are all wealthy and putting up in star-numbered hotels. Do you ever think of the ordinary ones, who, hounded out of their homes in Mogadiscio, are hopelessly wanting to reconnect, discover their way back to their sanity to recover it?'

'What about the ordinary Somalis?'

'... who are molested, deported and detained in Kenya!'

'This is a corrupt country,' she said, as if this was enough.

'A country with an attitude problem?'

She said, 'As a country and a people we have an attitude problem towards Somalis, wily shifters, cattle-rustling *shifta*-bandits, poachers, bad, bad, terribly bad! When we put together all we know about your people, which is precious little, and add to this the mean descriptions to be gleaned from the self-savaging Somalis of your Republic, and then, for effect, throw in all that we read in the Western media, the result is despicable, no doubt about it.'

I agreed that one would think that the peoples of our two countries were not neighbours, and that we had had no rapport with one another before plane- and boat-loads of Somalis fled from Mogadiscio and Kismayo to seek refuge in Mombasa and Nairobi. I asked her how much she knew about the violations of the rights of Kenyans of Somali origin, during the months of November and December 1989, when they were rounded up and made to undergo a humiliating screening exercise, ostensibly because the Kenyan government wanted to determine which Somalis were legal, and which illegal.

'I have a vague idea,' she said.

'Why have Kenyans never concerned themselves with what their government is doing to the Somalis?'

'I will admit I haven't concerned myself,' she said. 'It is as though we were dealing with another country, like somewhere else. We pay little attention to it, maybe because the Somalis are not relevant to our anxieties, and many of us do not have friends among them. I am ashamed about our lack of concern.'

I remarked that she did not look me in the eyes when she spoke.

She went on, 'Maybe we agreed in part with the propaganda our government puts out: that you can't tell apart the Kenyan Somalis who are legal from the newly arrived illegal Somalia Somalis from across the border. But we have no right to harass those already with Kenyan papers and passports, or submit them to an exercise meant to humiliate them as a group. We should err on the side of justice, and perhaps not bother distinguishing Kenyans into two categories, one of them always a second-class citizen. But then I can understand the Kenyan's worry about Somalis who, as a general rule, inspire us with fear, with self-doubt, with racial hate.'

For her benefit and for mine too, I went over the details of what happened in 1989. I explained that fifty-odd checkpoints were set up across Kenya, and all ethnic Somalis over the age of eighteen were required to present themselves with their national identity cards, a passport, if they had one, together with their birth certificate within a period of three weeks, and no later. Anyone who failed to be screened was subject to arrest and detention. A 'Somali Probe Committee' to produce a secret registry of all Somalis in Kenya was established in the President's Office, with the cooperation of the Immigration Department.

'Remind me,' she said, 'how did we come to that?'

I explained that, in a bid to wipe out of existence the Somali Patriotic Movement (SPM), the militia movements at war with Siyad's regime, the army attacked its bases. Following a confrontation between the militia movement and the army, several hundred civilian non-combatants fled the fighting into Kenya. The refugees were subsequently infiltrated by pro-Siyad elements, who engaged in banditry within Kenya. The refugees were deported in their hundreds into Somalia. This being what Siyad wanted, it was felt that President Moi wished to give *carte blanche* to his fellow president, who invaded the SPM bases. Again, people fled. And Siyad sent his soldiers across the border, to engage in further banditry. Kenya reacted by setting up a screening policy to identify the origin of all Somalis. That meant that all ethnic Somalis, including those whose territory lay in Kenya and who were Kenyans, by right, were reduced by this discriminatory decree to humiliated second-class citizenship.

She asked, 'And the result of all this?'

'All Somalis are to produce, on demand, a red card to security personnel,' I said, 'cards reminiscent of apartheid, cards meant to distinguish the Somali-Kenyan from all other Kenyans. Do you recall how the British colonial government annexed the Somali territory then called Northern Frontier District to Kenya in 1961? Or that these voted in an overwhelming majority to join the Republic? You see, since then the North Eastern Province has been under a sort of state of emergency, run by Kenya's security.'

'It seems', she said, appearing disturbed, 'that the destinies of our two countries have been woven into one another via a webbed history of entanglements, the way a history linking two colonized peoples is plaited with ruses of colonial motivation.'

As she gave me a lift to my hotel, Jeane Mugo asked, 'Tell me what the Somalis say about us?'

I said, 'They believe that you Kenyans are neither magnanimous in your offer of hospitality to refugees, nor are you noble in your generalizations. And that you think the worst of all Somalis, whom you believe are either loaded and arrogant, or poor refugees and corrupt.'

'Do you think they are not bellicose?' she said, with a touch of mischief in her tone of voice. 'Or not quick to pick quarrels with one another, clan against clan? Or as a government with the neighbouring countries, now with Ethiopia, now with Kenya?'

'Read your history!' I suggested.

'Which history would you advise me to read, yours or ours?'

'Let's say', I said, 'that history between neighbours is a living thing, more like a festering wound, runny with pus, without chance of ever healing. In Somali, we have a proverb: that the closest to each other are the tongue and the teeth and even they fight.'

'I agree with you that our history was determined by a third party,' she said, 'the colonialists. Until the 1960s, the authority of the entire region was not in the hands of the Somalis or the peoples of Kenya, but the British and the Italians, the one ruling Kenya, the other Somalia, colonial oligarchies with a licence to decide for us. As Kenyans, we are catholic in the inviolability of the boundaries bequeathed to us. This makes our history richer in controversy and contradictions. But we ought to treat our Somali-speaking population with the same dignity we treat all other citizens. For your part, you ought to give up your claims to what is essentially an inalienable segment of our land. Now,' she paused, 'tell me, why did the screening disturb you so?'

I replied, 'Because, from then on, it determined the future status of all Somalis. Do you wonder why we feel uncomfortable in your country?'

'I don't mean to be insensitive,' she said, 'but I am confident that the Kenyan Somalis are nowadays counting their blessings, grateful to their lucky stars that they did not join your Republic. One of them, an acquaintance of mine, put it succinctly when he lamented, "What a sorrowful way for a country to go!" Let us hope our own country does not go the way yours has.'

Perhaps because I knew where the Somalis were coming from, I could tell, in a matter of minutes, the refugees apart from the upstarts and the middle-class category of Somalis who were using Kenya as a halfway house between Somalia and their places of refuge, in North America or Europe. Most of the refugees were poor villagers, or migrants from the hinterland, semi-literate, uncultured in the ways of cities and at home among the disenfranchised. They were hopelessly uprooted, as if a sense of alienation had lain in wait to ambush them, a feeling of unbelonging accentuated by their cast-me-downs, their nails dirty and dwarfish, skin parched, their gazes highly unfocused. Sad-looking, they appeared uncared for, unloved. Those of upstart provenance, with connection to the deposed Siyad oligarchy, were altogether a different matter. These would display a sense of thrill, like a child discovering a bodily function. And the spoilt children they were, they enjoyed Nairobi as if they were on a weekend outing. They threw jokes as expensive as a delicatessen at one another.

Somewhere in between were the Somalis of the educated, middle-class variety. These were quieter, working on ways of getting out of Kenya. They lay low, seldom broadcasting their intentions. They stood the horrid conditions of the camps, or if in Nairobi gave themselves time to gather their fragmented selves, as they planned their next move. Some were busy arranging for a safe way out on a sponsorship scheme to destinations in North America or some other intermediary European stopping-off point. They were on the threshold of a new life, and they knew it. Somalia did not always form part of their future imaginings.

It was unsettling to meet them. It was unnerving to interview them. Their eminence of mind on occasion went no further than air tickets or visas to enable them to leave, their destination 'Anywhere but Kenya!' or 'Anything but a refugee.' The absence of choice was implicit in the hopelessness of their condition, a condition consequent upon the urgency of their cry for help.

They kept Mogadiscio afloat in their memories of it.

And a river of stories poured out, their memory flowing out of their mouths with the zigzag downward motion of a kite with a broken string. The rivers of those not quite certain of the ground rules ran dry of tales as soon as you came, maybe because they had no wish to share their views with someone who was from a different clan.

Meeting many whom I had known before made me only too aware that a lot had changed in the twenty-odd years I had been away from Mogadiscio. For there was now a generation of illiterates known as 'Siyad's children', a species of layabout youths spoilt to the core, morally wicked to the marrow, arrogant to a person, good-for-nothing lazybones. These contrasted with their age-mates who swelled the ranks of the youth gangs in Mogadiscio. Both groups were known as '*Keen!*', in reference to their constant use of the word 'Give!' Outside Mogadiscio, these youths kept asking for more things; in Mogadiscio, serving as members of an irregular militia, they robbed.

There was also the generation in their late twenties and early thirties, go-getting, ambition-driven men and women lording over falsehoods, lickspittles prepared to clean up the political mess others had created as long as their needs were met. These were different from the generation in their fifties. Reared on a diet of nationalism, this otherwise kosher generation lost their faith in nationhood, because Siyad used them, then abused them. They now headed armed movements, their nationalist aspirations of yore reduced to a memory, disowned.

As I moved between these groups, I thought about how Somalis seemed drawn to one another in the attitude of two dogs sniffing at each other's whatnots. You saw them in a huddle, speaking in conspiratorial whispers. When you met them a second time, they were sworn enemies, shunning one another like needles. Their distant stares focused on a distant land, their attention centred on the lure of peace and prosperity elsewhere, any place that was sufficiently peaceful for them to unremember Somalia.

Why some ended up in Nairobi and some in Mombasa depended to a large extent on the mode of transport by which they arrived. The wealthier ones flew into Nairobi; the poorer travelled by boat to Mombasa. I flew into Nairobi, from Kampala, where I was based. And then went overland to Mombasa.

Chapter Four

Mombasa was founded by Omani Arab traders in the eleventh century. Since then it has had more than any other Kenyan city's fair share of aliens, coming, seeing it and conquering it, or being conquered by it. Ibn Batutta, the fourteenth-century Arab chronicler, is among its notable visitors; so is Vasco da Gama, who, in 1498, tried to bring the Portuguese into its trade potential.

I too was conquered by it, once I got to know it better. I was lucky to have been introduced to the Mazrui family, who took excellent care of me. A nephew of Ali's fed me, provided me with all the help that I required, including ferrying me to and from my appointments, and plying between my hotel and the Utange refugee camp. In the city, I was heartened to watch these most cosmopolitan of Africans going about their business in a peaceable manner, and to listen to them as they engaged my fellow nationals in friendly banter.

Mombasa changed hands several times. At one time, it fell to the Persians, then the Portuguese and, in 1840, to the Turks. A sister state in more ways than one to Mogadiscio, it too was under the sovereignty of the Sultan of Zanzibar. The two city states accounted for a great deal of the cosmopolitan market specializing in the transit of goods to Arabia and India. The Zanzibari suzerain first leased Mogadiscio to the Italians in 1892, and in 1895 sold Mombasa to Britain, which made it the capital of the East African Protectorate until 1907, when the headquarters of the administration was moved to Nairobi, until then a mere colonial railway settlement.

One of Africa's most pleasant cities, Mombasa has a very long cosmopolitan tradition, boasting a Portuguese-constructed Fort Jesus, now a museum, and Anglican and Roman Catholic cathedrals, not forgetting a Hindu temple with a gilded dome. To cater for the largest concentration of Muslims in Kenya, the city has an extensive number of mosques, plus a lavish touch of pronounced Arab architecture, a maze of alleyways and a most impressive set of tall buildings with carved ornamental balconies.

Mombasa's trade links with the peoples of the Somali coast go back a long way, to the twelfth century, when the city states were engaged in a three-way commerce with Arabia and India, trade within their respective hinterlands and trade among themselves. If Mombasa as a port developed faster, it is because the British were determined to compete with and eventually outdo the German East African colony of Tanganyika, now Tanzania, in trade. As a result of this rivalry, the British imported Indian labourers to link Kenya by railway to Uganda.

Mombasa sits on a coralline island in a bay in the Indian Ocean, and is joined to the mainland territory by causeway, ferry and also bridge. The refugee camp where the Somalis are housed is located outside the city centre, near a village called Utange.

Only once did I travel overland between Nairobi and Mombasa, a distance of some 480 kilometres, the road narrow and potholed, the countryside drab, monotonous and hot. There were many checkpoints, each offering justification for the Kenya police to raise twice or thrice the equivalent of their monthly salary from the Somalis they intimidated. I was very much exercised by what I heard or saw, exercised like a man troubled by something about which he could do nothing.

I sat way in the back, across from a Somali couple and their two children who, for some reason, appeared ill at ease every time the bus stopped, and we were told to get down and stand in a queue to be bodily frisked, our identities inspected, luggage searched. Without fail, the man would be taken away, now into the bushes and now into a police vehicle, and he would be gone for some time. I was sure he was being worked over, and would be released after payment of a tribute to his Kenyan captors. Every so often, he emerged looking the worse for sorrow, and displaying physical stress.

What was it that made them pick on him?

I was travelling on a Somali passport with a visa issued at the airport. In addition to a Makerere University identity card, giving me the title of 'professor', I had my residence in Uganda. I never found out why they did not pick on me, or why after locking eyes with me they returned my papers, as though apologizing.

I knew that most of my fellow travellers, being asylum-seekers, had no papers, and the Kenya police at the checkpoints seldom bothered themselves with them. But why this man? The woman accompanying him shrugged her shoulders, giving away no information to the curious inquisitors who, from the way they asked her questions or the way they looked at her, were dying to know the background of the man in whom the police were interested.

At one point he got back in, appearing roughed up. It was then I introduced myself. He recognized my name, and told me that he was travelling on a genuine US passport, and was escorting his widowed sister-in-law and her children to Mombasa for them to be registered with the UNHCR and the local authorities of the camp as asylum-seekers. I gathered that registering with the UNHCR was a prerequisite to their papers being processed for resettlement in the States. Curiously, the policemen were making life difficult for him because, believing his documents to be forgeries, and assuming at any rate that he was sufficiently loaded to get himself out of trouble, they would insist that he pay, and he wouldn't. I asked him for his thoughts, and he said, 'A Somali in Kenya, whether with or without papers, has no option but to be humiliated or to bribe. Now look at the way they bow to the American to your left.' I did. That the Kenyans treated the white youth deferentially did not escape my notice. No more than twenty, and most likely doing Africa on the cheap, he was bowed to by every Kenyan. It was absurd how, without fail, they addressed him as 'Sir', whereas all we got was a 'You, there!', index finger pointedly wagging, voice a notch up the ladder of indifference to our status or age.

From the bus depot in Mombasa, I took a taxi to Manor Hotel, where I put up. The hotel had the formal air of the colonial era, the manager extending to me much warmer hospitality on discovering that I was a friend of Professor Ali Mazrui, Mombasa's most famous native son.

After a decidedly hot, long shower, a taxi arrived to take me to the Utange refugee camp in Mombasa, where my father, my son, my nephew and my sister had their allotted space in a rooming set-up, a maze of ill-designed facilities organized along the lines of gender, family affiliation and age-group.

It took a lot longer than I had imagined for the Mombasa city authority to decide if I could move my family out of the camp and into rented accommodation in town. Not wanting to break the law of the land meant that I had to go back and forth between various local and central government authorities, from a low-ranked corporal at the refugee camp, to Mombasa's Deputy Commissioner, and right up to the Permanent Secretaries of the Ministry of Foreign and Internal Affairs. For I wanted my son to resume his university education in Nairobi, wished my nephew to find an Arabic-language school in Kenya. I was of a mind to free my sister from the responsibility of looking after our father, so she could pursue her professional career as a nutritionist. I had a hard time, and accomplished little on all fronts.

As I sat in the taxi going to the camp, I thought how much remarkable change Mombasa had undergone since the first lot of fleeing Mogadiscians came to it a couple of months back. The Somalis were now a feature of the town, you saw them everywhere, a frontispiece to this ancient, many-doored city. The Mombasans, as a people, were now keyed up as though in earnest for a future which was far more outreaching in its boldness than anything they had done. If only ... !

For the government of Kenya and the people of Mombasa were not of like minds, at least not in the early days when the first boatloads of Somalis arrived. Because of this, there was something temporary about the Somalis' presence in Mombasa. Many might have made the city their permanent place of residence had they been given the option to do so, and if they could find a self-sustaining way of remaining a Somali-speaking island mass in a rugged humanity of Kenyans. Mogadiscians and Mombasans are by nature as well as inclination rumbustious in their dealings with one another, loving and hating, the consequence of pique with the habits of a neighbour one does not know well. A proverb has it that by not departing while you are still welcome, as a guest you begin to smell like rotten fish after three days.

My arrival in the refugee camp caused unprecedented stirrings. I suppose people in the camp assumed that, just because I had come from the larger world, I knew more about the happenings than they did. At the time, the news had broken about a boat with several hundred Somalis from Kismayo, which was not allowed to dock. My questioners had no knowledge that this was all news to me, as the tragedy had unfolded during the hours I had been on the road. In fact I had less information than those huddled around the radio, who now confirmed that women and children were suffering greatly, some fainting and dying, others on the verge of starvation.

'To flee a city in the siege of a strife,' said my sister, 'and then try to dock in a harbour where you're not welcome and where you are humiliated: this defines the sad state of a refugee's life. I didn't know Mombasans could be so indifferent to the sufferings of fellow Africans, who are also fellow Muslims.'

I thought to myself that the fact that the boat was not permitted to dock pointed to the otherness of the new arrivals from Kismayo. There was a time early on when Mombasans felt more hospitable towards the fleers of Mogadiscio's strife, but things were taking a different turn now that politicians and non-politicians alike were airing their opinions on the topic. The time had come for the 'refugees' to be blamed for the city authority's failings to deal with all manner of shortages. If a cutpurse ran off with a tourist's handbag and he was not caught, this was blamed on the Somalis. There was so much ill-feeling that the Somalis were accused of being the thieves, the rapists, etc.

They remained on the boat for a good week, the newly arrived refugees, as troupes of briefcase-carrying UNHCR executive men went back and forth, from the boat to the Police Commissioner, as telexes were sent back and forth between Mombasa and Nairobi, as the Head of State was consulted on the matter. Meanwhile, several women were delivered of dead babies, and the sick became sicker, the needy needier. Hopeless, helpless but angry, the Somalis in the camp waited for their fellow nationals to be authorized to disembark. The truth lay hidden in the unsaid: the Kenyan government was squeezing as much as it could out of the UN bodies for hosting the newly arrived 'boat people', whom it didn't accept as refugees.

There was a solemn silence among the Somalis, their language having failed to cope with this indescribable sorrow. In their quiet, I imagined them to be mourners awaiting the delivery of a dead body wrapped in their country's flag, a corpse in a hearse, ready to be interred. In their peregrinations, the carriers of the hearse were not to put it down or even stop anywhere, because the authorities had not assigned it a grave in which to be buried.

Now I made note of a question in my mind: How well do Somalis know their country and its people? I doubted that they knew Europe, other parts of Africa or the Middle East, where many would end up if they couldn't get where they intended. I put these questions to my sister.

She replied, 'Not knowing your country is what dictatorship does to you.'

'What other evils does dictatorship do to you?'

'Dictatorships alter the character of the disenfranchised.'

'In what way?'

She said, 'You are like a concubine, who is deferential to her paymaster, but insolent to all the others without the wherewithal to corrupt her.'

Whereas some of the refugees were determined to find a useful occupation on which to focus their minds, some were not blessed with that sort of noble resolve. But then, some vocations are easier than others to pursue in the absence of a purse. Film-making is a very expensive affair.

I met Abdulaziz Sheikh in Utange. He was one of Somalia's well-known cineastes, and I had last seen him editing a documentary in a cubicle in London's Soho. I asked him if he was thinking of making a film about his experience as a refugee in Kenya.

He said, 'It's virtually impossible to hold a thought long enough in your mind and to develop it creatively in the horrid conditions of a refugee camp. As you may know, it was not easy to make worthwhile documentaries during those last few years in Mogadiscio, because one was not entirely in touch with one's sense of self. Because, in Mogadiscio, I was preoccupied for a greater part of the day or night with my own survival and my family's, living on a pittance of a salary. I read somewhere, I cannot recall where, that if you live in a country where starving is commonplace, you begin to think often about food, you dream about food, you wake up with food on your mind.'

'You are thinking about peace, now that you don't have it?'

He said, 'I fled in an overcrowded boat to come here, fetched up with the refugee's folly, and with the reflection of our failures, abandoned as we are on the shores of our misfortune. And ever since landing here, I've been going over in my mind many thoughts, which are to do with this: that what happens to nations and to the cities serving as their citadels is no different from what happens to you or me, when we wake up one morning, and decide, knowing not why, that there is no point in getting out of bed any more.'

'Is that what you're thinking now?'

'I am thinking, how do I alter my miserable condition?'

'And how will you?'

'I'm working on several options. I suppose you could say that all my waking thoughts are subordinated to the ambition of getting out of *this* refugee camp before becoming irreparably damaged. I catch myself imagining myself happy with my family and my children playing joyfully as contented children, and planning a documentary.'

'Why did you flee?'

'We fled, I think,' he said, 'because Mogadiscio was emptying, and we didn't want to be caught up in the battle for its control. We saw our friends and families packing, and we couldn't think of a good enough reason to stay. So we took off.'

'Any idea what would have happened if you had stayed?'

'Maybe we would've been killed.'

'Or maybe not?'

He considered that for a long while. He said, 'Then we would have had to bear the awesome responsibility of first pronouncing our beloved country dead, and then of burying it. It is possible that we fled because we did not wish to perform the final rites of Somalia's internment.'

'Will you ever go back?'

'Go back?' From the way he spoke the two words, you would have thought that he did not know what the words meant. He thought for a long time, not speaking.

'Will you?'

'There is no "country" to return to, is there?'

'Why, whatever has become of Somalia?'

'Chaos, anarchy, rape, insane deaths, internecine madness.'

'But why run?' I asked. 'Why did you not get yourself a gun, and fight it out to the bitter end, in a bid to preserve your family honour, protect your properties against the madness all round, even in the name of a clan? Why leave one uncertainty, with which you might have coped, for another equally ugly uncertainty: that of exile, or of becoming refugees, or migrating to another land?'

He said, 'No matter what our starting point may have been, some of us have lived a semblance of a middle-class life, with no room for the kind of anarchy which turned the whole country into a casualty. But the anarchy in Mogadiscio was so extensive no number of hired guns would have saved us. It was everyone for himself, with frightened people fleeing in self-contained family units abandoning their homes for the armed gangs to loot them. We count ourselves among the lucky ones, because we were not harmed physically; and in Mombasa we have gained a timely refuge. I can think of many who did not make it to the boats, or could not afford the steep prices calculated in US dollars and in cash. Some drowned.'

He had known a couple of the UNHCR staff, then based in Kenya, former Western colleagues with whom he had worked in Somalia in his capacity as a documentarist. It was curious how those with whom he had been acquainted before never bothered to look him up in Mombasa. Putting up in luxury hotels with extensive swimming and other extra-mural facilities, no wonder they didn't remember ever knowing him.

At his own prompting Abdulaziz Sheikh explained, 'A state may be said to have collapsed when power and the wealth accrued to it is not distributed on the basis of a high standard of social justice to all, but according to a primitive plebeian plan, along clan lines. We are the casualties of a collapsed state, victims of an accident of history. I am not at all surprised that these foreign friends have not bothered to look me up. We cannot be worth more than our country, a nation at a low ebb, in inordinate disorder. As things worsen and as more and more of us pour outwards, fleeing, we shall have become the proverbial mendicant with no friends among the well fed. A nation in distress is accorded no respect among other nations.'

'I cannot imagine you not wanting to return,' I said.

He said, 'By the time I do, if I do, the country will have changed its character, and status too. And I will have become another person altogether, changed with my altered conditions, conscious that I am no longer invited as an equal. The civil war has marked us for life, reducing us to lowly thoughts in other people's minds. You mention the name of Somalia, and foreigners think, so that is anarchy, man-made famine and infamy!'

'Did you ever think this might happen to Somalia?'

He answered, 'I was privileged enough to travel out of the country and see for myself what was taking place in our country with the experienced eyes of a journeyer returning. And I worked with foreigners, who, although they may not have a very deep understanding of our condition, observe things from a different perspective. Things were really bad before they became very, very, very bad, and then suddenly collapsed into total anarchy.'

'Did you share your worries with others whom you trusted?'

He spoke slowly, with a cynical smile at the edge of his mouth, 'You saw Mogadiscio and imagined the proverbial mad dog with the clanking tin tied to its tail, a dog stoned, unloved, hungry and uncared for. One knew the end was closing in, only one did not anticipate it to be so self-destructive.'

I asked, 'What do you think has become of our enfabled self-image, the only country, etc., etc., unique in Africa bla bla bla, a land with a homogeneous people having one language and culture, one religion. What went wrong?'

All he said was, 'When too many persons are impassioned about something, whatever this may be, a kind of war erupts. That is what has gone wrong.'

I felt dissatisfied with his answer, and I said so.

He said, 'If you are asking, what are the features which brought forth the civil war in Somalia, the list is endless: centuries-old injustices; decades-old political feuds; Siyad's tyrannical state, and its indifference to the ordinary people's genuine grievances; the nature of post-colonial set-ups. Suffice it to say that these may be some of the reasons why high principles have been pushed aside and why, in their place, people have begun putting their faith in the pornography of a warlord's rhetoric, holding forth and reciting chapters and verses of clan mythography. Civil wars do not wait for reasons. They erupt, they happen, and may the rest be damned.'

INTERLUDE

I will not serve what I no longer believe in ... silence, exile and cunning.
James Joyce

Chapter Five

For various reasons which I hope eventually to go into, it seems appropriate to mention that for a little under twenty five years I have dweltd in the dubious details of a territory I often refer to as the country of my imagination. I find it daunting to attempt to explain or elaborate why I've had to weave a country out of the intricate web of a need, why I've felt that the construction of this country was necessary through a score of troubled years. For one thing, I've had to parley with my anxiety all these troubled years; for another, I cannot help assuming that it would be something close to a miracle to get across the workings of such a denizen's mind in an idiom accessible to other people, many of whom have always lived in the same place, who live where they were born, who have resided in a country with a physical existence as prominent as the international boundary lines on a map.

Maybe such communication seems difficult because I've always considered countries to be no more than working hypotheses, portals opening on assumptions of loyalty to an idea, allegiance to the notion of a nation: a people pledging their eternal vows to a locality which happens to be where they were born and which they choose to call home, a place with whose climate, physical geography and vegetation they are familiar. Alternatively, one may pledge allegiance to another, equally valid idea: a putative idea, a hypothesis brought forth by a dream, something to do with one's ambition; the seed-bed of migration; a wealthier probability for one's own economic self-improvement, for one's family's well-being or for one's immediate safety. During the long travel out of one hypothesis to another, one journeys further away from one's self. And somewhere between fleeing and arriving at the new destination, a refugee is born: who in effect is the citizen of a country too amorphous to be favoured with a name but one delivered out of the womb of sublime hope, a country whose not yet spoken language is imbued with the rhetoric of future visions.

I ask what becomes of a person – indeed what becomes of a people – when the country-as-a-hypothesis ceases to function. How full of tragedy, how full of inexpressible agony is the instant when it dawns on one that one's country does not exist any more, either as an idea or as a physical reality! I can remember when Somalia, the country of my birth, became dead to me in the construct of my logic, like a postulate that has been discarded. In that instant I felt at once displaced and incredulous, as though a mirror had broken. Eventually I would ask myself if on account of what had taken place, I became an*other*.

I remember standing in a flat in Rome and holding a dead telephone receiver in my hand. I was leaving for home, and had rung my elder brother in Mogadiscio, requesting that somebody please pick me up at the airport; he advised me not to return. His words have stayed with me: 'Forget Somalia, consider it buried, dead, think of it as if it no longer exists for you!' A few minutes later, still clutching the dead telephone receiver, I felt as though something live was surging up from inside of me: in that moment another country was fired into existence, a new country with its own logic and realities. Born of psychic necessity, this new country stole in upon my senses as quietly as a moth approaching the lit window to one's world, quietly, like the moth of my sanity. And this moth became of necessity a butterfly, circling the crystallizing fruit of my exile: an exile which perforce jump-started the motor of my imaginative powers.

Still, I must ask what becomes of a man or a woman upon whose sense of imaginative being, upon whose night, no moths tap at the window to the universe of his or her creativity. What if, at the portal of one's cosmos, no imagined fruit is given a crystalline form and no butterfly pays a visit? What becomes of any man or woman whose economic and professional position does not afford the privilege to create another country out of his or her sense of displacement? In other words, what happens to a people who cannot go back to the hypothetical reality of their homes, nor to their actual residences? Is this the clay out of which refugees are moulded?

Given the suddenness of the decision that had been imposed on me, I wondered if I would manage to cope, an African writer stranded in Europe, just thirty and barely known outside his 'former' country. I found myself combing the arid brush of my memory, recalling my young years in the hope that these might somehow help me better to see my predicament; I had hailed from a region in the Horn of the continent with a history of tumultuous dislocations, a region that has known more years of civil strife than it has stability and peace. And I remembered: I remembered how my family was caught up in a war of attrition between Somalia and Ethiopia; remembered how my whole family had fled across a border whose existence we, Somalis, had refused to acknowledge; remembered how in Mogadiscio, our new place of refuge, we started to reconstitute our identities from an idealism that had its ideological correlates in a sense of nationalism. At the time the newly minted idea of the nation was in the heart of all Somalis, and none of the recent arrivals from the war zone were treated as refugees: we were welcomed most warmly as though we had *come home*. (In those days all Somali nationals had the birthright to claim citizenship in the newly constituted Republic, which had not recognized the frontiers between itself and Kenya or Ethiopia.) As I reminisced I recalled the games of invention I had played in my youth: how, as a boy, I would mentally assume animal forms, metamorphosing into new states – birds, crocodiles, lions and snakes. I wondered if I could hold triple citizenship, migrate from one country to another – from that of my birth, say, to that territory newly fired into existence by the need to remain loyal to the ideals of the writer's vocation, and thence from there to the Rome, my new home. Thanks to the kind intercessions of friends I was able to fulfil the obligations of my triple citizenry, with the moth flying here and there, its shadows falling on the window to my creative energy, past the opaqueness of a writer's self-doubts.

It was during this period of self-questioning that I ran into an old friend of mine from Denmark, to whom I explained all that had taken place, adding that I intended to keep my country alive by writing about it. My Danish friend was of the opinion that no matter what the economic, political or asylum status of a novelist – whether he or she has papers or not – a writer is no refugee. We parleyed, she and I, and agreed on defining a refugee as a person who has lost the ability to express the fullness of his or her nature, and who flees across borders if necessary in order to articulate the essence of his or her being, his or her human nature.

Perhaps the year I was born had a turning-point influence on the question of Somali identity, and hence nationality – the question of a Somali's future status in the world. I was born in the southern town of Baidoa, which remained for a good number of decades in Italian hands, although the whole southern portion of the Somali-speaking peninsula would go to the victor in the Great War, the British whose army defeated the Mussolini-misled Italians. In a matter of months the colours of the triumphant colonial power would be hoisted to replace that of the vanquished, in a farcical game of vaudeville preposterousness. And whenever the European powers were absent from the scene, the Ethiopians would resolve into a tangible presence, heavily armed, to exact tribute. They ran the imperial show, an empire fielding famished soldiers in moth-eaten uniforms, ready to loot. Because so many flags flew in the Peninsula, our Somaliness became prefixed with a hyphenated identity: British

Somaliland, Italian Somaliland, French Somaliland, Ethiopian Somaliland. Then, in the early 1960s, another hyphenated identity came into being: Kenyan Somaliland. Two years after my birth my father would leave for the Ogaden, where he worked as an interpreter for the British administration running the affairs of the Somali-speaking region, and my family would stay in that area when the British quit. I've often compared the status of my nationality and that of my cultural as well as political identity to that of a Triestine who had become part of the Ottoman Empire, and then the Magyar-Austrian one and eventually a Yugoslav or an Italian, depending on who invaded the city; or to the Kurd who had to contend with the total absence of the hyphen, and therefore his Kurdishness. And what of the Palestinian Arab, with whose refugee status I became acquainted very early on in my life, when a number of them sought refuge in the riverine town in the Ogaden where I was growing up? Kallafo's townspeople managed to raise funds to help these destitutes. I may have been too young to comprehend the complexities of the Palestinian dislocation, although I could discern and sympathize with the immense tragedy of their plight; as a Somali I could identify with their loss of pride and identity. It was probably then that I started to think of a person's country dying inside him or her long before the individual is legally described as a refugee. (I've often wondered what became of the boys of the three Palestinian families with whom I was acquainted; or their older sister, whom a Yemeni from our town fell in love with, the Yemeni going insane when these families left for elsewhere.)

I came to understand that colonial subjects die a kind of death when they lose the birthright to define themselves in the terms of their birth, as they are made to respond to the multiple identities imposed upon them by others: when they are forced to see themselves as someone else's invention. We've all borne witness to the events currently unfolding in the region, the tragic civil strife, the cut-throat savagery. Indeed, we've seen the typical neo-colonial reaction to the complexities of the nationality question, as the Kenyan government created refugees both within and without its borders with policies inspired by a crude form of racism based on ethnicity. There is a perverse ingenuity to these invented identities, the malefic effects of which can often go unnoticed for great stretches of time. Only when things go awry do people take notice: whether in the Middle East or the former Yugoslavia, in the Indian subcontinent or the Somali-speaking peninsula.

Whenever or wherever new empires are created in place of old ones, a mass of humanity necessarily are made refugees. The Kurd, the Somali, the Cambodian, the Vietnamese, the Tamil-speaking Sri Lankan and the Palestinian share a common condition: their peoples have all been coerced into becoming part of an empire, and then cast off, and recast again as a new empire is constructed in place of the one that has been dismantled.

In drawing arbitrary imperial borders, builders of empires create a network of political and economic tensions, with a legacy both explosive and implosive. I do not have to remind anyone of how in the Horn of Africa the implosive nature of the crisis helped to engender tensions among the different nationalities in the region; how the explosive tendency of the conditions would every now and then prevail, bursting outward in a full-scale war between countries. The 1977 war between Somalia and Ethiopia claimed at least two and a half million lives in squabbles over the Ogaden; a great many more were displaced, swelling the statistics of the dislocated, both in the two countries and outside the artificial frontiers.

I would further suggest that the histories of tension-ridden empire constructions obscure crucial questions of agency as well as responsibility. Can we surmise the state of affairs between Somalia and Ethiopia on the one hand, and Somalia and Kenya on the other, had they not been soured over the boundary lines inherited from, and drawn by, the European powers?

Cast in the role of a belligerent expansionist, and incapable of asserting his or her identity — that is, his or her humanity — Somali is pitted against Somali in the internalized combustion, that vast implosion which produced Siyad's tyrannical regime, and its sorry aftermath. The authority to define relationships, name areas after royalties or a so-called discoverer, the authority to draw lines dividing peoples: these powers rested with the Europeans who defined our identities for a long time. But we've had thirty-odd years of flag independence and have failed in constructing our own images in ways with which we are delighted.

This makes the European world only partly responsible for the African continent's failures in liberating itself from the neo-colonial bondage. In forming an unhealthy alliance with the empire builders, the Africans — actors in their own right — have struck a deal with the devil within and that without. Of course, there were intimations of the disaster to come, of the conflicts that would take place twenty or so years after 'independence'. In the same way that Africans of different cultures and languages were often put together by empires concerned solely with wealth, one might argue that the Somali people were held apart by that same imperial greed. Ironically, the Organization of African Unity (OAU) never challenged the arbitrariness of these frontiers, and now, owing to popular sectional sentiment in the north of Somalia, the supreme craftsmanship of the European empire has been vindicated. For the border between the former Italian and British Somalilands would run precisely where it used to when the two Somali-speaking territories were colonies of Italy and Britain.

In Somalia, language is the linchpin of identity. The British Empire ran its East African possessions together as though they were one economic concern. The southern part of Somalia, which bordered this region, was not linked to that world, nor did Mogadiscio have anything to do with the Somali-speaking northern region known otherwise as the Protectorate of British Somaliland, or with the Ethiopia-administered Ogaden or for that matter with the French-held two-nation state, nowadays the Republic of Djibouti, but once upon a time known as French Somaliland.

Eastern Africa has not experienced empires of the scale of those in North and West Africa. Even a miniature empire – say, that of Shaka – was more expansive than any imperial venture in East Africa, which perhaps explains why there was no *lingua franca* until the British imposed Swahili. In the south of the Sudan, beyond the reach of the Arabic-speaking empire, there is a proliferation of Babels of every manner, dialectal tonality and description. The very idea of empire, it seems to me, is based on question of identity, whether at the rhetorical, philosophical or cultural level. It is no accident that we are heirs to the linguistic hegemony of those who at one time in the past were or are presently at the helm of empires. Nor do these tongues cease to occupy a central position in the lives of those who speak them, even after the total disintegration of the empire.

It has become increasingly obvious of late that the world is going through a radical transformation, and that these profound changes are making us take a fresher look at ourselves and our neighbours as everything falls around our ears. We cannot take anything for granted any more. Most strikingly, one sees in the expressions of one's interlocutors a distinct unease, the tincture of distrust. Values of humanity and decency, the humane principles which have held many a community together the world over, are increasingly devalued. New times have brought along new anxieties for many of us. An ugly temper is rising across the West European capitals, as a sense of gloom, paranoia and unjustified dread unsettles these citadels. The newspapers describe the 'human flood', tributaries of asylum-seekers, rivers of refugees, flotillas of boat-people, ramshackle rafts bearing bogus men and women arriving at European ports of entry in search of a haven, as immigrants or refugees.

Twenty-seven years ago the British Conservative Enoch Powell warned that increasing immigration would lead to 'rivers of blood'; we listen today, with the same predictable horror, to the ugly noises coming out of respectable quarters of France and Germany, not to mention the rhetoric of the neo-fascists and their acts of savagery, as they throw petrol bombs at specially designated hostels housing asylum-seekers to intimidate them. The presence of these migrants touches on the political and economic anxieties of the so-called developed parts of the globe, anxieties that are spectacular in their far-reaching implications. These fears are comparable to those of the beginning of the twentieth century, ironically the very period when the legal shape of the present-day world was determined, the period when the undeveloped world was divided into unequal portions among European powers, boundaries assigned by the inexact but grand design of capitalist zeal. Two world wars and a century later the inhabitants of that world are standing at the crossroads yet again. Where now are the architects of empire? Or do we now confront a world divided, a world of desiccated empires and small minds, islands of insularity?

Or are we witnessing a sorrier spectacle, one in which the West *abandons ship* at the 'end of history', at the moment that it claims to be its undisputed captain? No doubt we are seeing a radical change in the attitude of empire-building at the very breaking point when the wounds caused by Europe and North America have not ceased to run. For centuries, the European world had as its basic policy an aggressive, relentless imperialist expansion. Europe invaded, looted and colonized the rest of the world, transforming the worldviews and tampering with the cultural values and identities of those whom it subjugated. Europe prospered, its cities became cosmopolitan centres. Africans were brought as slaves, Asians imported as indentured labourers, destitute people the world over admitted into Europe as migrants, or guest-workers. And now that the rest of the world has been turned into a collection of shanty towns, cramped cities of cardboard and zinc, slums compared to Europe – now, Europe has lost interest in the rest of the world.

The Soviet Union no longer exists as an empire; it is not even a geographic entity. The disintegration of that empire threatens to send a great flood of displaced humanity moving westwards. The trajectories of empire, and its attendant identities, can only be understood against the backdrop of shifting political situations which informed the construction. But the closing of European and North American minds and hearts to the question of refugees precedes the Soviet Empire's disintegration. The laws curbing freedom to enter Western Europe differed from one country to another, but the legislation limiting the possibility of coming into Europe was in place long before the arrival of Somali, Sri Lankan, Ugandan or Ghanaian refugees to those shores.

In Britain this sentiment was first codified in legislation in the early 1970s, following Idi Amin's expulsion of the Ugandan Asians. The Home Secretary of the day introduced legislation limiting the number of aliens to be granted entry into the United Kingdom, whereas for hundreds of years there had been 'recruitment drives' aimed at enticing blacks to immigrate, to swell the ranks of the menial working class. Unskilled labourers from the West Indies arrived in boatfuls, and although these were not treated with civility, they were none the less allowed in and given the right to stay in the country. Many more came from the far-flung corners of the former Empire, and restaurants opened to the joy of this Kingdom's citizenry, and one at last began to eat well and cheaply. All the same, it soon became clear that there was a racist logic to the immigration laws, for one was treated differently if one came from what was referred to as the Old Commonwealth. In short, one was treated humanely if one was of European stock, whether or not of convict ancestry. Ready to join another empire of a more sophisticated order, the European Community, Britain has lately negotiated away its imperial responsibility.

The key words are 'integration' and 'disintegration' of empires, and both notions challenge the old ideas which they aspire to replace. Empires and alliances have largely been eclipsed by a series of exclusive clubs – the G7, the European Union (EU), the nuclear club – with membership limited to nations with the right credit-rating. One is left with the impression of a political establishment bereft of vision, lacking the ability to deal with the intricacies of the situation at hand. Nor are the questions any easier. For how does one explain this 'return' to 1930s politics; how does one explain the rise of the neo-Nazi right? How, indeed, can one explain the recourse to blood, the cultivation of ethnic absolutisms?

Even as the European Union is the single most cohesive transnational economic unit the world has ever known, the wealthiest and most powerful entity in world history, the peoples of this empire are barricading themselves in, aided in this by the rhetoric of fear and helplessness: fear of the nameless, foreign flood, helplessness at the escalating violence taken to staunch that flood. But if refugees are a challenge as well as a reproach to our humanity, if refugees are a lament raised, a cry spoken, if refugees are the bastards of the idea of empire, then how can one blame this highly disenfranchised, displaced humanity for all Europe's ills?

PART III

Every Italian, even the poorest wretch, is privileged. Nobody is a nobody. ... A logician might object that a society consisting exclusively of the advantaged, in which each person is 'doing better' than everyone else, as it were, is an impossibility. But the Italians have made this miracle — somewhat akin to the Indian rope trick, or squaring the circle — come to pass.

Hans Magnus Enzensberger

Chapter Six

I arrived in Rome in July 1976 as a traveller. I had come from Paris, intending to continue my journey to Mogadiscio. In Paris I had said no to the possibility of a half-offered teaching job at a university in Canada, because I was clear in my mind that I had unfinished business in Mogadiscio, and with writing, the *métier* of my commitment.

I changed from being a homeward-bound traveller, in transit, to an exile, and became the proverbial hunchback who must get used to his misfortunes. I made do with my meagre means. Attentive to history's flagstones linking Italy to Somalia, I tried to trace Mogadiscio all the way back to Italy through my writing. I might have felt more at home if it had been I who had chosen Rome as the city of my exile, willingly exchanging the status of a journeyer for that of an *émigré*.

Never having known what it meant to be an exile, I did what I could. Poor, young, Somali *qua* African *qua* black, ill-educated, unemployable, I accepted what employment opportunities I could obtain. The Lord knows there were few openings available to an illegal black alien with no intention of performing menial tasks in someone's kitchen, duties forever associated with my race, the nightsoil-men of Europe.

I had to reinvent myself. I made the self familiar to me take a back seat, and another, of recent manufacture, come forward and occupy the frontispiece. Then I buried myself in a burrow of self-hypnosis, and had to train my emotions as an exile, who needs must draw no attention to himself, nor point to his covert activities. Serving a higher order, I had to be part of the Somali world, and even though immersed in it, remain separate from it. As an exile in a country I had little direct knowledge of, I soon became mindful of a wisdom upon which I stumbled: that perhaps the proper study of Mogadiscio was Italy.

My experience in Milan took me into the disparate universes of the exile communities, of whom a large number hailed from one or another of the Latin American tyrannies. I envied the recognition afforded to these exiles, whose conditions were better documented than my own, especially from the standpoint of the host country. They were perceived to have genuine reasons to flee persecution, and were accorded more humane treatment. Moreover, very few of the exiles in Italy were Africans. And of the Somalis, many had not come out of their political closets then, nor made public their opposition to Siyad's tyranny.

I discovered in the first three weeks of my exile that I was up against a multi-pronged attack. Some of the detractions had an ideological thrust (a couple of my Italian friends reacted so hostilely to my description of Siyad Barre 'as a pillager of socialism' that they refused to talk to me). Other detractions originated from within my immediate family (my father being inimical to the position I held, and saying, 'Why must you take it upon yourself to challenge the authority of the state?'). I was pilloried in public and in private, and ignored in certain quarters; these unfair criticisms were meant to convince me that I was wrong in my assessment of Siyad's regime. While I did not back down, I learnt a useful lesson: that combining politics and writing is a lonely business; and that, as a writer, in order for me not to be reduced to the status of a pariah, I must not engage my detractors with rhetoric, but publish writings worthy of respect. It was then that I wondered if I had the ability to win my detractors over to my argument, my fight for social justice, against the unhealthy tenets of corruptive clannism.

By then I had published only two novels in English and a half-serialized one in Somali. I wrote my only novel in Somali within the first year of the language being supplied with an orthography. But the censors had discontinued its publication. Because I had dedicated my interest to the vocation of writing half-heartedly, pursuing it whenever the circumstances permitted, my income from it was minimal. My gut reaction to writing is comparable to my attitude towards money: you know how much you are worth when you have done a little of one, and have a small amount of the other. I knew how much money I had in cash the day I decided not to return to Mogadiscio, so meagre a sum I could have calculated it in cents.

Jobless and moneyless, I relied on the kindness of friends, of whom there weren't many. Some of these helped to arrange employment for my subsistence. I did translations, I worked as a substitute teacher of English at the Banco d'Italia. Suspecting that the authorities were keener on being in Siyad's good books than in mine, I tried my damnedest to remain 'legal', not when it came to employment but with regard to my stay permit. I had to leave every so often, and return with a three-month visa issued at an Italian consulate abroad.

Shortages were prevalent in my life in those days, paucity of money and of trust in humanity. Where, a month or so earlier, prior to the telephone conversation with my eldest brother advising me not to return, I might have planned a novel *pronto* in a matter of days, I was now so preoccupied with earning an income, and remaining within the law, that I did little serious writing.

I spent a lot of time travelling to Zagreb, Belgrade or Vienna so as to re-enter Italy with a valid visa. If I were based in Trieste, the border-town *par excellence*, for close to half a year, it wasn't that I had chosen it, but because Professor Marco Guadagni, a former colleague at the National University in Mogadiscio, needed a housesitter to look after his flat, while he was teaching in Somalia. I seldom went away for weekends in Ljubljana because I was in need of exit and entry visas. These made travel a cumbersome affair.

As I filled in the visa forms in triplicate or stood in a queue to acquire one or another of the permits I needed to get on with my life, I reminded myself that I was not a writer as much as a man marked by life's worries.

I remember a lot of heckling too. My acquaintances on the left had the habit of being rude to me. Charmed by Siyad's Marxist jargon, the Italian left, then the shapers and vocal arbiters of the country's postwar cultural and political framework, preyed upon someone like me, whom they defined as an alienated *petit bourgeois*. A casual acquaintance would have the gall to come up to me and say, 'Why don't you return to Mogadiscio where a socialist miracle is happening?'

I took to depressive moods for the first time in my life, lying in bed longer and longer, and waking up in utter dread of the morning's coming. How I dreaded sitting at my work desk, overwhelmed with worries, producing not a sentence worth preserving. I remember interrogating my misfortune, and wondering if the day would come when I would manage to put pen to paper.

I hoped that battling for a kind of moral truth would in the end help me to remedy the unease with a writer's block. Meanwhile my creative neurosis fed on the empty pages lying before me, with the unfilled spaces pointing to losses, not gains. I would revise yesterday's writing, fully aware that I would unwrite it on the morrow.

It occurred to me that I was not living in Italy as much as I was dwelling in the country of my imagination, an ideal land with no correlation between it and any land mass known to me. A part of me prayed for the movable barrier to lift, and for the writer's curse to go elsewhere, so I could produce a couple of sentences a day. Another part admonished me not to rush, not to force closed doors open; that I should not do anything impulsive. I woke up every morning, praying Eureka, let there be, and there was not. Not until I had sorted out the question of my *soggiorno*!

Writing novels compares easily with marathon running. Both activities require perseverance in the face of immense difficulties. Every time I left and then returned with a three-month visa, the 'stay permit' came out at me like a wounded beast returning with murderous vengeance. The ill-effects this was having on my state of mind were becoming more pronounced, to the point that a languorous mood kept me constant company, my nights merging into the torpor of my days, my daylight hours filled with the insomnia of blood-red eyes, and my nocturnal wakefulness marked with the weariness of stupor.

Then the phone rang late one night, and the voice of Nadia Spano, a woman I had been introduced to through her nephew, and whom I had met a couple of times at the Italian Communist Party's head office, where she worked, asked that I present myself on the morrow to Dr So-and-So at the Rome Questura. Speaking ominously, she said, 'Tell him Laura Diaz and I sent you!'

I was 'legal' in a matter of days, and was *compos mentis*, prepared for the first time to enjoy Rome. I remember the day my passport was returned to me stamped with a one-year stay permit. I got down seriously to the business of confronting my depression head-on. I was so imbued with the robustness of my self-confidence that in no time I was out of my dark moods, writing.

A friend lent me an apartment for several auspicious months after the concierge of the building in which my French partner and I shared a tiny apartment with a Maltese woman reported that a couple of suspicious-looking characters had paid me a visit, possibly from Siyad's security services.

The men called round several times and, finding me gone, asked about my movements. Getting nowhere with the concierge, a new lot came, who had a different story. They claimed to be cousins of mine, and that they had a message from home. What no one told them, because even the concierge had no idea, was that I had gone into hiding, and did not emerge until after finishing *Sweet and Sour Milk*. I never felt safe in Italy, and I left it at the first opportunity.

Somalis have always occupied an ambiguous territory of the colonized in the consciousness of Italians, ever since Italy staked its initial claim to the land along the southern coast of Somalia. It first leased Mogadiscio from the Sultan of Zanzibar, the then sovereign of the territory, and subsequently turned its inhabitants into subject peoples. It took several decades before it extended its authority into the hinterland, going as far as the *de facto* border with the British Somaliland Protectorate to the north of the territory, the Abyssinian-held

Ogaden to the west, and the Somali-speaking North Frontier District of present-day Kenya to the south. As conquerers, the Italians were citizens, the Somalis non-citizens in their own country.

Italy's colonialism is full of disasters, of humiliations, a tragic history ending in colonial culs-de-sac. In their self-assessments Italians are of the opinion that their colonialism was less brutal than the French or British subjugation of other African peoples. I doubt it, given that, as colonists, they were belittlers of the people over whom they ruled, whom they never saw as humans, only 'Negri', uncivilized primitives, on a par with the beasts in the jungles.

Italy consolidated its grip on Somalia only after failing to expand the *colonia* westwards, in order to create an empire of the Horn of Africa. Then it entered into agreements, and signed treaties not with the local Somali sultanates whose suzerainty over their own land it disregarded, but with the other imperial powers with which it shared in the carving up of Africa into spheres of future disorders. Somalis were but a mass of subjects subordinate to its colonial might, subjects to whom no concessions could be made, only a dastardly designation.

Little has changed in the Italians' attitude towards the Somalis. There was a time, not long ago, when all Africans were assigned the generic name 'Marocchini'. The Senegalese, who are engaged in petty trade all over Italy, are known by the pejorative appellation 'Vous comprez?', in allusion to their question in French, 'Would you like to buy?' For good or bad, Somalis had not earned themselves a name in Italian word-making, or a space in their minds, until the civil war. It is as if the Italians are taking a fresh look at the Somalis now because their country is front-page news the world over.

Perhaps no one should be surprised that they had no idea about Somalia. After all, those stationed in Mogadiscio lived apart from their subjects in more sumptuous circumstances. In *Arrivederci Mogadiscio*, Mohamed Aden Sheikh, in his book-length conversations with Italian journalist Pietro Petrucci, says that he was 'truly surprised' to discover that Italy's colonialism was hardly known or talked about by the natives. Elsewhere he confirms that there was 'no contact [between Somalis and Italians], no channels of communication, no places or possibilities of encounter, and no social occasions to make this feasible. They were two societies, in parallel existence, neither taking account of the other.'

Where, in their homeland, the Somalis were seen as subhuman by the colonists, it appears that they are not doing much better in Italy, not after the collapse of Somalia. They are not classified as refugees. Senator Mertelli's decree makes it explicit that on presenting themselves at any frontier, 'All Somalis are to be considered as "visitors" and granted entry into Italy, and if they so wish they are entitled to employment.' But what kind of job is open to them?

The majority of the Somalis do not qualify for refugee status, according to the Italian authorities' close reading of the 1951 Refugee Convention and Protocol, because they have no tangible evidence that, as individuals, they are fleeing persecution in their land. Hence their provisional admission into the country as 'visitors'. Senator Martelli's decree affords all Somalis the right to work or reside in Italy on the issuance of a stay permit, to be renewed every two years, until the situation in Mogadiscio changes.

Only a handful of Somalis have been granted refugee status, because of their clan affiliations. By defining them as 'visitors' and not acknowledging their presence as a refugee population, Italy deflects all the budgeting and expenditure-planning requirements. Italians argue that Somalis have come to Italy for years, long before the recent influx of Senegalese and other Africans from North and Central Africa, and there is definitely no need to alter their status at the exorbitant expense of a redefinition.

It was during my 1994 visit to Italy that I conducted most of the interviews analysed here. I spent my first two weeks in Milan, staying at a hotel conveniently equidistant from the apartments of my friends, of whose cuisine and generous hospitality I partook with much relish.

I discovered that appointment-making was in itself an exercise requiring delicate handling, because of the *'sistema clannica'*. Often someone known to me interceded on my behalf. Even when they agreed to be interviewed, there were conditions attached, the most common being that I should not bring along a tape-recorder, or not mention their names, or that I interview them in the presence of friends.

To supplement my news-gathering prowess I did not hesitate to descend on a group of Somalis not known to me, in the environs of Milan's Duomo, or at one of their points of encounter, a restaurant or a bar at the Cordosia underground stop. Making contact in this way meant pushing my luck. When it worked, and it often did, I did not regret my immodesty, because it was thanks to these men that I picked up hard facts about the refugees.

They explained the meaning of the words which have enriched refugee culture, terms including *xambaar*, in reference to the 'bringing in' of illegals into Europe and on to America. With regard to unmarried women in domestic employment, the word *tagsi* kept recurring. The term did not refer to a vehicle on hire, but to men allegedly 'rented' by women for their companionship.

There are several categories of Somalis in Italy. There are the 'ex-students', who since coming on bilaterally funded scholarships in the 1960s and the

1970s, and more recently of their own accord, to pursue their university studies, have stayed on. A very high percentage returned home on completion of their university education, and no more than 2 per cent have stayed on as partners of Italians. A much smaller number merged into Italy's underworld, remaining unaccounted for. No more than half a dozen have stayed on without Somali papers and without qualifying for Italian residence. The ranks of the 'ex-students' have of late been swollen by returnees to Italy, thanks to freemasonry remittances from Canada or the USA.

Other recent returnees to Italy come as 'fellows' of institutions of higher learning. These are known to have held positions at the University in Mogadiscio before the collapse. As fresh arrivals from the civil war, and at least for the first two years, the returnees were offered fellowships by the Italian government, grants which have since been discontinued. To survive, some of these receive meagre handouts as research assistants, their attitude one of wait and see. The luckier ones land more lucrative assignments with international consultancies, which commission from them research on their subjects of specialization. Many are awaiting sponsorships to North America.

The largest group of all comprises the domestic servants, more women than men, whose presence in Italy precedes the civil war era, in fact goes back to the 1970s, when many Italians on Technical Assistance assignments in Somalia recruited them as nannies, cooks or minders of elders.

The difference between the domestic servants recruited in the *before* and *after* civil strife periods is this: the recent arrivals are educated. Many of those coming *before* the civil war came from the underclass: women (and a few men), barely literate, with no chance of better prospects, who pursued this kind of vocation first in Somalia, and later, to improve their situation, followed their bosses to Italy. Of late things have changed.

The *domestiche* (servant) category accounts for the second single largest group of Somalis arriving here. This has the highest turnover: women of marriageable age, who could hold their ground with women anywhere if it came to family status, education or other advantageous attributes, have recently joined the market. The influx is a consequence of the current strife. Unlike the domestic servants of old, the recent arrivals have brought about a change in the way Somalis in Italy look at themselves: a sorrowful lot, with no country to return to!

The third category of recent arrivals is very small but also exceptional, one of a dubious clan-based provenance, consisting of twenty or so families on whom the Italian government has bestowed the status of the refugee on the basis that they were persecuted because of their clan. This group made their asylum claim during the early months of the civil war when everyone was of the mistaken opinion that the civil war was a conflict between two major confederal clan families. They are the only Somalis ever accorded refugee status in Italy.

Italy is seen by many of the newly arrived Somalis as a stopping-off point, a country affording them time, the relative comfort of being guests of relatives already established there, not to speak of the calmness with which to study other possibilities of respite. With a foothold on European soil, the hope of reprieve appears nearer, almost palpable.

Many of the recent arrivals, especially the men who do not work as domestic servants, are planning to go on to some other country in the Western hemisphere. Meanwhile, the 'boys', as they are referred to in the familial jargon, live five, six or seven to a room in the *tolka* apartments, flats paid for by female domestic servants, blood relations of the men. These are different from the *tagsi* apartments, whose rent is paid for by 'lovers'. In either case, the women *domestiche* use these apartments as *pieds-à-terre* on their days off.

Chapter Seven

There are enough Italian families willing to employ African women as domestic servants, and a sufficient number of Somali females eager to earn a living. Italians needing *domestiche* prefer Somalis to others, believing them to be more honest, and unlikely to come to work drunk or dirty. It is the Somali men who have been described as layabouts and liars, sentiments with which many concur. Ever since a senatorial decree was passed to grant all Somalis the right of residence in Italy for a renewable two years, Somali nationality is seen by the Senegalese, the Nigerians and the Ghanaians to be better than gold. In Rome, the Immigration Service hired a Somali-speaker to ensure compliance. The women, being more honest, use the work permit to be employed; the men use it to enter into shady deals, selling their *soggiorno* to the highest African bidder.

Of the women, only a handful are in illicit businesses of any sort, many working as domestic servants, or as minders of elders. There are a handful who sell their own bodies. I met these women in Naples, camped in the area of the city nearest to NATO's military camp. These women are known in Somalia as the 'Gacalow', or 'darlings', in reference to amorous relationships between the women and their clientele, American GIs.

In the *tolka* apartments for the men, things are the reverse of what obtains in the flats for the women. I went to the boys' flat when I was not meant to. I ate a meal to which I had not been invited. I happened to be in the company of a visiting dignitary from Ali Mahdi's camp, a man I was interviewing. Not one to stand on formalities, I tagged along.

There I talked to some of the men who were more open with me. They eat badly, the boys, stretching a long way the little their working sisters supply them with, because they prefer spending their allowance on *qaat*. Their main meal consisted of soggy spaghetti, eaten with burnt bolognese sauce or *maraq bilaash*, a vegetarian variant of the same. They live unhealthily. For drink, they consume bottled orange juice, lots of cola in plastic 'family' containers and oversugared tea. And they sleep a great deal; and talk on the phone a mighty lot. I smelt unwashed dry sweat on the day I went into one apartment.

Someone told me that the men clean up the apartments on Wednesdays, preparing for the arrival of the rent payers on Thursday. But the noise level seldom changes, except at about midnight. The radio is almost always on all day. At times the TV is on too, at an ear-bursting volume, and so is the ubiquitous tape-recorder, playing Somali music. Now and then, all three are on at once.

In contrast to the women, a handful of the men work for the least number of hours, gaining in a matter of minutes as much as the women earn in a month of no Sundays. The boys are profitably engaged in selling Somali passports, with work papers, to other Africans, or they sell papers to Somalis needing to travel out of Italy to other countries where the prospects are deemed to be much brighter. The few who are engaged in these shady businesses seldom mix with the other Somalis. They have their own hide-outs, places to where they might invite you to chew *qaat*, which is grown in Ethiopia, Yemen and Kenya and flown to London, and from there smuggled to Italy. Selling *qaat* is highly lucrative, and is exclusively a man's domain.

A network of men organize the *qaat* delivery to Italy, by 'whites' from London to Milan, twice a week. Then the Somalis distribute it through other middlemen to all the corners of the country. The reason why they use a European courier to bring in a satchelful of the mild stimulant, which is frowned upon, is that a Somali would be stopped at all entry and exit points in both England and Italy, which would defeat the purpose of getting it fresh. The courier is met off the plane by the Somali agent, who picks up the goods and hosts the courier for the night. From the fees involved, one would assume that most of the carriers are in a low-income bracket.

In addition to the few dealing in fake as well as genuine documents, and those who employ European *qaat* couriers to deflect attention from their merchandise, there are many money-changers, men acting as agents of businessmen in Somalia who trade in currencies. In Italy, unlike Britain, where Indians with East African connections have the monopoly of this business, the agents are Somali. Raxmo Axmad Ali, who looks after an elderly widow in her seventies, and who has board and lodging where she works, sends a monthly remittance to Mogadiscio, almost three-quarters of her salary. The money-vendor charges her a dollar's worth for every hundred that is paid to her mother.

'It's cheaper to be charged more here where I can put pressure on the money-vendor, whom I know personally, than it is to trust travellers who

may or may not deliver your money,' she said, 'Moreover, my people have
the habit of telephoning me here whenever they do not receive the money in
time, and this costs a lot more, fifteen thousand Somali shillings every three
minutes, money to be paid by me. As you can see, the civil war has exposed
us all to insatiable sharks, launderers of money, vendors of the same in
whatever currency is required, non-working men relying wholly on the sweat
of women.'

As I waited in her apartment for Caaliya Muxummad to come, I chatted to
her brothers, 'the boys' in the familial jargon. These were men, their ages
ranging from their late twenties to early forties. There was a teenage girl in
the kitchen all the time I was there, cooking. Self-conscious, I wished I could
ask the four men why they lived in self-neglect, why they did not keep the
flat clean.

We expected Caaliya to walk in through the door at any moment.
Meanwhile, we talked half-heartedly in the way people waiting for something
else to happen do. I asked specific questions, and got general responses for my
pains. They confirmed that dissent would seldom issue from the lips of 'the
boys' biding their time, waiting for the opportunities to alter the
circumstances to their advantage. A bone of contention, which was rarely
picked in the open, even though it was often alluded to, in my conversations
with the men was whether or not the women had the right to do what they
wanted with the money they earned. In Somalia, men held the purse strings of
the income they generated, and power accrued to them. The roles were
reversed in Italy.

One of the brothers told me about a younger brother who had the gall to
question his elder sister if she was a *tagsi*. When she didn't answer him, he hit
her, then picked a fight with the man on whom his sister was allegedly
spending her money. I asked Caaliya's brother, Bile, what he would do if he
discovered his sister was one.

'Fearful that she might cut off my allowance,' he said, 'or worse still, might
not help me buy the services of a *xambaar* carrier who would get me to North
America, I try to keep all the traditional questions about family morality under
wraps. A man in my condition, dare I say, does not speak of dignity, nor does
he ask questions.'

I asked if he would ever work as a *domestico*, considering that his sister, who
was older and more educated than he, was working as one, maybe to pay for
his air ticket to America?

He replied that he had never performed household chores or any menial
jobs in his life, and that a part of him preferred the kind of humiliation he

suffered at his sister's hands to that at an Italian's home. He concluded by saying that he had a better negotiating power with his sister than he did working in the kitchen of a white woman.

I asked, 'Aren't you smitten by a sense of shame, the shame of depending on someone else, no matter who this might be?'

'It is not done in our family for a man to go into a kitchen and cook,' he said, 'or to pick up a broom and sweep the floor. We had servants for these kinds of jobs, and women did them, at times in addition to their office hours. It is dishonourable and un-Islamic for a man to be sullying himself in this way.'

To my question as to how he got to Italy, he replied, 'My sister Caaliya paid a *xambaar* carrier the hefty sum of three thousand dollars for each of us, and there are six of us, her siblings. Because she put her mind to it, she was able to arrange for all our sisters, except the one who is in the kitchen, to be "carried" to Canada. If we, the boys, are still here and not working, it is because arrangements are currently under way for us to be "carried" one at a time to North America, where we will join two brothers and three sisters, who have Canadian nationality, or the USA, where a brother has a green card.'

I asked what his educational qualifications were. He had no degree. I wondered if he had ever worked in Somalia. He had not. I said, 'Do you realize that in Canada or the USA there are few jobs open to an unskilled person such as yourself? The best you could hope is to get a dish-washing job in a restaurant, or a nightwatchman. Why do you refuse to perform these menial jobs here in Italy, and pay for your keep and eventually your way to North America?'

'There is a difference between Italy and Canada,' he said.

I waited. He explained that the difference between doing these menial chores in Italy and Canada lay in the fact that the prospects ahead of one in North America are brighter. I asked him: how so? Because in Canada or the USA, there was hope of his being granted nationality, whereas in Italy there was no such chance. In other words, he didn't mind performing these lowly duties as long as he had justifiable aspirations of improving his opportunities for self-advancement.

We heard the lift stop at the floor where the apartment was. Then a key turned in the door. And Caaliya Muxummad walked into the silence her arrival created.

The atmosphere took on a different aspect the instant Caaliya Muxummad walked in. She was the mistress of this place, more like a woman used to giving orders. But as she was a domestic servant, I wondered what it felt like to receive instructions from her Italian signora, what it felt now to be the signora of this apartment, barking orders. The fact that she looked from the boys to the mess they had created, then at me, was lost on me. Shouting to no one in particular, she said, 'Who lives here, pigs or humans?'

When one of the men called to the one girl in the kitchen, blaming her for not clearing the clutter before Caaliya's return, the look in Caaliya's eyes was one of rage. She reminded the man who had spoken that 'the mess had better be cleaned up by those who made it'. Now she turned to me, not to apologize, but to say within everyone's hearing, 'Do you know what I think? I think Somalia is in a mess, because we refuse to act responsibly towards our communities.'

And then she remained standing and silent until all the men got up, to busy themselves with domestic chores: one to make up the bed in haste, another to pick up things off the floor, a third to go to the kitchen to help. By the time the fourth made it to the door, apparently to leave, Caaliya was saying to his back, 'Don't you come back into this apartment if you are not willing to give a hand in running it to everybody's benefit.'

Excusing herself, she left the room.

She returned half an hour later, after a shower, which revived her spirits. Caaliya strode into the living room, in a floral dress of exquisite pattern. No sooner had I seen her than I remarked the change in her gait-*qua*-personality. Among other things, she was no longer looking like a maid, which she did when she entered the apartment earlier.

I shifted uncomfortably on the edge of the unmade bed, where I sat, as I engaged 'the boys' in a futile talk, which wasn't going anywhere. I was impressed at Caaliya's metamorphosis into her own woman. I could sense that here, in her flat, she could assume the stride of her pride, her personality on her day off, a mistress of her own and other people's affairs. On her re-entry, everybody left the room in deference to her.

She said to me in a voice imbued with a newly recovered seelf-pride, 'You appear to be as surprised as someone who has just seen a ghost.'

I nodded my head, in silence.

'I am my own person here,' she said, 'a mistress of my moods, my own time, and I account to no one for how I behave or what I do with my time. And I await instructions from no man. However, you will discover that even though I am my own mistress, I am not always on top of things.'

'Why is that?' I asked.

'Because we remain subject to a male ethos everywhere,' she said, 'I put on the uniform of a maid for six days of the week to earn an income, which I spend on men, who insist that I clean up their mess when I return to *my* apartment. As a woman, I am forever subject to recriminations and reprimands if I do not serve men hand and foot all the time.'

After a pause, I asked, 'When you step out of the uniform and into your clothes, do these external transformations make you feel different inside?'

'Of course,' she replied. 'Here in my apartment, there are no-go areas. And I engage in a communication either with my equals or with my dependants. It is only natural that I feel different.'

'How do you feel as a maid?'

'I feel terrible,' she said. 'I feel humiliated.'

'I meant . . .,' and I trailed off.

'I am quieter for one thing,' she said; 'for another, because I am conscious of my status, my hands are often demurely folded behind my back in deference to my employers, my head a little bowed, my gaze downcast, and I drag my syllables in the attitude of someone with a slight stutter, when I answer my bosses' questions. In other words, my demeanour is calculated not to attract attention, but to please others.'

I knew from talking to 'the boys' that Caaliya had a room in the apartment for her exclusive use, a room under lock and key when she wasn't around. Occasionally her younger sister shared the room with her, whereas the four boys, one of them her senior, another only a half-brother, had two rooms between themselves. Female relations camped in the parlour.

'When the family who employ me go on a trip abroad or away on vacation in the summer,' she says, 'I house-sit for them, answering their telephone, making sure everything is all right, but I return here nightly. When my eldest brother is in Italy on a visit, he puts up here too. Then, rather than upset the boys' sleeping arrangements, I move in with friends, who have a larger apartment.'

I was amused to hear her refer to her brothers as 'the boys' when 'the men' would have been more appropriate. But then it sort of made sense as I thought of football coaches alluding to their mature players as 'my boys'. No doubt the diminution was meant to indicate the direction in which the scales of power were tilted. In Italy the Somali women were the breadwinners, and it was their prerogative to define the terms, or to decide who was put up where, when or why, decisions not challenged by the lie-abed men whom they supported.

Caaliya pointed out that one of the aspects the civil war had brought to the fore was the difference, in attitude to work, between our men and women. 'It appears', she said, 'as if there is a more overriding tension between men and women than between the clan-families that are at war at home. For although the clan divisions follow tensions of a trodden path, the tensions between men and women are newly manifest in salient ways, particularly now that their income-generating roles have been reversed, the women working, the men dependent on the women.'

Caaliya told me that women joined the workforce within days of arriving in Italy, whereas men groomed themselves to be kept in the style to which they had been accustomed back home. So, in addition to paying back the money they owed to the *xambaar* carrier, the women worked ceaselessly and untiringly to continue providing for the men they had supplied with air tickets to get to Italy in the first place, then to maintain them in grand style, while waiting either to go to North America on a sponsorship if they were lucky or well connected, or to cross yet another boundary within Europe, into Holland, Britain or Switzerland, countries where the men expect to receive monthly social welfare benefits. She concluded, 'But would they lift a finger? No way.'

As principal of a well-established secondary school in Mogadiscio, Caaliya Muxammad did not quibble about the kind of work she got in Italy, so who are these men to do so? She went on, 'No longer pampered with male power, especially now that everything is in a shambles because of the curse visited on our country, Somali men, compared to their womenfolk, have proven themselves to be worthless. After all, the cult of male supremacy has predominantly depended on an untruth: that in their self-centred way, men ruled the world. Bullies, brutes of the worst kind, sufferers from self-delusion, men have contributed less to the well-being of our societies. And whether men like to hear it or not, exile abroad, the difficulties inside, these have both shown the weak stuff of which our men are made. No longer the chosen heirs to temporal power, and no longer endowed with the benediction of being closer to God than the womenfolk, the men fall apart like toys a child has glued together.'

She continued speaking in that vein. Where the women employed an arsenal of God-given talents, the men stood around, doing nothing, busy tracing their line to the antiquated system of clan values, a system which guaranteed them continued financial and moral support from better-off relations. Such imponderables as self-dignity, one's personal honour, being true to a societal ideal: these give way to the exigencies of the day. And like beggars showing off their amputated arms, the men pointed to the harsh conditions consequent on the civil war. The idea was for the families to be held together at all costs, that those who could must work, and those who could not must be supported. Caaliya was viscerally disturbed by the sight of able-bodied men standing in groups almost any day of the week, having coffee in a bar, or loitering at one of Milan's underground stations or at Florence's, Rome's or any other city's principal railway rendezvous.

She said, 'If you are of a mind to, you can hear them pontificate on matters of war and peace, which warlord is doing what to whom and when, and who is winning. Winning what? Our men are not fit to sit in judgement on the ruinous affairs of a country they have been bailed out of. And the women? The women work day and night here as they worked day and night at home, they work harder to settle the debts of the pontificators, who fund more acts of attrition at home.'

I asked, 'What would you reckon would happen if the women stopped funding the men who fund the acts of attrition, or stopped funding the pontificators?'

'The day the Somali women decide to stop providing funding for these mad warlords' ambitions, mark my word the civil war will surely stop forthwith,' she said.

Once a week the women congregate at an open-air piazza not very far from the centre of the cities where they are found: to share the latest gossip about the land to which, unlike the men who set their sights on migrating to North America for good, many wish to return. You can remark the evidence of invisible tears and the toll taken in toil.

Caaliya Muxummad put it thus: 'It's very very very hard to work in someone else's kitchen, in obedience to someone else's instructions, cooking to somebody's order, in accordance with a menu of ideas that are not yours.'

I asked about the tallage the women pay in patience to raise someone else's baby, nannying them towards a healthier growth, to whom they gave better succour in life, the women who were pining to have one of their own and couldn't for one reason or another.

Caaliya Muxummad said, 'I am in my early thirties and I think how I might have had my own child if it had not been for the civil war. I think of how I might have settled down with the man I was planning to marry. But the strife saw to the termination of that dream, because it disempowered our men, making them into lesser persons!'

She looked away for a moment, her hand going to her face, as though she might have prevented a tear wetting her cheeks. 'My fiancé came here on a ticket I paid for, a ruined man. I parted ways with him, because he wouldn't stop getting involved in clan politics.'

She looked at her watch, but was in no hurry to show me out. I suspected that, it being Thursday, her day off, she was going to the piazza where the women met up late in the afternoon. I knew too that, unlike the men who had the gall to sit in cafes, consuming drinks they can ill-afford, and posing in outfits too extravagant for their pockets, the women were of humbler habits, seldom indulging in out-of-the-way extravagance. You would remark the odd expensive dress, or a necklace to be paid for in monthly instalments, or a brooch or a bracelet made of valuable metal set with gold or silver. Even so, the women bought these items of jewellery not to boast or show off, but as part of a *franca valuta* mindset, given that Somalis had little or no trust in banking systems.

Caaliya explained that the demands the families made on the women, because of their earning power, were resonant with the current reality of the country, demands firmly fixed in every kinsman's or kinswoman's mind as to the responsibilities to be borne by family members in these times of crises. She added, 'The burden the families place on the women is manifold. The women are expected to care for the ailing, the senile and the wounded. These burdens are increasingly becoming difficult to meet, the demands taxing their patience more, and making women question their uninterrupted loyalty to the family if the crisis continues.'

I asked if society demands less of men.

'Men give less of themselves to a crisis,' she said.

I nodded my head in utter agreement, and said nothing.

Caaliya Muxummad went on, 'You cannot imagine how painful it is to receive what I can only refer to as absurd requests: my septuagenarian father wanted to take a woman in her teens for a wife, and he asked me to fund his irrational lust.'

'Is your mother dead?' I asked.

'My mother is still alive,' she said, 'and if you want to know the truth is kicking harder than a she-donkey. And what about me, I am older by twenty years than the girl in her teens my father wants to take as his wife. The absurdities of these petulant male demands, you can't imagine the agonies they cause!'

What of her brothers and half-brothers? What sort of absurd demands did they make of her?

She replied, 'I have come round lately to the opinion that if any good has come out of the current crisis, it is that our exposed raw nerves have shown us aspects of ourselves of which we had no experience. But then we didn't know one another, did we? We didn't know one another as members of the same immediate family, or of the same clan, scattered all across the land, that we are, sharing nothing but a generic character. Nor did we know one another even as generic Somalis. I am glad of the chance to gain access to areas of our minds which had remained closed to us. My brothers, half-brothers ...?'

I waited, in eagerness, for her to continue.

She did, saying, 'It's sad but true that anyone reaching the mature age of twenty-something without ever earning their keep is bound to live in a world different from the one I grew up in.'

'How do you mean?'

'My brothers and sisters are no different from the majority of Somalis who have never earned a living all their lives, kept men, for whom women cooked, whose clothes were washed and ironed by women, and who ate the labour of a father, or that of an older brother when in Mogadiscio, and who, now that they are in Italy, depend on the sweat of women *domestiche*.'

Our conversation went off at a tangent as we linked work in Somalia with knowledge about the country. Caaliya, in her analysis, assumed that one had a better knowledge if one trained in a profession, or worked at a vocation.

She said, 'In this regard, my brothers had no more than a vicarious knowledge about our country, a few generalizations or clichés based on ill-informed hypotheses. Siyad's twenty-odd-year tyranny and the economic hardships which came with it caused the natural cohesion of the family to be as good as wasted, not worth a misspent coin. Which is why we, who trained in professions and worked at vocations before the collapse, have a double tragedy on our hands: the old generation, dependent on our earning power, is irreformably wrongheaded, the young ones unresponsive to the current challenges, not knowing the rightness or wrongness of their own actions.'

I shook my head in what must have been despair. I said, 'What are their aspirations, the dreams your brothers see, their ambition in life towards which they *work*? What future?'

'I look at them,' she said, 'and see faces that have known no regrets. I talk to them and hear them not admitting to any wrongs, or to having lived a life of utter failure. Theirs is a history of dependence, a chronic reliance on the income made by other people's sweaty brows. Lazybones, that's what they are, with no ambitions other than going to another country, where they will be the recipients of a refugee stipend.'

We left the apartment together, she and I. I gave her a lift in a taxi that was taking me to another appointment. Without my prompting her, she told me that the women *domestiche*, on their day off, on Thursday or Sunday, discuss matters of grave importance, topics to do with life-lines to their folks back home, and how to keep the bonds unbroken.

She went on, 'This being the only times they go out of the house where they are employed, and because they are not entitled to the use of the telephone, many of them find it expedient to see to it that they organize handing the money over in US dollars to the money-men, who arrange for the authority to have the money drawn in Mogadiscio, in shillings.'

'How much is their commission?' I asked.

'Ten per cent, paid up front here, and not in lire, but in US dollars. On top of that, they levy a 5 per cent commission on the money being changed in Mogadiscio into Somali shillings. They are sharks, these money-men,' she said.

I said, 'What do you think of women *tagsis*?'

'I think it sad that the women do not realize they are being taken advantage of. But what can we women do? We have no women's organization and no place to meet in order to talk about our problems, women to women. But when our conversation touches on men, our cynical attitude as women becomes apparent, both in what we say about men, and in the words of derision with which we describe them: exploiters, liars, lazy-bones. No love lost, eh? The men, for their part, refer to all women who are not related to them as women of low morals, or worse still as "*tagsis*".'

I asked if anyone has ever described her as a *tagsi*.

'I have been described as one by Bile, my half-brother, the one with whom I had lost my temper earlier in my apartment, because he wouldn't lift a finger,' she said. 'I suppose he described me as a *tagsi* not because he suspects me of being one, but because I put my foot down firmly and refused to continue providing him with cash for his own lavish ends.'

'Would he know if you were seeing a man?'

'Not unless I wanted him to know,' she said. 'The way I see it, men seldom have a kind word to speak about women who are strong-minded, and who stand up to their unfair maladroitnesses.'

The taxi stopped. She got out. Scribbling my notes in a shorthand only I could read, I continued my journey to my destination in the comfortable knowledge that I had done a good day's work, my first.

Chapter Eight

A Milan-based 'carrier' who wished to remain anonymous told me that not a month passes by without a newly carried Somali turning up at one of Italy's entry points, fresh from Kenya, Yemen or elsewhere outside Europe, countries where asylum-seekers' future prospects were deemed to be less promising. 'The refugees are fleeing from the persecution of the police and immigration officials of the host country. They leave their so-defined first country of asylum, and embark on journeys fraught with dangers, in the hope of entering Italy.'

Carrying illegals out of one country and into another is an expensive affair, requiring detailed planning. Before being 'carried' to Italy, most of the refugees would have spent no less than two cruel years in their country of first asylum, two years in which, as Somalis, they faced daily extortion at the hands of uniformed authorities. They might have stayed on in the land of their first asylum if, as bona fide refugees waiting for resettlement, many had not experienced daily humiliation at the instigation of the indigenes, who made them feel very unwelcome.

'Why do Kenyan and Yemeni officials make life unbearable for the Somali refugees in their countries?' I asked.

'It is as if the Kenyan or Yemeni police officers are envious of the Somali being resettled in Europe or North America,' explained C.A., the carrier. 'Otherwise, why should they place so many obstacles in their way?'

'Bribery?'

'The more bribery they pay, the more they are harassed.'

And where was a carrier's place in the scheme of things?

'A carrier makes these hurdles vanish.'

At airports between the city where they had begun their journey and Italy, in the company of their 'carrier', the refugees would be treated as though they were the world's pariah, every immigration officer proving to be as inimical to them as a Muslim to pork. Told in the crudest language to stand aside, they would be asked incriminating questions and their papers examined. The way they were dealt with, you would think they were in the drugs business. By C.A.'s reckoning, a third of those carried were sent back to the starting-point of their travel, returning penniless and in debt, humiliated and, on top of that, in chains.

In his opinion, the risks they took were the least of their worries. For they embarked on their trip in full awareness that staying on in Kenya or Yemen posed more problems; and that anyone travelling on a Somali passport was suspect, even if he or she had all the necessary papers in immaculate order, and had proper documentation to enter the country of destination.

Commercial airlines did not sell air tickets to Somali travellers without first putting them and the documents they bore through a most rigorous scrutiny. More spot-checks awaited them at every step of the way, hurdles put in their way at every curve. They could be stopped at will, their papers looked over at any point anywhere at an airport. And then they could be treated to more step-asides of an embarrassing sort every ten to twenty metres. Once aboard an aircraft, they might be asked to hand over their passports to a stewardess, who would hand them to an immigration official of their country of destination, an officer waiting to receive them at the steps of the plane. C.A. said, 'Somali travellers are treated like unaccompanied children, only no one is kind to them. You would think they wore an invisible label round their necks, pointing them out.'

'Are you saying', I asked, 'that Somali asylum-seekers and their carriers are engaged in a battle of wits with the immigration authorities in the countries they leave and the ones they plan to enter?'

'It is as if they are saying to the authorities who think up all manner of legal constraints that they, as refugees, are equal to their dare. Yes, that's what I am saying.'

'And they come to Europe a hardened lot?' I said.

'And having suffered at the unkind hands of heartless Kenyans and Yemeni, not to speak of the representatives of UNHCR, a most insensitive lot of mercenaries.'

'Then they pay a high dividend to a carrier, like you,' I said, 'who contracts to bring them to Europe, in exchange for a sum of money which they can ill afford. How can they be equal to anyone's dare?'

'Maybe if only to show these Europeans who frustrate their desire to leave a hell-hole of a country, like Kenya,' he said, 'by placing spectacular obstacles in their paths all the way from the starting-point of our journey down to the cubby-holes which they call home here, in Milan.'

'Has it been well worth your while?' I said.

'You know, I am not certain any more,' he replied.

'Why is that?'

It was then he told me a story about a European scholar of Somali language and literature with a penchant for tirelessly asking his informants one question too many, as he paid attention to the minutiae of Somali. The questions had to do with details of the tongue natives either had not given much thought to, or had no knowledge of, in the sense that they had not studied it, or had never bothered to research into the epistemological significance. The scholar had the habit of putting the same question to everyone he met, never feeling satisfied with the answers given. The villagers thought him insensitive, and self-centred too.

'One day,' C.A. went on, 'at a meeting of the elders' council, someone suggested that they played a prank on the tiresome scholar. The idea was for each of them to answer only a portion of his query, and then send him on an intellectual goose-chase of the kind that would make him go further from the point with which his inquiry had begun. In this manner, riddles led to more well-bred puzzles, allegories gave birth to parables pregnant with the foetuses of spiritual truths, which in turn brought forth proverbs, which begat rhetoric, poetry and so on and so forth. In the end, the scholar ran out of the energy to ask any more questions.'

I wondered aloud what he meant.

Apparently I was being sent on to another carrier, with the initials M.D., whose address C.A. provided me with, but not before writing and giving me a brief note of introduction. Was he playing the same prank on me?

'We started on a draught of innocence,' said M.D., 'a draught taken, dregs and all, in full trust of the humanity of our Kenyan and Yemeni neighbours, and of those who are better off than we are. We could understand Europe closing every opening in the refugee law with restrictive modalities aimed at discouraging *the vermin* from Africa to arrive.'

C.A. concurred with M.D. in his assessment of the refugees' mood and stamina, and agreed that a battle of wits was being played by all those involved, the refugees doing callisthenics for their dignified survival, the European immigration officers well aware that the higher the bar to be scaled, the more fatal the fall.

'As carriers,' he assured me, 'we contribute our fair share to making the exercise worth our while finally and to the refugees in terms of safety, so that the falls, if they occur, are not as dangerous as the European authorities predict.'

Why did he think Europeans wanted to keep the Somalis out?

'Because of our dark skin, and our religion,' he said.

Did he have the evidence to prove this?

'Do you think me naive?'

He looked at me for a long, long time, and rose to his feet, in the hasty manner of someone about to tell me that the interview was over. I wondered if he would advise me to consult another carrier, with whose address he would provide me.

'What matters is that the doors are closed,' he said, 'and we, as carriers, are determined to open them at the risk to our lives and our business concerns in order to afford the refugees the possibility of pursuing their ambition, a future, in their minds, painted the colour of bright hope. Somebody compensates us for the dangers we take, and we carry.'

By 'somebody' he meant not the refugees themselves, but their better-off relations, who were tired of coughing up enough funds to maintain them in camps in Yemen, Kenya and Ethiopia. Ill-run and neglected by corrupt UNHCR officials, the camps were a bedrock of the international community's indifference to refugees. The carriers brought them out of these hopeless countries, on the payment of a commission upfront. He added, 'If a refugee's life points to an effort of survival, then escorting them to Europe will make their survival less expensive to the relatives supporting them on their meagre savings.'

'What's been your success rate?' I said.

'Exemplary,' he boasted.

'Can you be more precise?'

'Eighty-five per cent of those I carried arrived without a hitch,' he said. 'In fact, in the two years that I have been in the business, only three families have been apprehended.'

Did he know what had become of them?

He was deliberately economical with the details. 'It was the fault of the head of the family, who, against my advice, decided to replace one of the boys with a woman much older. I warned him of the dangers involved. The man was so stupid he argued that whites could not tell black women and boys apart.'

'What happened to them when they were apprehended?'

'The last I saw them, they were in a cubicle in Orly, Paris, waiting to be interrogated,' he said. 'Most likely, they were sent back to Yemen, at no immediate risk to myself or my business. Once I got home, I rang the relatives and informed them what happened, that we made the detour to France, because our starting-point was Djibouti.'

'Since you did not deliver, did you return their money?'

'Of course not.'

'Why not?'

'We contract to escort people to Europe,' he explained.

I asked if the carrier and his clients travel together or sit apart, and pretend not to know one another. Do they travel on the same document? Had he, as a carrier, discovered where the bottlenecks were? Where were the difficulties – at the points of exit in Djibouti, Addis, Yemen, prior to the journey being embarked on, or at European entry points?

Understandably, he did not want to answer all my questions. He said, 'We do as thorough a research as possible before accepting a commission, at least I do. And we take into account that each assignment has its uniqueness, and requires us to adjust to its circumstances. The variables revolve around the number of persons to be carried, the ages of the offspring, their distinguishing features, the height, the width or narrowness of the woman's girth. Each carrier has his own style. I prefer carrying two refugee travel documents, one to be used, another to fall back on in the event of unprepared-for bottlenecks.'

'Where do you and your "quarry" meet and when?'

'We meet at an appointed place and time,' he said, 'to rehearse possible scenarios: problems and what to do about them; no-problems, and how to proceed, so as not to create problems. Once aboard the aircraft, I sit furthest from them.'

'And if there are difficulties?'

'Difficulties outside Europe are easily spirited away the instant a wad of dollars is exchanged. But, as I explained before, problems inside Europe are of a different nature – not that they are no concern of the carrier's, but that he will walk away from them, because of the risks to himself.'

'Why is your success rate higher than the other carriers'?'

'Because I am better educated than most of the others in the business,' he said. 'I speak several languages, including Dutch, English, German and Italian. And before finding myself stateless in Kenya, I was a professor in biochemistry, my degrees having been conferred on me by universities in Germany and the Netherlands.'

'What European papers do you hold?'

'I am registered as a resident in one European country, and as a refugee in another,' he said.

Did he look for a job in either country?

'Because there is no chance for me to obtain employment as a biochemist,' he said, 'I have never bothered looking for one. I have found jobs as a dishwasher, or as a cleaner.'

What were the other features contributing to his success?

'I bring reason to the execution of my assignment,' he said, 'not emotion. I set about my job of a carrier as though I were rehearsing the role of a difficult character in a play, now playing one role, now another, forever truthful to the role of a carrier.'

'What do you do when you sense danger?' I asked.

'I change my nationality,' he said, 'and fall back on my other papers, confident of not being linked to those I had carried. In any case, I admonish those I am carrying to stay away from me, because on the whole it is safer for them if they do not associate themselves with me.'

'You said earlier you rehearse with them?'

'If they are to be registered as "residents" in my own travel document, then at entry points they may be asked questions about the city they are supposed to be residing in,' he said. 'For this reason, I teach them the ins and outs of the area in which they are domiciled, not to mention the streets and alleyways of the ancient city. I train them in knowing the answers to the leading questions an immigration official might put to them. If they are entering as "refugees", the questions are different.'

'Why would anyone ask them where they live?'

'Because Somalis are suspected of travelling on forged documents anyway,' he said. 'To ascertain that they are genuine residents, they are asked to write down their addresses, and to give their telephone and social security numbers from memory. You would be surprised to know how many of them fail to pass this elementary questioning. But from this, you will gather that someone has done good enough research about Somalis, who are often incapable of spotting the snares laid for them. Likewise, we do our research.'

'Does that mean,' I asked, 'that everyone in the carrier business must have such sophisticated backups as you do before being certain they would not be apprehended?'

'Some do, some don't,' he said. 'I have more backups than most, backups in at least three countries, including Italy. I ply other routes too, London and Paris included.'

'I am impressed,' I said.

'We are professionals,' he said.

By this I understood him to mean, when I thought of it, that he would be a fool if he did not take the necessary precautions against possible financial losses, or if he didn't distance himself from a passenger proving to be a liability; I understood him to mean, too, that it was only apt that he demanded all payments upfront. Cynical and wise enough to know the risks involved, he was cognizant of the high price that he would pay if he failed. 'Can you imagine where I would end up if I were apprehended?' he said.

'How did you become a carrier?' I asked.

From the way he looked at me, then stood up to his full height, I could tell that our interview had come to an end, and that it was high time I was introduced to another carrier, who might or might not answer all my questions. The thought occurred to me that I was being sent on yet another goose-chase. However, I was gracious enough to thank him for his time, and for the suggestion that I speak to A.N., a carrier.

I met A.N. the following day, and asked him what had prompted him to enter the carrying business.

He remembered with sorrow that something had gone wrong when his sister was being carried to Italy, before Senator Martelli's decree, which gives Somalis the right to stay. He went on, 'Our whole family was stranded in Nairobi at the time, including two sisters, a younger brother, my wife and myself. My wife and I had hopes of a sponsorship to North America, and while waiting, we thought we might as well fund one of my younger sisters to come and work as a domestic servant. The idea was to set up a base in a European country, possibly for the younger ones to go to universities, etc.'

'How did you go about contacting a carrier?' I asked.

'I contracted one via an acquaintance,' he said. 'A single phone call sufficed. He rang his contact in Kenya, with whom I spoke in turn. The contact received the kill, the hefty sum he demanded, four thousand US dollars upfront, on behalf on the carrier. He flew into Nairobi, we met at an appointed place at the airport, the contact making the presentations. The following morning, the Kenya immigration rang to inform us that our sister was back in Nairobi, on a deportation order from Italy. She was in handcuffs.'

'Your money was never refunded?'

'We took the loss of the money, which we could ill afford, as part of the risk taken,' A.N. explained. 'That wasn't our problem. Our problem was that the carrier failed, because he panicked at the last minute, and gave in to the intimidation of the Italian immigration authorities, who would not allow my sister to disembark at Fumicino.'

'Did you ever discover what happened?'

'Apparently because the carrier we had commissioned had refused to cut his Nairobi contact in,' he said. 'Miffed, the man in Kenya snitched on the carrier by phoning someone who phoned the Rome immigration. A reception committee was waiting for my sister.'

'What became of the carrier?'

'No one has heard of him again.'

What did A.N. do then?

'I became a carrier for a dare,' he said.

How did he do that?

'I borrowed money to set up a one-man carrying concern,' he said, 'just for a dare. First I evacuated my immediate family to Italy, an intermediate point from where I despatched a sister to Britain, two brothers to Holland and my wife and child to Canada. To supplement our income, my sisters worked as domestic servants.'

'Just for a dare?'

From his viewpoint, he had to make one of two choices, neither salutary: to remain in Kenya, or to go to Italy, with no job prospects. He discovered that dealing in the illicit business of bringing illegals into Europe, with all its gains, had its attendant risks, too. But at least he stood a chance of improving the condition of his immediate family.

How did he recruit his first clients?

He said, 'I found the rich potential of recruiting young women. Put simply, I paid for a woman's travel and relevant expenses, claiming she was my wife, which relationship granted her entry into Italy, once I organized my own papers, on the basis of a forged document. The woman entered into a deal with me by signing an IOU affidavit. On arrival here, I put her in a *pensione* and found her a job through an employment agency, which was in on the deal, their cut guaranteed. They deducted their commission at source, and ensured that the woman reimbursed my money with interest.'

'Has any of them reneged on their promise to pay back?'

Firm in tone and gestures, 'We wouldn't let them.'

'How did you make sure they didn't?'

He said, 'Italy being a corrupt country, everyone is corruptible. I know what I am doing.'

How did he expand his business?

'I moved, regrettably from my viewpoint, into carrying families of five to seven members,' he said, 'with mothers and children and so on. I would not have contracted to do so, if it had not been for the pressures placed on me by my sister-in-law. How I have hated myself for caving in to her demands! Because I nearly got caught the one time I did this.'

'Why?'

'Because more things are likely to go wrong, the larger the contingent to be brought in,' he said. 'Moreover, there is less of a chance for a woman and her children to be deported forthwith without their case being heard, and more of a chance of the carrier being apprehended. To save herself and her children, a woman would talk. If she is believed, you are in deep trouble.'

'What are the ground rules then?'

'Not to take unnecessary risks,' he said.

I asked if he could elaborate.

'Bringing in a family of illegals runs counter to my idea of risk-taking,' he said. 'The other difficulty is that at the best of times the people who contract you to bring in the members of their families may not give you precise information. And then you may not discover the discrepancies until you are in an alien environment. You run higher bills, bribing local officials, the slightest hint of something going wrong putting you in peril. Also you are blamed if something goes awry, you are not sufficiently rewarded if everything works out. Because I don't like to fail, whatever the odds against me, I put my life on the line, to make sure I don't.'

'What are your future plans?' I asked.

'I will retire as soon as I complete a contract I am working on now,' he said. 'The carrying business has not been good for my heart, and my mind is not at rest day and night.'

Listening to him speak of quitting the lucrative business of carrying, A.N. put me in mind of a gambler who, having won a rich hand at roulette, promised to abandon the awaiting wealth.

'Would you like to meet another carrier?' he said.

I nodded my head. He gave me the name of another carrier, this time not in Milan, but in Florence. As a matter of fact, he rang the man, and made me speak to him. Although I had no intention of doing so, I promised I would get in touch with him when I was in Florence. I didn't.

Chapter Nine

After a two-week stint spent in Milan interviewing domestic servants and carriers, I embarked on a gruelling journey across Italy. I took night trains going south, to Naples, then came back north, to Turin, or Venice, and after a couple of days' lecturing, returned southward for a commitment in Rome, only to leave on a night train yet again, waking up in Milan. I was seldom left with time for leisure.

The Somalis were citizens of a sorrowful country, a number of them with passports to other kingdoms. When many had a love affair with 'abroad', Italy happened to be where they went. But Somalia remained their abiding passion. Only one man, whom I met in Florence, a medical doctor specializing in gynaecology, struck me as having made up his mind to take Italy for better and worse as his permanent love.

And what did they talk about when they met, the Somalis? History interested them, living history, their place in it, their contribution to it from exile. By our meandering discussions, we paid visits, some of them and I, not only to specific periods but to events. Commenting on and remembering what happened or didn't, they called on aspects of the oral tradition upon which some of them based their argument. Rarely did they have evidence that would stand up in court.

A medical doctor, who had attained the rank of major in Somalia's national army before coming back to Italy to take up residence in Florence, where he had studied, told me with knowing cynicism that he nearly married General Aideed's daughter. A little nervous, most certainly self-conscious, because we were in his apartment within possible hearing of his current wife, with whom he appeared to be happy, he chuckled, 'Imagine having Aideed as your father-in-law?' His mother, sitting there, wisely pushed aside her son's tawdry remarks by admitting that, although it might be a daunting prospect, the General may have been a different man in close familial quarters.

Others took me down into the caves of ancient history, where I felt lost, since I could not discern what they saw in Somalia as they reinvented it. At one point, feeling rather gullible, I felt as if I were walking on the hillside of history, trekking up the trodden footpaths of their memory, tracing history to its linguistic as well as to its archaeological beginnings. Another interlocutor let go a volley of names, ancient and modern, names of cities and settlements, proof that Somalis were a confederation of professional communities, not clans. Abdurahman Salad Dhorre said, 'Clan is the outward expression of an insecurity native to the mind of someone wanting to worship at the shrine of individualism, while speaking in the forked tongue of the communalist.' I remember remarking then that we address one another in cognate terms that are a perfect fit for a society organized along blood kinship lines, terms with a political significance, like 'brother', 'sister', 'auntie' or 'uncle'.

Suldaan Gaarane is a patrician traditionalist. He is a charming man, his mannerisms pleasant, but odd, friendliness exuding from him. A medical doctor working as a consultant in one of the biggest hospitals in Florence, he was generous in giving me *carte blanche* use of his contacts. Now and then he arranged my appointments, and did what it took to facilitate things for me. Such was the respect he was held in, doors opened in other people's minds and hearts at the mention of his name.

We met, he and I, in cafes, or at a bus stop, and walked to get to his favourite haunt, an off-the-beaten-track hideout, where we would indulge in talk, the waiter coming with more *espresso*. Once he took me to a restaurant at its closing time, the chairs upended, and the owner having his meal.

'As people who bring little to life,' said Suldaan Gaarane, 'we cannot hope to gain much from it. Our targets are increasingly becoming unrealistic.

I asked, 'What are you talking about?'

'Tradition is a target, an honourable goal worth achieving,' he replied. 'I view peace and truth-telling as other targets worthy of our endeavour. So is family honour. Ask yourself, 'Whom do the warlords represent?" They represent a streak of anti-tradition, and they are the product of a plot to dishonour our centuries-old culture. And they break every single tenet by which Somali society is held together. Morality, the idea of kinship, of blood and belonging to lineages. As a society we have not stood up to them, because we lost touch with these tenets ourselves. No society can walk away from its age-old traditions, and expect not to be plunged into insane blood-letting.'

'What brought about the erosion of tradition?' I said.

'The mixing of clan-politics with a generous dash of *kutiri-kuteen* rumours, without credible foundation,' he argued, 'that is where the problem lies. Corruption of history being endemic, we are suffering from an overdose of viruses, which we mix with our home-grown ingredients.'

Did he think that Siyad is the major culprit?

'If the sky were to fall around the ears of a nation,' he said, 'could it be argued that the collapse of the heavens was the responsibility of one person? I agree he was an evil dictator, but he alone is not responsible for what has happened to our country. Tradition ennobles one, there has been nothing honourable about dishonourable behaviours, since we, as a nation, did not safeguard our sense of nobleness. If many of us hadn't gone along with him for our own selfish ends, we wouldn't be where we are today.'

I asked him point-blank if he was mourning the loss because he needed to be accorded a more special place, higher than the roles allotted to those of plebeian beginning?

'Ours is different from most other Somali clans,' he said. 'It is better structured, one person being the representative of the community, someone in whom everyone has trust. The ruin lies in this self-centred gangsterism: like householders not knowing what's happening inside their domains. Chewing *qaat* has destroyed our morality, with many dwelling in irrealities. They chew *qaat* and dream, and out of that dream they build a house. They wake up, and the house they have built in their dream is gone.'

Is it not rather naive to think that tradition is everything?

'The absence of tradition has resulted in the absence of a structure guaranteeing harmony between the members of our society. But because the youth owe no loyalty to the elders, the women have no trust in the family they are supposed to raise, the father does not enjoy the respect of his offspring, there is so much rot! Fear has suddenly called on us, fear of what we might have been turned into, a nation in peril. We live in a world in which the adults are afraid of the dark. Now when children are afraid of the dark, the grown-ups are there to assure them of their safety. But when the adults are themselves afraid?'

'All because of our disregard of our age-old wisdoms?'

'We are journeying in the direction of a void,' he said. 'The trouble is, we like to accumulate: accumulate wealth, accumulate power, claiming to ourselves everything, every power, and leaving nothing for the others. Siyad was an "accumulator": power, wealth in himself and in his immediate family, all the good things of life in himself or in his immediate clan.'

'If you returned, would you be a king of your clan?' I asked.

He said, 'I would not be king, MP and a minister in a cabinet all at the same time. I must share these with the others of my family in the way God's bounty is divided between people. After all, these provisions are meant to belong to all of us.'

Dottorando Mohamed Abucar Gacal is an intensely intelligent man. He was in the armed forces of Somalia long before the institution was discredited. Gacal was a professor *manqué*.

He said, 'The definitions "refugee" and "non-refugee" with regard to Somalis in Italy do not tell the whole story. And if I hesitate to come up with an alternative term for them, it is because despite their being inadequate, there isn't a word that would cover the various shades and differences, statuses and so on and so forth of the Somalis here.'

He arrived in Italy to train as a medical doctor. He was in his fourth year during the 1977 Ogaden War, when, to do his internship, he worked in one of the Mogadiscio military hospitals for one month. He said, 'The flare of a matchstick could have started a huge fire. We were certain there would be a civil war, but were unprepared for the ugly form it would take.'

He lost heart because he could not bear to remain loyal to his professions, as an army officer and a medical doctor. A man with a visitor chatting to him during off-visiting hours would bleed on his bed, the mattress unchanged and unwashed. He added, 'These were the signs of moral decay. A society that mixes blood with defecation doesn't take care of its sick. Such a society is as dead as dead wood.'

'Perhaps you've been away too long?' I wondered.

'I was saddened by the ugliness of what I saw, realizing along the way that I didn't know our people,' he said. 'No one likes to admit that other societies have better prospects of dignity and honourable survival of the human species than one's own.'

Was that why he left Mogadiscio, never to return?

'On returning to Italy,' he said, 'I made the resolve to take a deeper interest in the humanities, if only to understand my people. This, after it dawned on me that there was no point in becoming a doctor, no mileage in attempting to cure people of their ills if you cannot diagnose their ailments with help from their culture. I found it imperative to understand where the patients came from, what turned their stomachs, what made them tolerate dirt, corruption.'

He felt no close affinity with the majority of those he came into contact with, those who did not know wrong from right, evil from good, or who appeared not to be keen on cleaning up their own mess. 'And the hypocrisy of it all,' he said.

'What hypocrisy are you referring to?'

'The hypocrite's immoral behaviour, their trust in their doctored reactions,' he replied. 'In public, they ride the high horse of justice-for-all as they speak in impeccable tones of moral rectitude. In private, however, they speak differently, hypocrites with mouths reeking of the filth of lies they utter.'

I said nothing; I listened.

He said, 'The hypocrites, with their porcine tendencies as they wallowed in excrement. I am glad I left when I did, because I was getting unbearably obsessed. Somalia was reduced, in my mind, to a porcine image, in which all our ills were gathered in its singular glob of spittle. The image has remained imprinted on my memory.'

'In plain speech, what is your life like now?' I asked.

'My life is on hold,' he replied. 'I hope to go back to it when the authority of our nation, which has been commandeered by madness, is returned to us.'

'Meaning?'

'I will return when peace returns,' he said, 'to contribute my share as a medical doctor and as an intellectual in the cleaning-up exercise. The Lord knows we have plenty of cleaning up and self-cleansing to attend to.'

'To most Somalis,' said Dr Abdulqadir Salaad Dhorre, whom I met in Naples, 'the future is a responsibility many appear unprepared to shoulder, the past a lament they sing, with the refrain of regret "*If only!*" The present is a dirge. If we knew our history, we would confront the challenge the civil war is posing to us!'

Abdulqadir Salaad Dhorre has an inexhaustible energy, a desire to leave his imprint on everything he touches. An expansive man, he punctuates his speech with stresses, emphasizing his words, at times repeating himself. This made me wonder if he was hard of hearing, or if he thought that I was. Passers-by turned round as we walked, and stared at him. Unperturbed by all the attention he drew to himself, he spoke on, a man sure of himself and certain of the rightness of the positions he takes. Dhorre struck me as someone in love with the idea of uprightness, a posture he cuts with utmost ease, as if it were his second skin. As for his personality, it is as if he had the habit of depositing it in the trusting indulgence of those with whom he conversed.

He is a highly read man. Bright-eyed, wakeful, passionately intelligent, he is peripatetic in his research interests, taking on to himself the challenging task of demystifying Somali history via the study of the country's language. He was the kind of man who benefited from being met more than once, for at first, I imagined him to be full to the brim with untested ideas that are at best fantastic, and at worst naive. He was so intense you remarked that he took himself seriously. He told me in the initial ten minutes about his hobby-horse, 'Somalia's history'.

Then he told me about his achievements in geophysics with a sobriety that belied his successes. He took his doctorate in 1989. Since then he had been engaged in research and in publishing his findings, no mean achievements, considering that he landed a job with the Italian multinational AGIP. He edits a monthly journal in Somali, and is at work on a book about Somalia, 'paying attention to the language spoken by the people of the peninsula, a language with historical intricacies that have been turned into ugly inaccuracies'.

He told me he had migrated first to Canada, but quit it after discovering that he could not pursue his professional interests. 'I didn't want to be the big, but dead, tree trunk,' was how he put it. 'I wanted to be a living tree. In Canada, I would have had to devote much of my thinking to waitering, and to earning enough to live on and maybe earn more than I earn here in Italy. I chose to return to Italy where I have the possibility of working as a freelance in my field, working with Italian and other European firms on geophysical expeditions to other parts of the world. My profession is close to my heart. I live in Italy, because this makes it possible for me to be nearer the nerve centre of my preoccupation, Somalia.'

In his spare time, he runs a mosque principally for the Somali community in Naples. He helped to raise the funds for it because he was displeased with the manner in which clan loyalties and qaat-chewing were playing negative roles. Since religion transcends most of these differences, he put a great deal of effort into setting up a mosque.

He said, 'Somalia informs my days with intelligence as well as compassion; it provides the dream content of my nights; it is also the incubator of my incubus, supplying my memory with the verse and chapter of my daily and nightly prayers in the mosque so I can communicate with the soft centre of my humility, and come into physical contact with the perimeters of my failings, which are as solid as my own certainties. Even though I am far away from it, Somalia offers me the possibility of earning what meagre livelihood I make.'

'What of Somalis?' I asked. 'How do you relate to them?'

He replied, 'We are united in ignorance, in the smallness of our minds, embodying a narcissism, a self-centredness, which stresses non-existent differences, in these times of attrition.'

'Any extenuating circumstances?' I asked.

'They are innocent in their knowing,' he said. 'They are also knowing in the nadir of their pretentiousness. Give them your attention, and in return they might offer you earfuls pointing not to their innocence, but guiltily to their knowledge.'

Was it possible to cure Somalis of their clannishness?

He said, 'It's something to do with circles being squared, with an epoch of despair being born, a mood of the times guiding or misguiding our actions. A Somali wisdom has it that a people cannot be wrong.'

I kept silent.

'The *Muuryaan* marauding a building and then defecating there put me in mind of children unable to control their bowels,' he said. 'but the warlords, their partners in crime and mayhem, are like children in that they run home in panic, straight into the bosom of the clan, the instant they are in trouble. Of course, when they are riding high and winning, and everyone is singing their praises, they behave like grown-ups, and claim all the credit to their cunning.'

'Could you define the warlords for me?'

'They are the smelly fat which rots the rest.'

And what advice would he offer the Somalis living in Italy and rooting for the warlords? Or those who are funding the war of attrition from their own pockets?

'When it rains in Mogadiscio, the clan umbrellas are opened in every city, town and hamlet in Italy,' he says. 'Now what advice would I give to the openers of their umbrellas in Italy when it rains in Mogadiscio? I cannot think of any.'

I asked Dhorre, 'Do you think Somalis are Muslim?'

'They are Muslim, of course they are,' he said, firm in his conviction. 'Even so, their faith is infested with self-derision. But they are Muslim.'

I repeated my question, rephrasing it thus: 'Do you think that a people behaving as un-Islamically as the Somalis have done can still be called Muslim?'

'I am in no doubt that we are Muslim,' he said.

'And yet?' I say, waiting for more clarification.

He said, 'We are *essentially* Muslim if only because we are not adherents to other faiths. If we had revived our interest in our ancient myths and sky-gods and *Waaq*, the residues of a vaguely remembered system of beliefs that have given way to the Islamic onslaught, our position might have been different.'

'But you would agree our behaviour is un-Islamic?'

'We are a prodigal Muslim nation, with a penchant for choleric temperament,' he said. 'What's more, we do not behave in keeping with the Islamic tradition a great deal of the time, more specifically during the man-eat-dog epoch of self-savagery. The thing that is most un-Islamic about our behaviour is that we are egregiously unrepentant. We are prodigies of human nature, sinners waiting to acknowledge their sins so they may be pardoned.'

'Do you think ahead of the day you will return?' I asked.

'I do,' he said, 'day and night.'

I met by chance an Italian who ran a farmers' cooperative in the southwest of

Somalia before the onslaught of the civil strife. He was travelling with his Somali wife in the same train as I between Turin and Naples, and said, out of the blue, after he had stared for a long while at the clear heavens, 'Somalis are a heartless evil to one another, but hospitable to the foreigner.'

How naive of him, I thought, as we introduced ourselves. They told me they had gotten married recently, after a long separation. They had met in Mogadiscio, where Saida worked in the office of the cooperative Luigi managed. According to her, they had planned to announce their intention of becoming man and wife to her parents when the crisis in Mogadiscio came to a sudden fatal head. They met hurriedly, each fleeing in a different direction, each certain that their affection for the other was sufficient to warrant their hope in a future together. He flew to Nairobi, she fled first to Kismayo, then Mombasa, thanks to Luigi, who provided her with funds to take her parents and herself to safety. From Nairobi he went to Mombasa, turning up at the refugee camp one late afternoon. He asked around and was taken to where Saida and her family of five roomed. Her father put his foot down, forbidding her to entertain Luigi. The old man said to his future son-in-law, in his broken Italian, 'Mia bambina *buttana!*'

There was an ugly scene, Saida got savagely beaten, and her mother was frog-marched out of the room. A crowd gathered outside to hear the story told of a family which fed for weeks on money earned by a 'whore'. 'Can anyone believe that my own daughter is a *buttana*? Or that I am no better, given that I have eaten foods bought with money made available to my daughter by a man who has been sleeping with her?'

With broken bones and every muscle aching, Saida lay on her back for almost a month, her bones refusing to mend, her muscles in abject agony, tense, hurting every time she thought about what her own father had done to her, or how little her mother had helped to restrain the old man, and how her two younger brothers had taken her father's side: while they all spent lavishly the money that the Italian had provided her with. For his part, Luigi, humiliated and pained by what he had heard his putative father-in-law say, remembered how he flew into a rage, nearly hitting the old man for calling his daughter '*puttana*', when God knew that they hadn't touched, much less made love. 'I am a virgin and will stay one until you make an honest wife of me,' she had said to him time and time again. They never even kissed. All along, he planned to convert to Islam.

He returned to Nairobi, a heartbroken and depressed man. He spent many miserable days in the house of a fellow-national then on leave. The house was big enough to accommodate Saida's entire family; in fact he had borrowed it with this in mind. One Friday afternoon, he went to the Italian Embassy to pick up a fax, and there he met a Somali housed in the same refugee camp in Mombasa as Saida, his beloved. The man had applied unsuccessfully for a visa to Italy. Luigi got to talking to the man, who knew Saida. Yes, the man had heard of the sad story, and he showed, more than any other Somali had shown, an instance of commiseration. The man had said to Luigi, 'It was no business of the father to humiliate you.'

Luigi and the man went out of the embassy together, and sat at a bar where they had drinks, and later went to a restaurant. Luigi hosted the man for a couple more days. When he got to know him better, he asked if there was any point appealing to the senses of the old man. Or would all his intercessions come to naught? If so, would the man assist Saida in getting away and coming to Nairobi, to be with Luigi, who loved her? The plots they hatched that night resulted in the Somali getting his visa to Italy, and Saida joining Luigi.

'He was a witness at our wedding,' Luigi explained, 'and is our neighbour. A typical Somali scenario. I can't think of any other country where people's moods, as in a see-saw now going up and now down, have such high and low swings.'

Out of discretion I didn't ask for the man's name, nor did I want to be told the name of the city where they all lived. 'But what are your current thoughts about Somalia?' I asked.

'I long to return to it,' Luigi said.

'What about you?' I addressed myself directly to Saida.

'I don't want to see that country ever again,' she said.

To Luigi, 'What do you say to that?'

'In my cynicism,' he said, 'I tell myself that I have gained a woman, and in the process lost a land I love. Who knows, maybe the years will have removed all traces of bitterness, to enable us all to visit Somalia, at peace.'

PART IV

England lay before us, not a place, or a people, but a promise, an expectation.
George Lamming

Chapter Ten

My trip in the month of May 1993 from Kano, Nigeria, to Munich via London was fraught with all sorts of humiliations, because I was travelling on a Somali passport.

At Kano International Airport, a British Airways ground staff member, her behaviour consistent with the cautious attitudes airlines take towards passengers of 'deportable' nationalities, announced on the sound system that she had 'apprehended' a Somali among the travellers bound for London. She might have been reporting the presence of an undesirable alien in our midst.

Soon after this announcement, no fewer than three of BA's ground staff began to move round, to apprehend the alien. I doubt that they had any idea what a Somali looked like, much less what he might or might not do, if approached. The BA ground staff had in attendance a hefty man in the Nigerian immigration uniform, as they paused now in front of an Arab-looking passenger, whom they asked, 'Are you a Somali?', now towering over an Indian, sitting. If I did not bother to point them in my direction, it is because I knew that sooner or later they would get to me.

When the entourage trooping the colour of authority finally got to me there was the menace of attrition in the tone the ground stewardess used as she stretched her hand out, shouting, 'Please give me your passport if you have one!' It is not unusual for one to run into snags at Nigerian airports, small obstacles put in one's way by officials desirous of levying their standard fee. Nor was it unheard of for Africans employed by European airlines to be overzealous, seeking to impress their bosses. I suspected, however, that this was of a more serious nature. As I handed over my passport I remembered a similar incident at the same airport several months earlier when my wife and I were travelling out to Britain together. On that occasion the unbearable ugliness of an unnecessary confrontation had been defused by a ground stewardess who had known my wife almost three-quarters of her life. My guess as to what this woman might do was as good as a bet placed on a horse that has never run a race.

Half an hour or so later a man in BA uniform returned my passport, which he gave to me, saying, 'You can travel now.' But not a word of apology. I wondered if as a Somali I ought not to feel rancorous towards airline staff who lack civility.

I was going to Munich via Britain because on an earlier visit in April 1993 to the German Consular Section in London the Second Secretary Mr Robert Müller informed me that Bonn had decided no longer to stamp visas into Somali passports, but that the Embassy was awaiting a special dispensation from the Minister of the Interior which would authorize me to enter Germany without a passport.

Talking to me from behind a glass fortress, Mr Müller told me that since it would require at least ten working days for this special permission to be prepared, I could return in a fortnight to pick it up. To put pressure on him, I reminded him that I was off to Nigeria. He thought it easy to collect it on my way from Nigeria to Munich via Britain. From his genteel manner you might have thought that Nigeria was a taxi ride away from Munich, and that London was on the way.

Mr Müller was as good as his promise, the dispensation ready when I presented myself to him. He welcomed me warmly as if we had been long-lost friends, and handed me a suspicious-looking document, a mere lose sheet of German Consular Section letterhead on which my particulars had been typed, and at the bottom his name. Somewhere to the left, there were some twenty to thirty words in high authoritative German dispensing to me the status of a Somali allowed to spend several weeks on the soil of the Federal Republic of Germany.

After meeting my commitments in Munich, I flew back into Heathrow, intending to break my journey in London for a couple of days and pick up a computer for my wife, before returning home.

When we landed, my brain was busy going over what I had to do, including seeing my literary agents, having a meal with my sister, buying a few books and a present for my wife and child, maybe taking in a film or a play, calling up a couple of friends, picking up my wife's computer and so on. All of a sudden, a man not much taller than me was blocking my way. And he was speaking to me, his words deliberately running into one another as though they formed part of a riddle. 'Where have you just come from?' I was taken aback, and didn't answer at once. Assuming that I didn't understand his question, he repeated it faster, making the letters run into one another, like bad ink.

Only when he asked if I had a passport, and if I could show it to him, did it occur to me that he might be from the Home Office. Obliging his request, I was not curious as to what made him take such an interest in studying it, knowing he suspected my visa to be forged. I remembered hearing of Somalis arriving with no passports, which they had disposed of in the aircraft lavatory, for them to become stateless, undeportable, refugees. Satisfied, he let me get on with the remainder of the bureaucratic rituals at Heathrow, saying, with a touch of sarcasm, 'Welcome to Britain, my Somali friend!'

Perhaps it is apocryphal to claim that a Somali 'community' existed anywhere in Britain at the beginning of the twentieth century. I have no problem with the assertion that an odd assortment of Somalis, predominantly male, settled in London's East End, or Cardiff's Butetown, or Liverpool's Toxteth at that time. But I would not describe this assorted collection as a 'community'. Nor, if one were a stickler for correct definitions, were they seamen, but firemen, whom maritime historians, like Thornton, do not think of as 'genuine seafarers'. Recruited as cheap colonial labour at a time when desertion by British seamen constituted a grave threat to the maritime industry (as many as 57,861 British seamen quit in 1900), the Somalis, together with Lascar Indians and others, were hired on 'coolie' wages, at 25 per cent below the British standard pay. The reason for the British seamen's desertion had to do with the change from sail to steam, and from wood to iron, innovations which reorganized the work around the marine boiler and coal, making an already hazardous job a more deadly affair. Shovelling coal into a furnace in a temperature of 50°C is one of the dirtiest, most arduous tasks one can undertake. In the opinion of the white seamen deserting their positions by the thousands, the firing of the boilers was not seafaring. It was a job fit for blacks.

The Somalis worked in the aptly named 'tramp steamer trade', so called because the ships relied on telegraph contact with their head offices in the British Isles, which directed them to ports from where they would pick up cargoes, not necessarily for Britain, but for other destinations. On occasion the steamers did not call at any of the so-called tramp steamer ports, like London or Cardiff, for almost a year. Not considered British subjects, although born in the British protectorate of Somaliland, the Somalis formed part of the low-paid ethnic gangs, subject, according to the 1894 Act, to humiliating conditions of labour, to repatriation on termination of contract and to their occupation being restricted to the 'seafaring' industry. Unless they jumped ship, they were not entitled to be domiciled in Britain, since residence gave them, in theory, the same rights as other Britons.

Even so, some of the Somalis managed to set up and operate boardinghouses in which others of their kind lived, somewhat sheltered from the racism of the Mosleyites and other burgeoning fascist forces. Much of English society was either alien to them, because they wished to have nothing to do with it, or forbidden to them by the laws of the land. Theirs is a truly tragic story, as sad as the guttural sorrow of present-day Somali refugees.

We won't know until relevant research is done what damage this brawn drain did to livestock production and family relations in the far-off British protectorate from where these men came, or to the mental balance of the recruits themselves. If anything, their life histories prior to their arrival in the British Isles serve as pointers to a deterioration in the protectorate's skilled manpower in the field of livestock farming. Yet these men were worth less than a bit of dirt under a British farmer's fingernail.

For reasons which partly had to do with segregationist policies and partly to do with the fact that they often appeared proudly obsessed with their own identities, almost to a man refusing to assume any other nationality, the Somalis remained consigned to the bottom of Britain's heap. A large number of them served in the British Army, Navy or Air Force, contributing to Britain's war efforts during the First and Second World Wars as well as in the Falklands, some receiving medals, some earning the highest honours, their status an unenviable one, the most deprived minority, a deprivation resulting from the authorities' total neglect of the needs of the Somalis. I remember meeting a returnee to Somaliland, who spoke with pride about his days as a seafarer. This man was looking after a few camels bought with his meagre savings from working as a fireman on tramp steamers.

There is an outstanding autobiography by one Ibrahim Ismail, a Somali seaman from the eastern part of the then British Protectorate. This extraordinary document was completed in 1928, but not published until 1977. Ibrahim Ismail worked as a ship's fireman for a number of years before quitting this arduous occupation and joining the Whiteway Colony, where he enjoyed the patronage of a Belgian named Gaston Marin, the colony's formidable secretary. In her book *Whiteway, a Colony on the Cotswold*, Nellie Shaw, who gives to Ismail the name Sala, describes him as 'a nice fellow, rather like an Arab in appearance, and soon won all the hearts'.

Ismail Ibrahim remembers that he and his friends had just arrived in Cardiff when a house on Millicent Street belonging to a Somali named Abdi was attacked by whites. Too young and inexperienced to fight, Ibrahim was sent off to the boarding-house of another Somali, and speaks of a mob with soldiers at its head surging from street to street, searching for Blacks to kill. The way it went: the police would first locate the Blacks, then the crowd, numbering about a thousand, would pursue the black man. Although outnumbered and not protected by the police, the Blacks fought with whatever weapons came to hand: frying-pans or pokers. Ibrahim also talks of a Somali with a European wife, who, although ready to face the mob, was dissuaded from doing so by his friends. The man cuts a tragic figure, as he hides in a burning house, maybe hoping that he will be saved.

In the late 1880s, there was an all-male seafaring 'community' of Somalis, numbering between fifty and sixty. Cardiff was their transient home, where they lodged in the docks area when on shore leave or during 'downtime'. Aside from the Egyptians and Yemenis, they were the only Blacks. The Somalis were respected or hated, depending on your view, for their financial acumen, being astute businessmen, mindful of what they spent and conscious of their responsibility to their homeland. Every seafarer remitted money to his home community, helped to construct houses, acquired livestock and paid for an assortment of his immediate family's needs. Of every gang working the same ship, only one of their number was expected to have a smattering of English. Uneducated, the others spoke only Somali, and a handful of these were literate in Arabic, the language of the Koran.

During the First World War, some of them were in active service in the Merchant Navy. The depression following the war hit the Somalis harder than it affected many other Cardiff residents, who were also unemployed, as the shipping industry was in decline. Some of them starved to death, because, with no English and no contact with the local residents, who were, on the whole, racists hostile to the presence of Blacks in their midst, they had no idea of the existence of soup kitchens, or other state-provided benefits.

All the seafarers who survived the depression were employed in the Merchant Navy when the Second World War broke out. They fought as Britain's colonial fodder in Burma and North Africa, on the same terms as fellow-Somali recruits, as part of the native force from the Protectorate. Those recruited in Britain and those from the colony were so numerous that HMS *Somalia* was launched.

After the war, there was a fresh arrival of Somalis, some being returnees to Cardiff, some joining their relatives already based in Butetown, others trying to find employment. The 1950s would see another rise, this time an influx of able-bodied youths from the Protectorate as a direct consequence of Britain's post-war economic boom. Not until the 1960s, after the independence of the country, did women and children move to Cardiff to join their husbands.

The 1960s witnessed a turnabout, with many Cardiff Somalis returning home. The reversal was, in large part, because of the community's nationalist sentiments being high, and the economic well-being of the Republic. This situation obtained until the middle of the 1980s, when the growing political unrest in the country compelled the families with bases abroad to arrange for their extended families to join them where they were. The new inflow was the first of a series of influxes that would alter the composition of the Somali population in Britain. Following the massacre in and destruction of Hargeisa and Burco by Siyad's ruthless army of mercenaries, nearly the entire population of these cities fled to refugee camps over the border. Many of these ended up, as refugees or as dependants of families, in Cardiff.

The arrival of refugees in 1989, and more recently, even if made an already bad situation much worse, the precise figure is not known. However, it is thought that the number of refugees from the civil war is equal to the number long established in the area. With 95 per cent unemployed in an estimated population of 4,500, it is easier to count the persons with jobs. The old community is as much a victim of unemployment as the new one. If they pose a significant problem to the housing section of the local authority, on which they wholly depend for their council accommodation, it is because, on the one hand, the old settled community always remained the most deprived one in Britain. On the other hand, the newly arrived refugees, who have good degrees, competence in English, and skills, are downgraded to the unskilled workforce, on account of their qualifications not being recognized.

British newspapers run stories of racist attacks on the refugees, a situation reminiscent of mobs ruling the streets in Cardiff, as Somali settlers hid in fear of being flushed out by the police and then killed by angry crowds.

I visited the Somali community in Cardiff, and suffered the sorrowful spectacle, the misery, poverty, lack of opportunities that is Butetown. In all the years in which I broke my journey in London, for me a vantage metropole from where I proceeded to other European and North American destinations, I never bothered to do a study of the Somali presence in the British Isles. London remained the city of friends, where I left my winter gear or picked it up on my way elsewhere; it served as the watering-hole of my media campaign and a very useful one at that. I wrote for the British press about Somalia. All the same, these stopovers, at times no more than a brief visit lasting a day or two, and spread over twenty years, did afford me many an opportunity to get to know about Somalis in Britain.

Deferential to a writer's calling and more than ever cognizant of the desire, especially after the civil war, to record things while one can, I found Somalis in Cardiff and London helpful in introducing me to the elders of the community, and sharing the little they had.

I was pleased to talk to an elder like Mohamoud Qalinle, in Butetown, Cardiff, who got out for me to see the five medals he had been given by the Admiralty. Among these honours were the Atlantic Star, the Italy Star and the Africa Star. Born in 1916, Qalinle moved to Britain in 1937, just before the Second World War, in which he served. He is married to a Welsh woman, who, having provided us with tea, left us to talk. At my prompting, he pulled out his British Seaman Identity Card. A few minutes into our conversation, he told me how he met James Callaghan, the former British prime minister, in 1942 as a young MP, and how the two men continued exchanging visits until recently.

In his Certificate of Nationality and Identity, issued to him as a 'Colonial Seaman', Qalinle's clan name is mentioned. When I pointed this out to him, his handsome face beamed with a charming smile, and then he said, 'We never had problems with one another, as Somalis. It was always with others whom we fought, never amongst ourselves.'

I asked how many of them there were when he came to Cardiff in the late 1930s. He estimated there were several hundred Somalis, a figure close to a thousand, or maybe eight hundred. He nodded his head twice, as though confirming the figure. Then he explained that when hired, the seafarers worked the ships in gangs of nationalities, ships for whites, for Somalis, for Arabs and so on. Then, as was his habit, he turned to his friend and fellow-seafarer Mohamed Aden Qaar-Libaax, whom he asked to show me his Aliens Registration Card.

Some of the Somalis I met in Cardiff were as inhospitable as Qalinle was welcoming. They refused to be interviewed by me, because not only am I a non-belonger when it comes to clan politics and affiliations, but I am from the south and they from the north. They were a miserable lot, these, playing cards in a tea house which was ready for demolition half a century ago. But I was looked after, and very well too, by Abdulkarim, an enthusiastic young man, dynamic, healthily energetic, who made life pleasant. Abdulkarim ran the Somali Relief Association in Butetown.

It was in London that I first saw the sad aspect of the Somali refugees, dressed as they were in cast-offs which had known better days in warmer climes. Damaged before fleeing their land, hunchbacked from years of carrying unseen burdens, stooped because of years of economic worries, disfigured like the squat form of a tree stump in the dark: no brightness illuminated their eyes, and there was no spring in their gait either, and no laughter issuing out of them. Europe was a mystery to them, although they may have lived in it now for almost two years, because their kind of living hardly made for understanding a continent with which they were not familiar before arriving as refugees.

The late Xassan Gurxan said that the refugees reminded him 'of cows recently watered, but then denied the joy of rolling in the hot sand'. Seemingly uncared-for, maybe because their minds are either not at peace with their condition or busy elsewhere, they walk, their stride slow, their feet clumsily housed in sandals with broken buckles. Their teeth, unseen by a dentist, are brown from their bad diet, their eyesight impaired, their hearing likewise. In short, theirs is a life of provisional living in a while-you-wait place of refuge. They take masochistic delight in suffering. The Somali is a refugee, *malgré lui*!

Their voices and general aspects are livelier when they are delighting in the company of their family and friends, with their wisdom spoken in the crescendo of mutual self-trust. In their hovels in the East End of London or in the ghettos of Liverpool, Manchester and Cardiff they re-create Somalia in all its details, in the music they play, in the prayer-mats hanging on a nail on the wall and the women running the homes, the men making politics their business. The food they eat is the food the poor eat anywhere, foods eaten not to please the tongue but to fill the stomach. I ate it, and it did damage to my constitution, not robust at the best of times. From then on, I called at non-eating hours of the day, and still they prepared ghee- and butter-rich meals for me, which got my stomach a-running.

The presence of other Somalis whom they trust brings a good deal of chatter to their tongues, which are astir with tall and short tales. With Britons, suspicion and silence cloud their countenance, because many hardly speak English, and they do not feel genuinely welcome there. An English friend of mine explained that the gutturalism of the language perhaps puts the European in mind of desert noises, as if, in place of saliva lubricating their vocal cords, the Somalis had sand in their voice boxes, which, sounding gritty, makes one keep one's distance.

Sorrow stays in the neighbourhood of the Somalis in much the same manner as moths hover in the vicinity of a just-lit Tilley lamp. But the Somalis do not do savour the honour of welcoming it. They chase it, as though it were a dog of mongrel beginnings, saying, 'We have our fair share of sadness, why can't you go somewhere else, why not call on someone else?' Do the British keep their distance for fear of being infected with a dose of Somali sadness?

The first Somalis to arrive in Britain as asylum-seekers came as a group, as supporters of the Somali National Movement (SNM) militia grouping, which had been defeated by Somalia's erstwhile dictator Siyad Barre. A substantial number of those who turned up in the late 1980s claiming to be refugees belonged to the top leadership of the SNM movement, which exiled itself to Britain, where their children were to get on with their education and their wives received allowances, and they received British-issued refugee documents for the convenience of travel. They were joined by the SNM's rank and file.

More recently, however, other Somalis of plebeian beginnings, and coming from Mogadiscio, formerly an Italian colony, or from the Ethiopia-administered Region Five, formerly Ogaden, have arrived, swelling the Somali refugee population to the exaggeratedly estimated figure of 75,000.

Chapter Eleven

She said, 'A refugee is a person who is a country worse off.'

Asha Haji Mohamoud was one of the few Somali refugees to hold a moderately decent job. She was a Students' Advisor at East London's Tower Hamlets College. Born in the former British Protectorate of Somaliland, she was sent away to an all-girls' school in the Sudan, because the colonial government had not bothered to see to the educational requirements of females in the colony. Later, she went to France for further education after marrying and giving birth to a son and two daughters, and more recently, in 1990, to Britain to pursue a specialization in education.

I asked, 'Are you a country worse off?'

'I am not.'

'So you are not a refugee?'

Her gaze scanned the surrounding area as if she might receive inspiration from what her eyes fell on. She said, 'I do not see myself as a refugee, nor do the authorities in this country wish to treat me as one, because to date I am not officially recognized as one.'

I kept silence, for fear of repeating myself.

'I am biding my time here,' she said.

'How do you mean?'

'I have sought temporary shelter here,' she replied, adding after a thoughtful pause, 'Think of me as a person who, caught up in a storm, takes cover and stands under an awning, a woman standing under a shelter, not because it is hers, or that she chose it out of so many others. But because the awning happened to be there when the storm broke. That's important. The awning was there when the storm broke!'

I asked, 'Do you have the privileges which come with being acknowledged as refugees?'

'I do not,' she replied.

'What do you have?'

'Like all Somalis,' she replied, 'I am granted a leave-to-remain in Britain status, and my papers are renewed every so often, the understanding being that when Somalia is at peace, even the privilege to stay on will be withdrawn.'

'How do you feel?'

'I feel insecure,' she said, 'but my insecurity has to do more with our self-derision than with the fact that I have not been granted all the privileges which come with being a refugee. In any case what is a refugee, a person whose space of manoeuvre is no bigger than the space which my Adam's apple moves up and down in? Refugee space is circumscribed even if they have the host nation's benefaction.'

'As Somalis, we don't have the temperament for it?' I said.

'I cannot see Somalis operating in relative comfort within the refugee's confined space,' she said. 'Maybe something to do with our rebellious spirit, I don't know. It is the regimented existence of a refugee that we cannot take, whether we are of nomadic or urban stock. We are as unfamiliar with the pristine uncomplicatedness of an idyllic life as a cat no longer mousing!'

I asked her to define the loss when Somalia collapsed into stateless anarchy, in fact a few months before completing her postgraduate course.

'We are all the poorer,' she said, 'for no longer being active contributors to our culture, because of where we are, cut off from the land of our ancestors and planted in alien soils from which we receive no cultural inspiration. We are active consumers of alien views, the unmourned personages in a tragic tale.'

I reminded her that if there *is* refugee culture, which there is, then she, as a Somali in Britain, was contributing her fair share, whether she acknowledged being a refugee or not. We all put in our dividend daily. I explained that Somalia's culture before and after the collapse was daily mixing with new 'appreciations', accretions that were essential for the dynamic character of living cultures. 'Aren't we learning new ways of doing things daily, while appreciating the culture of others, here and elsewhere?' I said, 'If you wish to hear my opinion, you sound very much like a refugee to me.'

She shook her head in disagreement, saying, 'In concert with the admission that you are a refugee, you succumb fully to the conditions which the wretched status imposes on you. I don't wish to have anything to do with *that*!'

'What do you do that the refugees do not do?'

'Let's say I have not celebrated other people's history, or deferred to my hosts because they are at peace with one another and with who they are,' she said. 'Let's say I have not mourned the death of a part of myself at the expense of my self-pride, negated my Somali identity, self-servingly broken with my past or unenlightenedly severed links with my homeland.'

'What have your reactions been to the Euro-patrician tongues of prejudice,' I asked, 'a prejudice informed by racism, racism imbued with hate and slander?'

Asha Mohamoud replied, 'I won't deny that it worries me that some mad bigot might waylay me as I hop on a bus after work, or as I come to work. Other than that, they are not my concern, and I am not bothered by them. They can say what they please. Like I said, I am standing under an awning where I sought shelter from a storm. When the storm blows over, I will leave the awning. As I stand under the shelter, I keep asking myself when I shall be reunited with my land, ultimately my protection.'

I wondered if it had ever crossed her mind, all the time she lived in the Sudan, first as a student, then as a working mother, or later in France or Britain, that the day might come when she would not be able to go home.

'Perhaps it is because I had never considered this as a possibility, or what this might mean,' she said, 'that I could not, at first, define the loss when it dawned on me that I might not.' Then I watched her as she clasped and unclasped her fingers. I thought she might have been picking at the wound that was Somalia!

His alias was Ali Ahmed. He was from the north of the country, partial to the Somali National Movement, especially in its inception days.

He told me that he fell out with the SNM, of which he was a supporter, long before arriving in Britain. Because of this, he felt he could not apply for asylum status on the SNM ticket, nor for being a member of a clan which became a target of victimization. He believed he would cut a dubious figure doing either. I had known of him, coming as both of us did from a country with fewer members of the so-called elite than a millipede has feet, but that was our first meeting.

'We came as refugees from a life of uncertainties,' he said, 'uncertainties to do with who we were, members of Clan X serving in Siyad Barre's regime, while the going was good. I arrived at a time when there weren't many Somalis in an asylum-seeking racket. There were a few of us who quit Siyad's boat just in the nick of time, together with the rats, so to speak, to set up fighting militias. I fell out with the SNM leadership over the way a militia ought to be run, just as I had fallen out with Siyad over the political modality and how to run a modern state. Then I left Ethiopia, and came to Britain with a visa in my passport.'

He suddenly appeared ill at ease, in the attitude of a man who had unwillingly imparted a secret to the wrong person. I pretended not to notice his discomfort, and asked him to remind me of his last ministerial portfolio in Siyad's regime.

'Suffice it to say, I was prominent enough,' he replied.
'Of the category that conferred with Siyad often?'
'Daily.'
I asked him to tell me more.
'We used to report to his anteroom on a nightly basis,' he said, 'unless we were out travelling, and even then you would let one of his minions know where you went, and so on. We were on duty all the time.'
'And once you were in the anteroom?'
'We met there, the twenty or so of us in his coterie, and waited to be invited in and spoken to,' he said, 'Every now and then, we had a letter to sign, authorizing us to hire or fire. And even when we didn't have urgent government matters to be placed before him, or there was no cabinet meeting, we went there, maybe to socialize with one another, pariahs with no friends among the terrorized Somali populace.'
'What happened if you were not seen for two nights?'
'You would be questioned as if you were a truant, when you next turned up,' he said. 'Siyad had his way of knowing, how to displease you, belittle you, niggle.'
'Was that all?'
'Actually,' he said, 'I was one of those who saw our nightly visits to his anteroom as though it were part of a ploy to construct an alibi, in case a plot to overthrow him, assassinate him or destabilize his regime were uncovered. At least you could account for your movements, that you were present in his anteroom all the time, as if this were proof of your innocence.'
When did he start taking his distance?
'I can only speak for myself,' he replied. 'I hadn't the guts to face him. Being a coward I quit quietly. And before doing so, I arranged for my family to go to Ethiopia, where my wife originally comes from. And when the opportunity came for me to be out of the country, on a government mission, I travelled out of Mogadiscio in full preparedness that I would not go back, and went straight to the SNM based in Ethiopia.'
'Where were you when the cities of Hargeisa and Berbera were razed to the ground, and their residents massacred?' I asked.
'I was in Addis Ababa,' he said, his voice trembling, 'as a member of the group entrusted with pursuing the interests of the movement in an underground sort of way.' He paused, as though he were affording me the time to remember that Siyad had hatched a conspiracy with his evil counterpart, Mengistu of Ethiopia, the two agreeing on the destruction of those opposed to their rule.
'And when did you fall out with the SNM?'

There was more than a touch of sorrow in the tone of his voice as he said, 'I fell out with the ideology of the movement once the Executive Board declared its secessionist strategy. I resigned, saying I wouldn't be part of it.'

'And when did you fall out with the oligarchy of your family?'

'When I argued, and in public,' he said, 'that all Somalis did suffer from wholesale tyranny at Siyad's hand. Most likely because someone had reported me to the authorities here, the man at the Home Office who interviewed me on the expiry of my visa repeated to me verbatim the words I had used. I can only think that someone who did not want me to be granted the asylum excommunicated me from the clan or its movement, since in the early days, it was essential that, as a Somali entering Britain, you could identify your clan and the militia you support.'

'Then what happened?'

'The man at the Home Office suggested I return to him.'

'And did you?'

'To date I haven't.'

'Are you or are you not a refugee?'

'I have no papers to prove either way.'

'Why did you take an ideological stand on the issue of which clan you belong to here, in Britain, where it doesn't matter,' I asked, 'when you did no such thing in Somalia, where it would have mattered?'

'In Somalia,' he said, 'I am born into a clan. In Britain, I am a Somali. I was a Somali when I lived in this country as a student, or when on government-related business. I insist on remaining one. It matters not what others think.'

I told him, 'A Spanish proverb has it that when three persons agree on calling you an ass, it is time you put on a bridle. As someone who held a prominent position in Siyad's regime, were you not dishonest?'

'Dishonesty is perhaps my second name,' he admitted, 'given that by hiding here, ensconced in this small basement flat, empty of comfort as my inside is dim with sorrow, I am not truthful.'

I asked, 'Who are you in Britain?'

He replied, 'I am a stateless person.'

'And why are you here? Why not somewhere else?'

'Like where?'

'Why have you not gone back to the Home Office?'

'And then what?'

'Become a refugee, maybe?'

'There is no salt in the tears a refugee sheds.'

I ask, 'How do you make a living?'

'I make enough,' he said.

'What do you do,' I asked, 'cooped up in this basement flat?'

'I earn as much as I require from ghost-editing and from translating complicated text into English, or from it into Arabic,' he said, his voice faint with humility. 'I make enough.'

'What of this accommodation?'

'I am on a sublet from a friend,' he said, looking around. 'This flat belongs to a friend who is away a lot. Since we don't stand on formalities, we share this cramped space when he is here, as my guest.'

'Does he move to the guest room, or do you?'

'Who says it is a he?'

I said, 'Please pardon my indiscretion.' Then, 'With whom do you socialize, if at all? I ask, because Somalis are affronted by those of their kind who act peculiarly.'

'My circumstances are rather unique,' he said.

'How do they view your condition?'

'We are as self-centred as only refugees can be.'

'To what extent does what they think of you worry you?'

'It is of no one's concern what my circumstances are.'

When I couldn't think of any other question, I left.

Abdullahi Omar was in his mid-forties. His family hailed from Djibouti, although they had resided first in the then British Somaliland Protectorate, and more recently in Mogadiscio. In clan terms, he, too, was a non-belonger, fitting neither into the rationale of the as yet internationally unrecognized breakaway Republic of Somaliland, nor into the cut-throat business in Mogadiscio, nor for that matter into Djibouti.

'Since becoming a refugee, I have come round to the view that almost all my life I have lived a life of pretence,' he said. Abdullahi Omar trained as a civil engineer on a bilaterally funded Somali–German scholarship, and had the habit of creating compound words in deference to the Teutonic influence on his speech pattern. He went on, 'Do you know, it has been exhausting, draining all my energy, this life of pretence: in the cities where I lived, at the schools where I was sent to, and then later in Mogadiscio, and now in Britain. I lead a life of pretences.'

'You as you,' I said, 'you as Abdullahi Omar?'

'I meant,' he said, 'I Abdullahi *qua* I as a Somali.'

'You mean we are a society of pretenders?'

'Yes,' he said, 'pretending to be socialists when we were not, singing the praise songs of Siyad when we hated him most venomously, humouring his paranoia so as to get on, pretending. When I joined the civil service I pretended to work for a state which espoused a pretend ideology, to wit socialism. We pretend to define ourselves exploitatively, as part of a self-promotion.'

'We are hypocrites through and through?' I said.

'And we dwell in a not-yet universe, in which hope is assigned to a not-yet-come kingdom, the heaven, the next world, because we are presently in hell; a not-yet cosmos in which the refugee has most things that make life liveable. It is in this not-yet-come kingdom that we dream we shall fully enjoy the fruits of our ambitions.'

I asked if at any time he knowingly abandoned the world of pretence for a true one. If so, what were the consequences?

'I abandoned it when I joined the opposition against Siyad.'

'And you were detained?'

'I was. For two years.'

'Was your opposition phase one of pretence too?'

'It must have been,' he said, 'otherwise we would not have been caught in a contretemps not only by Siyad but by a history full of betrayals. He made us rally to the clarion call of a clan, well aware that all our efforts would come to nought.'

'How did he do that?'

'Siyad's studiedly Machiavellian tactics, combined with our mistrust of one another, made our pan-Somali position untenable. And in our pretence, we played a two-handed game, having faith in the armed militia groupings, which advocated retaliatory action not against dictatorial tyranny, but against unarmed civilians of other clans, at the same time claiming to be working for the good of all Somalis.' He paused, and was silent for quite a while. He said, 'There is no avoiding the truth that if we did not live in a world of pretence, or were not dwelling in one now, we would admit to each of us being responsible for the devastation, the total disintegration of our civil society.'

I said, 'What's your status in this country?'

'I live in a world of pretence,' he said, 'which is not of my making this time. I have leave-to-remain in Britain papers, a refugee who is not accepted as one.'

'What of your family?'

'I have three boys and a girl,' he replied. 'They are all of school-going age, and they are relatively happy with their school. My wife, my children and I meet in a world of pretence: I am described in my file at the British Home Office as the head of the household, but they know where the votive offerings come from. The children go to school, I stay at home, days dawn, nights fall, and we continue living in this world of pretence, and hoping that some day soon the not-yet kingdom will reveal itself to us.'

I asked him when we would cease to live in this false world.

'When every culprit is named,' he said, the tone of his voice filled with the authority of conviction. 'When the Who's Who of the murderers is pinned on the wall, when these are tried, when they are judged for the crimes they committed, and when our society admits a global guilt, everyone a murderer.'

'Is this likely ever to happen?' I asked him.

'In a civil war like ours no one is innocent.'

I couldn't argue with that.

Where the Somalis from the north tended to be obsessed with the idea of secession and wanted to know your position within a few minutes of meeting you, those from the south tended to gravitate towards a miscellany of topics, including the place, if there was to be a place, of clan in politics, the warlords, peace and how to obtain it, with whom to compromise.

Ahmed Aqil, the editor of a broadsheet called *Somaliland Events*, was partial to the North seceding and setting up its own government, and for it to be recognized. I asked him where the borders between the two entities, the Republic of Somaliland and the Republic of Somalia, should be. He said, 'The frontier should be where it used to be, when the British and the Italians were colonizing us.'

I was being facetious when I suggested, 'Why don't we leave the borders where they were *before* the arrival on the scene of the colonialists.'

Quick on the uptake and smiling, he said, 'There were no borders *before* the British and the Italians came. The problem with this is that we tried it, and you burnt our houses. We prefer for there to be a boundary between us.'

He served in the national army in the 1977 war between Ethiopia and Somalia. He reminded me that he was the commander of the battalion which took Harar. And now? 'I am in London, and hope to rebuild *Somaliland Events* to respectability.'

Probing, I discovered that he had published only his first issue when *they* broke into the offices and carted away the computers and the printers. He didn't elaborate on whether the theft was an inside job, just as he didn't explain what he was doing in Britain establishing a broadsheet, when he might have done a more needed job of creating a readership in the Republic of Somaliland.

Idris Hassan was probably the first Somali to enter Britain as a refugee. He had come with refugee status from Germany, after being screened at the Zirndorf Camp by the American army stationed there. Because Somalia at the time was in the Soviet bloc, Idris Hassan was debriefed by a man from the CIA, who asked him detailed questions about the Russian presence in the country. He told me a humorous story about being offered a job as a window-cleaner, a job he couldn't accept because of his fear of heights. As a tea-boy, it took him six months to get his asylum papers in Germany processed, a far cry from what happens nowadays to asylum-seekers. He repeated the derogatory implication of the Somali word '*Is-dhiib*', to 'hand yourself over', as though you were exchanging your soul for the papers. In Somali, '*Is-dhiib*' means to surrender, and implicit in it is defeat.

He moved to Britain to work for the BBC Somali Section. And after three or four years, he exchanged his German asylum papers for British ones.

Chapter Twelve

Most Somalis from the south of the country arrived, in Britain, in smaller batches, never more than a family unit at a time. Many do not openly mention their affiliations, and which of the militias they support. Some came from Italy, a fact they did not declare to the Home Office, for fear of being sent back. Likewise, those who entered on forged documents did not publicize this in their claim for asylum.

In the case of one refugee I interviewed, I discovered that he had sought asylum in Sweden as a Somali and was granted it. Depressed, he left Stockholm for Mogadiscio and ran into trouble with Siyad, then flew to Britain, claiming to be a Somali from Ethiopia, and was granted it again. His name was Hassan Gurxan.

A few months before his death from liver damage, Xassan Gurxan rang me at the ungodly hour of three in the morning, his tongue audibly soaked in drink, to talk for an endlessly long time. I remember asking him what he missed most. His mind made detours before coming to a point. And he waffled a lot.

While he did, I reminded myself how, when we were at school together, he outshone us all; I reminded myself how several years earlier he had fallen foul of Siyad Barre's regime; then returned, having made peace with the erstwhile dictator, who promised that no harm would come his way if he returned. Soon enough he was in trouble with Siyad again.

He said, 'It is in my European exile that I have gotten to know myself, and I do not like what I behold when I probe into my subconscious.'

'What do you see when you probe?'

'A tawdriness in what passes for a life.'

'Have you told your friends what you have espied?'

'I fear loneliness, and prefer their company to speaking the truth,' he said. 'I am telling it to you, because I assume you will understand.'

I repeated my earlier question, 'What do you miss most?'

'I miss whirlwinds,' he said.

I thought that maybe three o'clock in the morning, when you had just been woken up, was not the best time to trade jokes. I asked if he could repeat what he had said.

'I have not seen a whirlwind since my arrival here in Europe,' he said, 'and this has affected my mood in a negative way. I am thinking that perhaps I left Sweden for Mogadiscio because I missed whirlwinds. It is as if there is something of a "mythical" side to whirlwinds.'

'And what's that?'

He said, 'Only in my memories and my dreams do I watch with fascination as the wind picks itself up, like a fast athlete raising himself to great heights before falling, and regains its upward motion before collapsing in on itself. What a beauty, a whirlwind whirling up and up and further up, then settling, sand to sand. I miss that. I miss mirages too, that vaporous haziness which comes with heat, and which has an ethereal quality to it, distant like a noon bright with sunshine.'

I said something to the effect that it was a pity he did not go home, for homesickness was blinding him to the humid scent of an autumn carpeted with the season's leaves; to the clarity of a winter's day frosted with a coating of snow; to the inspiration of a spring ebullient with the energy of rebirth. He retorted, 'You can keep your pity and pity yourself, and you can keep the autumn, winter and spring. To be pitied is what I hate, for pity is alien to me as whirlwinds are to a European.'

And he hung up on me.

The next time we met, I asked him what his status was.

'A refugee may be different things to different persons,' he said, 'but to himself, the African refugee is an offspring of the continent's post-independence derangement, of the fires of hope extinguished by despair, of several hundred years of enslavement, feudal, colonial and post-colonial. Every *fin de siècle*, Africans suffer a fresh sense of doom.'

Seized with the wish to engage him in a fruitful dialogue, I rehearsed the questions to myself, sifted through my thoughts and asked my questions until he answered them. He was that kind of man, he could waffle. Unlike most other Somalis, there wasn't a surreptitious sorrow that he communicated; nor did he surround himself with sorrow, for his self-preservation. But the odour of sadness was there all right, and I could smell it; when I got closer, it had alcohol as its base. Somalis were not as I used to claim: transparent as a spider's cable, visibly hanging down, balanced even on the rebound. I could find no way of penetrating his protective adhesive, the odour of his sorrow.

I listened to him. 'There is nothing as complex as human beings living a prosaic life in times of peace,' he said. 'No one bothers to celebrate peace when they are enjoying it, because it is there, much like a neighbour of whom you take no notice. But then I hadn't taken much notice of whirlwinds either, and had no idea that I would be missing them.'

We went for a walk in Islington. We walked past the street where I was staying with a friend, but I did not point the flat out to him, afraid that he would be a nuisance in future. As we strolled, we met Somali children on some errand or another to the neighbourhood store owned by the ubiquitous Asian from East Africa, the children's palms tightly closed on two fifty-pence coins or a pound, with which they would purchase a carton of milk or an ice-cold bottled drink for a guest. When his feet couldn't hold him up any more I hailed a taxi and paid a round sum, confident that it would cover the distance to his place.

And on my next visit to Britain, I learnt he had died.

'There are uncertainties you work into,' said Abucar Mohammed, 'when you are a refugee, uncertainties that come as a result of your divided loyalty.'

He was in Mogadiscio when it all exploded, and stayed on in the city after two-thirds of its long-term residents fled from it. He lived in a large house with several other men, in virtual isolation, not one of them ever daring to step out of the house, for fear of being killed. His wife and two daughters were in another district of Mogadiscio, safe in the midst of her own family, many of whom would not have spared him if they had laid their hands on him. He was unnerved by his children and his wife living in close proximity to, and daily contact with, insane marauders. His brother-in-law was reputed to have murdered many people, raped numerous women and tortured many others. The way things were, his wife and her mother were confident that they and the children would not be harmed, but they couldn't guarantee what might have happened if he went. No one's word of honour meant anything any more. His family and his mother-in-law's family were holed up somewhere, he and some of his clansmen elsewhere for six months.

'How did you spend the time?'

'I watched the day's shadows lengthening into nights, and the nights contracting into a couple of hours' sleep, that was how I spent the time. And fear was my insomnia. To while away the time, we did what we could to entertain ourselves, playing cards, reading the Koran, those of us who knew how to read teaching it to those who did not. We prayed more often than before, remembering Allah in hardship, vowing never to surrender to the kind of demonic avarice which had turned Somalia into a hell.'

'What did you subsist on?' I asked.

'Everything was available but at an exorbitant cost,' he replied. 'There was a sophisticated business arrangement, which transcended so-called enemy lines. The system operated with its own checks and balances, because you could receive credit through a third party and pay your money in hard currency to yet a fourth party, in the full knowledge that the marauders would put the screws on you, and dispossess you of everything, including your life.'

How did it all appear to him from where he was hiding?

'We used the system to our advantage,' he said.

'How did you do that?'

'My sisters, in Toronto, would transfer money to a couple of the parties representing the interest of one of the militia men then in control of the airport,' he said. 'I knew when they sent the money and how much before the instructions to pay me were received by the representative, in Mogadiscio, of the Somali in Ottawa. Some of my inmates had their passports taken out, flown to Nairobi and returned with a visa stamped in them. You could do anything in Somalia if you had money.'

I asked him how he went out, first out of the hideout, and subsequently out of Somalia altogether. He rubbed his thumb against his forefinger: money. 'And visa?'

'I had an Italian visa issued to me,' he said, 'with someone flying out of Mogadiscio into Nairobi and out again in a matter of days. There was no need to leave. Money did it all.'

One of his brothers-in-law hired himself out as an escort to some people on UN business. Later, he was into lucrative money-making ventures, paying a couple of underlings, and hiring them out, guns and all, to visiting Europeans and Americans. That was where you made a mint. Now and then you might branch out into hostage-taking too. So his brother-in-law, barely in his twenties, got to organizing the taking of an Italian hostage, a simple enough operation that took longer to plan than to execute in broad daylight, in the centre of the city. The hostage was a diplomat, and he was in a mess, because he was setting up his own business in Mogadiscio, when he was supposed to be in Nairobi, at his desk, working. As ransom, in exchange for his release: visas, hush, hush!

'What did you do when you got out?'

'I turned up at Heathrow,' he said, 'because I had no idea how I might be treated if I went to Italy. I was asked questions all right, and at some point was worried stiff. You see, I had no baggage, having had no time to acquire luggage other than a shoulder-bag and a few books, which I bought at Rome's Fumicino, where I parted company with my wife and children. It was the uncertainty as to when and where I would meet them again, or if ever, that was uppermost in my mind, not if I had baggage or not.'

'How long did it take you and your family to meet in Britain?'

'Another six months,' he said, his lips encircled with the smile of irony, as though he were remembering those six months in Mogadiscio, when fate held them apart, with him in virtual detention, and she and the children living so close to danger all the while.

Then he said, 'Do you know what I did on first coming here?'

'What did you do?'

He replied, 'I washed and washed every minute of the day and night, I showered more than a dozen times a day, and paid large sums of money to a drycleaner's, a hairdresser, all in the hope of ridding myself of the rank reek, emanating, in my memory, from Mogadiscio's unburied corpses at the initial stages of the civil war. Today, nearly four years later, I still feel as if that stench has clung to my hair, the bend of my arms and legs, in the hair growing in my nostrils, my pubis, my clothes. No amount of washing has done the job. I wake up every night, smelling of the odour of self-hate. After all, that's what it is.'

Hussein Mohamed was in his late thirties, at one time a supporter of the United Somali Congress. He came from Mogadiscio, via Nairobi, direct to London. I asked him what he expected to find in Britain.

'We Somalis "discover" countries in ways that put one in mind of the "explorers" of yore,' he said. 'It is in keeping with our nomadic tradition to scout around for green pastures, at times going off the beaten track, even risking one's life.'

'Do you remember who "discovered" Britain for you?'

He said, 'We hear a lot. The word going round, Somalis talking to each other will tell you what is what before you embark on an expensive journey.'

'What did you hear?'

'We heard money is bad, but education is good,' he said. 'We prefer education in English to any other European language. We know a lot about refugee policies in Europe, some liberal, some not so liberal, but education was the primary concern, and this for my children. I have three daughters.'

I too had gathered a bit of gossip about Hussein, whom I knew to have enjoyed the benefits accruing to a man of his family, being a cousin of one of the warlords severing Mogadiscio into two irreconcilable halves.

I asked, 'If you had everything, why did you leave?'

He said, 'There is no mileage in profiting from the misery of others, no point looting if you cannot enjoy your booty. I had my immediate family airlifted out of Mogadiscio. They went ahead to Nairobi, with bagfuls of looted dollars in cash. My plan was for my family to join me.'

'Could you tell me why you left?'

He sounded irritable when he said, 'I left Somalia when it became obvious that it had ceased to exist as a political fact. The country is there, no one is denying it, it is there in the finicky wind stirring in the brightness of its noons, but that is all. There is no more mileage to be made out of it until peace has returned.'

'You left when there was no more to loot?'

'What little education I have, I received while serving in the army. That I was a mercenary', he said, 'is a charge I wouldn't deny, a mercenary in the direct employment of a tyrant. I was one of his bodyguards. How I used to humour him!'

'How did Somalia cease as a political reality?'

'It did so without ceremony, right before our eyes,' he said, 'with all the related rituals pertaining to statehood coming to a sudden death. Not long after this, when it became clear that we couldn't revive the state going defunct right in front of our eyes, I began to loot. My intention was to take my family out, and educate my daughters somewhere safe.'

I asked if he was one of the first to break into the banks.

'Everything was up for grabs,' he said. 'Banks, people's safes at home. I took the opportunities which came my way. But then I hoped that peace would return, then I would enjoy my ill-gained loot, and this was not to be. Instead I fell victim to looters with more guns than me. They were under the direct command of a mightier warlord. I fled, not only to save my skin, but to salvage what I had plundered.

I had heard that he flew to Nairobi in style. And then?

'From Nairobi, with a bit of help from a Kenyan facilitator with contacts in the government, I was seen on to the aircraft to the UK, with visas and all, hardly any questions asked.'

I asked, 'How did you get hold of the facilitator?'

'In Kenya, dollars speak for you with such eloquence, you can relax,' he said. 'Everything was done for me in the hushed secrecy of corridors I had not set foot in. Seven thousand dollars cash did the talking. I saw no one in Nairobi, spoke to nobody except a waiter, who, unbidden, asked if I were Somali, and if so, was there anything out of the ordinary that I wanted done? It took five days for this waiter to organize my journey.'

And at Heathrow airport?

'No papers, we destroyed them before disembarking.'

'How were you received?'

'Hostilely.'

'What did they do to you?'

'We were humiliated,' he remembered. 'My family and I were kept apart and incommunicado for several days and given bad food and were generally treated miserably. In the end we were allowed in. Here we are, humiliated but alive.'

Was he planning to return eventually?

'Somalia of yore is no more,' he said. 'Another, stronger, is taking shape.'

I imagined, in my mind, that he was alluding to the protean nature of a rebirth, with its attendant problems. I waited for a long time, saying nothing.

At his own prompting, he said, 'Somalia is an orphan, but you can trust one of the warlords to have the gall to make the claim that the new country owes its life to him. Fancy the cheek! What a pygmy memory some of these men have.'

I asked him to tell what he thought about the warlords, and he spoke much like somebody quoting a poet. Chanting his words, he said, 'For every freedom won, a tradition is lost. With every gain comes a loss, in every loss a gain.'

When he wouldn't tell me if he was quoting someone, I said, 'How would you define a refugee?'

'I recall one of my daughters asking her mother, my wife, what her first delivery was like,' he said. 'She replied that it being a stillbirth, it was the worst pain she had ever experienced in her life, a pain so acute, she explained, that it pierced her body, entered the perimeters of her mind, numbing it. And when the pain was gone, what did it feel like, our daughter wanted to know. The pain dissolved like burning gas vanishing in the air around it. If she woke up with the pain returning and lodging itself in her eternal memory, it was because she felt the loss of the stillborn, buried without her getting to know him. A pain for nothing, the pain we suffered.'

And how would he define the losses or the gains?

'Because we set Somalia aflame,' he said, 'in pursuit of a personal gain, all of us have lost something. This collective loss, the nation's, is indescribable.'

I asked what he had been doing in Britain since arriving.

'I've been bartering one uncertainty for another,' he said.

'What uncertainties?'

'We are like people on a journey of self-destruction embarked on long before many of us were aware of it,' he said. 'Fancy this? We had no idea we were having a bad trip.'

Ready to return to Kaduna after conducting some of the above interviews, I rang my wife to arrange for someone to pick me up from Kano where the international airport was, nearly 250 kilometres away from our home base. Two days before the day I was due to depart, my wife requested that I collect her computer from storage in London, and that either I have it air freighted as unaccompanied luggage, which would be a lot cheaper but also riskier, especially as Nigerian baggage-handlers do not bother with cautionary inscriptions, warnings in large letters to *handle with care* or that the item is *fragile*. Alternatively, my wife suggested I try to take it with me into the cabin as hand luggage, having paid excess baggage.

As we spoke on a faulty line from Kaduna I saw myself dragging along a computer almost half my weight, the heat of Kano so intense that my shirt stuck to my back, my glasses nervously poised on my nose-joint and about to be knocked off by one or another of the numerous passengers colliding with each other, or by uniformed immigration or for that matter customs officials who were presently in the hallway acting in their informal capacity as facilitators in exchange for a meagre gift, all the better if this was offered in the form of cash. Thinking ahead, I saw myself at Kano airport, where there were so many people who had no darn business to be there and who somehow found themselves in the international airport's hallway, men and women who milled about in congestive disorder, standing in one's way, blocking one's progress to the small window through which you hand in your passport and wait: in preoccupied panic, not knowing when or if at all you would see your travel document again. I would allay my anxieties about pickpockets beforehand by secreting somewhere on my person any item I did not wish to declare, but I felt weighed down by a general anxiety concerning my legal standing: would I be allowed to re-enter Nigeria, even though I had all the required documentation? My wife gave me advice on how to go about packing up the computer so as to secure it against possible mishandling. As we spoke, I wondered if I would see her again, in Nigeria.

In Kano we have close friends high up in the state government who intercede on our behalf in matters of bureaucracy. We do not see them as often as we would like to, and on occasion call on them whenever we are passing through, not only to help us enter the country without bureaucratic hassle but so as to make our unpleasant re-entry palatable by encountering and exchanging a few words with them, before we head for Kaduna, three hours away. My wife agreed to alert them to my impending arrival by giving them a ring. The plan was for her to come to Kano a day earlier, spend a night with our friends and their children, of whom we are very fond, and then meet my plane the following day.

I got cracking on packing up the computer first thing next morning, and had to go to a couple of shops specializing in packing things up before finding what I was looking for in a Baker Street outlet. My hostess in Islington took me to Gatwick, where I approached the check-in desks with studied caution. I felt betrayed by the trolley on which I had heaped my baggage, now going this way, now that, because of the clumsy weight I was pushing. There was no way I would not be charged excess baggage, I knew, but I tried to persuade the ground hostess to allow me to take the two boxes into the cabin, within view of me if possible. I talked and argued and tried to charm the ground hostess to see things my way, but to no avail. I paid a lot of money as excess baggage, and the boxes were sent into the hold.

The instant I was seen to my aisle seat, before we were airborne, I got talking to a British Airways steward with a view to having the computer brought out of the hold. I argued that not only was every other passenger bringing on heavier stuff than mine, but that given its fragility and the recklessness with which things of that nature were often mishandled at Kano airport, it would give me, a frequent traveller on this route, peace of mind if it was brought into the caring hands of the crew. When he failed to bring it up into the cabin, he promised to do the next best thing: allow me to enter the hold of the aircraft before the Kano porters were allowed to bring anything out of it.

Upon landing, I was asked to follow BA's deputy manager of the ground staff, who told me where to wait. Some twenty-five minutes later, I was on the heels of a Kano porter, assigned to balance the two boxes on his singularly agile head with an expressive eloquence I often associate with an Africa tolerantly bearing the mixed burden of its ancient and modern history. I remember very little of the long walk, but I remember what the man wore, and that he had several days' unwashed sweat, which translated into BO of the kind one gets used to in Africa. In addition, there was an inconvenient tear in the bottom of his trousers, but he moved indifferently forward, the goose spots on his unwashed behind making me conclude that in all probability the porter was not of the clean habit of Muslims, who perform ablutions in which the body is ritually cleansed of all impurities.

Following on his heels, I emerged into another hall, through a hole in the wall. I paid him off after he placed the two boxes and my suitcases on a wobbly trolley that had seen better days, and I got to pushing my way in the direction of what I took to be Immigration. With no porter to be apprehended, I learnt to my great shock that by coming into the hall through the hole in the wall, I had avoided both immigration and customs too. And I now had the attention of several uniformed officials with lips besmeared with dirty expressions. The long and the short of it was that I had entered Nigeria illegally. 'What are we going to do about you?' said one of them, my passport in his hands.

Word travelled fast: about a Somali, with smuggled goods, who had knowingly and unlawfully entered Nigeria. In no time some of the officers tried to dispossess me of my suitcases and boxes, ready to handcuff me, put me in a Black Maria, my belongings as good as theirs once I was spirited away to an undisclosed location. I wouldn't let go of any of my property, insisting that I speak to the most senior officer, to whom I would explain myself. I must have mentioned on several occasions my wife and my friends' names, with worrying repetitiveness, because suddenly two men from the State Protocol Division appeared, vouching that I was a guest of the state government. Passport stamped, my suitcase and computer boxes chalked without my opening them, I was seen to the exit of the airport, where a driver welcomed me with a loving note from my wife, who couldn't be there, because she was down with fever and in bed.

Bemused, I told the story in Kaduna, where it was received with utter disbelief.

PART V

A giant tree, uprooted by a storm, fell across a path that ran along the shore of Lake Ki-Chi-Saga in Chipewa Indian country. It remained where it had fallen, an obstacle to those who used the path. No Indian had ever thought to cut it in pieces and roll it out of the way. Instead a new path was formed which bypassed the tree; instead of removing it the Indians moved the path.

Vilhelm Moberg

Chapter Thirteen

I had not much knowledge of how the land of the Swiss lay before I arrived in Lucerne early one October evening by train from Zurich, as a guest of Caritas. But although I didn't know the lay of the country or much of its geography, and precious little, in a concrete sense, about its tormented history, the truth was that I knew a lot more about Switzerland than most Swiss knew about Somalia. What's more, I had a passing familiarity with the polyglot writings of this plurilingual European nation, and had even had the pleasure of shaking hands, and exchanging a few words, with some of its world-renowned authors.

I had been to Switzerland on brief visits before, to give the odd lecture or a reading. I had attended a writers' conference in the Italian-speaking canton of Ticino three years earlier. A little over a year before, I had spent a fortnight in the German-speaking cantons, where, with my wife and translators in tow, I had travelled the width and breadth of the country, to speak to relatively large audiences in theatre halls and cultural centres in Berne, Basel and Lucerne. I even got to meet secondary school students keen to hear about their peers in civil war-torn Somalia, some wondering if there was anything they could do. The journalists interviewing me were clearly more interested in my comments about Mogadiscio than they were about the German translation of my novel *Maps*, which I had come to promote.

To get my visa for Switzerland issued, my wife and I drove from our temporary residence in Broadstairs, Kent, to London's Montagu Square, where the Swiss Embassy was situated. I recall remarking how very few Europeans were capable of distinguishing the migrant sludge entering their continent from the clear oily attributes of bona fide refugees. My wife pointed out that I was neither a migrant nor a refugee. At any rate, she assured me, my hosts, since they had already pledged funding for the research trip, would have seen to the bureaucratic end of the visit, air tickets, visa and so on. Although I did not divulge my suspicions, part of me doubted that Caritas had worked out ways of obtaining a visa, to be issued by the consulate in London, for I was sure my Somali nationality would have presented them with unprepared-for obstacles. Never mind the fact that the Director of Caritas, with whom I had spoken on the phone a fortnight earlier, from our Kaduna base, had assured me that all had been taken care of.

My misgivings were confirmed by things going sadly wrong just as I had suspected. I had to pay no fewer than three visits to the consular section and ring as many as four or five times, and still had to wait in humiliating conditions for over five weeks before being issued with a visa. That even the bonus of having Caritas as my hosts was not good enough made me wonder if there was more to things than a mere bureaucratic delay.

My suspicions took a worse turn when I was made to fill in the application form, in triplicate, each with a photograph. Years of international travel on an African passport have sensitized me to the number of application forms one is obliged to complete: the more numerous, the longer the wait for approval. I have known what it feels like to be told to step aside so that the papers of those behind me in the queue may be processed at a speed commensurate with the respect in which their documents are held – while I am made to wait!

I knew from observation that everyone else in the waiting room of the consular section had been given one application form. Why did I have to fill in three of them? Although I was now sure I was in for a longer wait than usual, I was equally surprised when Mr Boehii, a most courteous visa official who knew me from previous visits to the consulate, made an informed guess that the process might take four weeks, if not more.

On impulse, I wanted to cancel the whole trip. However, my wife's wise counsel persuaded me to keep faith with my fate, that of a Somali exile writing about Somali refugees. Being more pragmatic than me in such matters, she advised that I disregard the onslaughts on my pride. She reminded me that the research, once it was done, would be for the general good of Switzerland and Somalia, an ideal worth pursuing. And then she made me remember a vow I had made: that I would remain loyal to the ideal of writing about the destiny of the Somali nation, no matter what the obstacles.

It was just as well that I went to Switzerland, because once there, I was received most cordially by those I ran into, and with whom I had anything to do. People helped as best they could, some going out of their way to welcome me. A couple of officials from the immigration service talked to me on and off the record.

I stayed in St Beat Seminary in Lucerne, courtesy of my hosts. I had two rooms to myself, one serving as my bedroom, the other as a workroom, two rooms separated by a corridor, each with its own telephone. I had two unobtrusive neighbours, an elderly woman, a most gentle soul, who had just turned seventy-five and, down the corridor, past a fire door, a man, probably much older than the septuagenarian nun. He had the habit of making throat-based noises, whether awake or asleep. The director of the theological college, the student seminarians and the nuns who ran the place vanished into their respective wings after we had eaten our suppers. Only once, when I got in rather late from Geneva, did I meet some of them chatting away about non-religious concerns. Otherwise, we stayed out of one another's way until after their morning prayers.

I recall getting to Lucerne around eight in the evening on a train from Zurich as soon as I cleared the immigration and customs formalities at the international airport. I saw very little of the countryside from my train window on account of the fog. When my first day dawned I woke to a mix of anxiety and joy. I hoped that in addition to the work I had come to do, I would see enough of this metropolis of fountains and lights. As it was, wherever I went I rubbed shoulders with camera-carrying Japanese, Taiwanese and Hong Kong visitors on package tours, and you can be sure the ubiquitous American doing the world in a week was there too. On my way down the steep hill that led to the offices of Caritas on the first morning, I was barely out of the church complex when I chanced upon a gargoyle with a penis protruding from its gaping mouth, a penis emitting a jet of drinking water to assuage a climber's thirst.

As I contemplated the image I wondered if my initial reaction of mild shock pointed to the prudishness of my own upbringing as a Muslim, because Muslims most definitely would not have countenanced the idea of permitting such a grotesque image to have pride of place on the premises of a mosque. To find out if my response was out of the ordinary I sought the opinion of Ali Samater, a fellow-Somali to whom I showed it after I interviewed him (see below). The man stared dumbfounded at the pissing gargoyle. It was a long while before he regained his tongue, only to say, 'Now what sort of a deity do the Swiss pray to?'

Why did I think about peace, when my friend's remark was nothing to do with peace, but concerned the Swiss? I did not share my self-questioning worries with him, keeping them as a secret close to my chest. I reminded myself that for over two years now, ever since Somalia collapsed into a self-savaging anarchy, I felt as though I were more or less bereft of the notion of sin, as if the distinction between evil and good were no longer obvious to me. Not that I thought I was like a just-born baby clutching the world in the clasp of its fist, or a senile person past sinning, who chewed his gums while reminiscing. It was as if the horrors of Mogadiscio helped to rid me of the idea of sin, like someone who knew not what the word meant. Even so, I did not allow the unsettled nature of my thinking to graze the tip of my tongue, which I bit hard to stop myself speaking.

For someone like me, born and culturally brought up a Muslim but also trained in the ways of the secular world, religion moves in the depths of a mirror in the manner shadows stir in the bottom of a still pond. Although I am no apostate, the fact is, I do not pray five times a day. So when I countenance the notions of evil and good I do this outside the theological parameters of wrong and right. Killing people is evil no matter what your faith; being accommodating to those seeking a safe haven even on a temporary basis is virtuous. I doubted if the youths who heckled me in virtually every Swiss city where I talked could work out where the gargoyle fitted in all my theological waffle. At one time, in Lausanne, things went out of control, when the youths whom my fellow nationals called *Ikhwaan*, an alias in Somali for fundamentalists of the Muslim Brothers variety, were so rude to me that Zainab Islan (see p. 152) intervened.

The idea of religion and what we make of it kept coming to me, now in the shape of the cross in the Swiss flag, now in the church bells ringing, now in the dawn prayers down below in the chapel, now in the grace said after eating our meals and now in the youths rudely heckling me for saying that the Islamic clergy have failed as much as every other segment of Somali society, and must share in the blame.

In the seminary dining hall at eating times, I stood upright and reverentially silent in the midst of my fellow residents of the seminary as they said their grace, their heads bowed, their eyes closed in deference to their deity. Because I did not join them, I felt a little embarrassed, rather like a third passenger in a train compartment in which two fellow passengers are busy kissing and petting.

Koranic verses strayed stealthily into my memory, verses which I recited as I walked down Lucerne Marina and over the principal bridge, heading for the railway station, to take a train to Zurich, Berne, Lausanne or Geneva. I often wondered if these verses called on me as if to vindicate my Islamic origins, because on the one hand the *Ikhwaan* hectored me, and on the other I was staying at the seminary where God's name was invoked daily. Or could it be that, as theologians were fond of purporting, I was seeing Him in the harmony of His creations, the breathtaking beauty of the Alpine greenery, and in the symbiosis of built-up land, lake, mountains and nature: a Lucerne of peace!

Wandering, my eyes fell on the recently burnt wooden bridge. The Japanese tourists so much loved the bridge that they donated huge amounts of yen towards its reconstruction. Lucerne's city authorities had difficulty deciding what to with the surplus funds they received. I wondered, would they donate it to Mogadiscio?

Private in my sadness I stood by the railing on the bridge and saw my reflection in the waters of the lake below, my shadow no bigger than a frog; and, *mon dieu*, how ugly I felt! Why? Because Lucerne's crystal blue waters merged with Mogadiscio's; and I am chanting random verses of the Koran and drinking the blessed ink washed off the slate on which the day's lesson of the scripture had been written. For a Somali, this has been a decade of self-doubt, I told myself, of doors opening and letting in a history marked by the extent of its maledictions. Is this why, in such trying times as these, my vision filters through a placenta of eternal destruction?

Perhaps life is incomplete, I thought to myself, if I am not able to tie the various strands of my history into a unified knot, the rich past fully complementing the impoverished present and the uncertain future. In Switzerland, God became the poem my awakened memory recited to its own unconscious. And I spotted evidences of Him wherever I turned. Bile Yassin Kenadid (see p. 158), a friend, gave me Allah's word, a welcome gift in the form of a translation of the Koran into Somali, the first specimen I owned.

Bile was aware where I was lodging, but I doubt that he was aware of the religious debates I engaged in wherever I went within the Confederazione Helvetica. All the same, I don't deny I was unsettled by a youth rudely asking if I believed in God. Did the fact that I hardly knew what had prompted him to ask it in the first place make the question difficult to answer?

For what it was worth, I engaged my compatriots in debates, as though we were battling with our own demonic spirits, little confident that we would regain the calmness with which remission would be granted to all Somalis. I wonder, do these God-related preoccupations point to a moral acceptance of a vacuum in which civil wars occur and madness reigns?

As I think of Lucerne, I think of the cross of my long exile slowly descending on me. Yet I can only conclude that the trip to Switzerland was well worth making.

Because of its fabled status, everybody has a pet opinion about Switzerland. Those who look upon it favourably, and there are millions of these, refer to its beauty and how technologically developed it is. Switzerland occupied a unique place until the recent recession, the economy functioning proverbially well, like a Swiss-made watch. Those with not a kind word to say about it repeat the clichés about the country and its people. They speak of sticklers for detail, of withdrawn and reticent people, orderly, and, to borrow an apt phrase from Friedrich Dürrenmatt, one of its most famous authors, 'obedient democrats'.

For good or bad, the country's unique feature is neither the lucre of its bank culture nor its watch-making industry, nor for that matter its natural beauty, but is centred on a tenet of governance unique to the formative history of its cantons. How these were formed, and how they have stayed in a union in which each part looks after its own interest and that of the whole, is part of the Swiss charm. Spared the savagery of wars, the land remained an island of peace at a time when the rest of the continent was ravaged by Nazi greed. Perhaps it was in this regard that another native writer, Conrad Ferdinand Meyer, contended that the Swiss live as though they are 'outside history'.

An acute observer, Dürrenmatt wrote that many of the things for which the Swiss are admired abroad are not what they seem. In his view and in the view of other writers living and whom I interviewed, the different peoples of Switzerland do not live cooperatively together, no. Tolerant of one another, they live side-by-side as if they knew no better.

In an interview in the *Guardian*, Professor Jean Ziegler, a controversial socialist MP and a pro-European lobbyist, argued that his country was built upon the outdated principle of neutrality, rooted in a profound fear of the outside world. According to him, the twenty-six cantons formed a union for self-serving practical interests. They formed a union which functioned well as long as there was sufficient threat of outside aggression. In the December 1992 referendum on whether or not to join the European Union, the Swiss voters were divided along ethnic lines, with the Germans voting against European integration, and the French and the Italians voting in favour. Maybe the problem of identity within the perimeters of Swissness is far more significant to the French and the Italians than it is to the German-speakers. Etienne Barilier argues that in each Swiss 'the uncertainty as to his identity and the doubt about his legitimacy arouse a certain power of interrogation. He who is not sure of existing may question existence itself.' Adolf Muschg, indubitably Switzerland's most famous living novelist in German, said that his country was built by European refugees fleeing persecution. Even the constitution of the land, a document thought to be as Swiss as Emmenthal, was drafted by Professor Schnell, a German refugee. With a touch of irony, Muschg told me how the four nationalities put him in mind of four persons who needs must share a single room, each having his own view of the landscape through a side entrance to which the other three have no access. 'But as behoves people who hate and are suspicious of one another,' he continued, 'the Swiss live in separate universes governed by a different ethos, different etiquettes, the German-speaker being the dominant.'

He went on, 'The Swiss authorities seldom bother with the source of the wealth crossing the border and entering their country, not as much as they are fussy about people coming in. And while keeping out the people they do not want, they admit a handful of highly talented professional men and women, who are welcome guests.' Muschg found it disturbing that many a Swiss conveniently forgets that until recently their own government used to fund outward-bound migration on one-way tickets to Brazil, where the newly arrived Swiss poor would establish a settlement named Nova Friborgo, after Fribourg. 'That a whole village migrated from the Canton of Ticino to the United States is nowadays only of folkloric interest, but there you are. Nor can anyone deny that the near-starving in Graubünden were helped to migrate to South or North America in their hundred thousands.'

'Maybe the Swiss don't like to remember how poor they were?'

'My mother, who is from a simple family, wanted to migrate to New Zealand, where she imagined there might be a brighter future,' he said.

'Or maybe the Swiss are marked by their fear of *the other*?'

'Nor are they comfortable speaking about their anxieties,' he said, 'now that two-thirds of Swiss society will have been on the dole in a decade or so. But it's equally important to affirm that there is hardly any bonhomie between the Swiss themselves, with the well-to-do striking deals with the wealthy from other countries who are guaranteed tax havens, and the poor looking rather askance at foreigners with a darker complexion. You might as well ask, "Whither the humanity of the Swiss?"'

Lukas Hartmann, who has written a book on the attitude of his fellow nationals towards the newly arrived refugees, wondered if the Swiss were tired of giving. 'The Swiss have had a history of caring for refugees,' he said, 'accommodating waves and waves of refugees over scores of years from so many Eastern European countries. It is possible that this has hit them, producing in us a plethora of indifference to the Somalis.' Hartmann recalled with pride how following the Franco-German war in the last quarter of the nineteenth century, some 60,000 refugees were taken in, given shelter and absorbed. A village called Burgdorf, with a population of 3,500, hosted 1,000 persons.

'Things were different in those days,' he said, 'in the sense that our society then was structured differently, on the charitable idea of neighbourliness, on the cohesiveness of families. Now there is no such thing as a caring, neighbourly society, and no family to speak of either.'

Hartmann put much of the blame on the current structure of the Swiss family, which, in his opinion, 'has been reduced to a community of singles living in singles' apartments. There is no need to bother with neighbourliness in a world in which the members of the family are self-sufficiently living a life isolated from the others, watching TV on their own, doing their own things alone, shopping and then going to work by themselves in a car. Often, the neighbours do not happen to be one's fellow-workers.'

'Like people in the Western Hemisphere?'

'Like all other Europeans,' Hartmann continued, 'the Swiss are looking more into themselves and caring less about the rest of the world. And they might as well, since they dwell in a world of lonely individuals. A lonely person is an unhappy person, without a family, and with no care in the world about other lonely people.'

Franz Holler, a cabaret artist of considerable stature, spoke with prophetic uncanniness about his people when we met at his home in Zurich.

'The Swiss', he said, 'display the proclivity to treat all foreigners with unqualified suspicion. Spared the ravages of all the wretchedness which comes with wars, the Swiss are alien to the predicaments of a refugee's life, never mind a refugee who is black and a Muslim, like the Somalis. And the hysteria being whipped up by right-wing extremists, the authorities paying heed to the hustings of popular resentment against foreigners.'

'Because they wish to deny the refugees charity?'

'I doubt if the impression that charity has gone walkabout in Switzerland is correct,' Holler asserted, 'because it hasn't. Many ordinary people are still caring, the French-speaking cantons being more generous-hearted than the Germans. It is the attitude of the government that is disheartening.'

I remarked on the dour silence with which my presence was received as I took the tram to his place. 'Why do they appear so hostile? What is it they cannot stomach about the refugees?'

'The Swiss are accustomed to order,' Holler argued, 'to things working well, to their comfort in their environment. Anarchy is kept at bay. What disturbs the Swiss is what they cannot understand, the life of a refugee, a symbol of the greatest disorder. The Swiss shy away from any form of disaster. They shun all contact with all shapes of chaos. You would think the world had come to an end, the way the Swiss reacted to the burning of Lucerne's bridge. The thought of an accident on the ski slopes on the Alps upsets them so.'

'What of the Swiss who arrived on a refugee ticket?' I said.

'These are worse,' said Holler, 'much worse. They wish not to be reminded of their origins, Hungary, Poland, Russia. They take more distance.'

'Is there a pattern to the way the authority responds to refugees?' I asked.

He said, 'This depends to a large extent on whether the refugees are fleeing a government in total control of conditions at home, or fleeing an internecine war. Maybe because the Swiss link anarchy with disorder. Anyway, the thinking behind the refusal to admit refugees fleeing a collapsed state is because internecine wars pose a challenge to their faith in governments, the Swiss being an orderly nation. Those escaping an internecine war are seldom recognized as refugees, only asylum-seekers.'

He remembered, with sorrow, how Jewish refugees were sadly turned away. As if to counter it, he now recalled how, when in 1956 the Hungarian uprising against Soviet domination yielded its harvest of refugees, the Swiss received the refugees with open arms; or when Prague exploded into an autumn of defiance, the refugees were received with garlands of warmth.

Holler believed that Switzerland 'colonizes' other peoples not by touting muskets, but through the Swiss franc. I asked, 'Who are the Swiss? Or rather, how would one define them?'

Holler said, 'It's becoming difficult to define a Swiss in the traditional way, because of the newly arrived migrants who have been incorporated into the Swissness of things. You even see a black Swiss in military uniform. Again, although I may not be able to say how I do it, I bet I can spot a Swiss from a distance.'

Then he told me about a short story he wrote about a Somali refugee invited to a Swiss village party for the boys who attain the age at which they are to be conscripted into the army. His fellow youths are so flummoxed that he does not know about fondue that they report him to the authorities as a foreign imposter, not a true Swiss, only for everyone to learn afterwards that the Somali refugee received a fluky invitation, owing to computer error. At a meeting, the villagers decide that from that year on, every youth of conscriptable age residing in the village will be invited to their annual gathering, even if they are not Swiss.

If eating fondue or speaking Schwyzerdütsch are considered essential in some of the cantons, François Piguet considered the passport to be the major reference point of one's Swissness.

Piguet continued, 'The Swiss self-definition is centred on one's tongue when it comes to the German-speakers, and culture among the French-speakers. To us, culture is tantamount to nationality, just as it is in France. The differences in language and culture apart, the Swiss passport defines us all, binding us to our Swissness, it being the document which ultimately determines if one is entitled to the privileges nationality confers on one. Whoever acquires it, regardless of the colour of their skin or the language they speak, is Swiss. The passport is proof of your Swissness.'

I asked François Piguet about the origin of the cross in the Swiss flag, and passport, and he replied, 'The Schwyz canton, mother to the idea of the nation, inherited it on the basis of its loyalty to the then German-speaking empire, the cross being the direct link between the Emperor and God. When the other cantons joined Schwyz in a Helvetic confederation, agreeing on a semi-direct cantonal democracy in which the citizen counters state decisions through his own initiative in matters affecting his own life, a new form of coexistence was brought into being. And the cross stayed!'

Dr Zakaria Farah, a Somali-born Swiss, told me how, in his travels across Africa, many immigration officials, on being presented with the passport, automatically assume that he works for the International Red Cross, in their opinion a good enough institution to issue a travel document. 'It doesn't bother me,' he said, 'especially since I am welcomed warmheartedly.'

I asked Bile Yassin Kenadid, who was sitting across from me, how the Somali refugees in Switzerland were described. 'They are described as "asylum-seekers",' he replied, 'a term with no precise juridical definition, so vague that those to whom it is applied are lost in the legalistic jargons invented by lawyers.'

Dr Zakaria Farah concurred with him.

Bile Kenadid continued, 'This is a country run by jurists, working in cahoots with bureaucrats. And woe betide any refugee arriving from Africa, because no sooner do they consult a legal pundit than they are told that the law is as slippery as a wet cake of soap, and anyone foolish enough to stand on it will fall flat on their broken backs.'

'When it suits them,' Zakaria said, 'the Swiss authorities use the first-country asylum clause in the Geneva Convention, of which they are a signatory. The argument goes that, not being their immediate neighbours, the Somalis must register with and apply for the status in a country adjacent to them, where they must seek asylum.'

In contrast to the Organization of African Unity's Refugee Charter, which allows for more room for the refugee both as an individual and as a group, I reminded them that the 1951 Geneva Convention is highly restrictive, elitist, discriminatory and exclusive. 'Implicit in the Convention', I said, 'is that individuals are entitled to refugee safe havens only after proving that they face persecution if they return. In Africa, an entire community may be classed as deserving of the refugee status, every single one of them, as Somalis, as Rwandans or as Liberians.'

A fellow countryman living in Zurich speculated, when I told him that I was off to Geneva, whether the French-speaking cantons had the kindness to accommodate more Somali refugees than the German-speaking ones. He had neither the statistics nor any other evidence to base his assumptions on, only a gut reaction. I too couldn't help remarking on the general ease with which Africans moved about their business in the French-speaking cantons after a week of being in Geneva.

France von Allman, Director of the Protestant Social Centre, pointed out that Geneva not only attracted foreigners but was most adept at offering them more possibilities.

'For one thing,' she said, 'Geneva offers the black person an anonymity the German-speaking cities don't, anonymity being a precious gift most highly appreciated by those wishing to effect a healthy *mélange*. Why, do you ask? Because Geneva is the city of refuge, and takes a kinder view of foreigners, especially refugees. Geneva does not apply the draconian Swiss laws to the letter.' She gave the example of the Zaïrean refugees whom other cantons deported soon after Berne decided it was time for them to be sent home. 'But not Geneva,' she explained with slight pride. 'It was only after discovering that there was no legal way of *not* deporting them that we sent them home.'

What about the Somalis?

'To qualify for asylum,' she said, 'every refugee must prove that his or her life is in danger. A great number of the Somalis have no such proof. Nor have they proof beyond any legal doubt that they have been persecuted or tortured by a government from which they are fleeing. *Because* there is no government in their country. Given provisional leave to stay, their fate is no different from the Eritreans', some of whom have been here for close to ten years, whose work permits have of late been withdrawn. You see, the Eritreans are at present being prepared for repatriation back to their home country now that it is independent, and there is peace there.'

'What will happen to them, do you have any idea?' I asked.

Mrs von Allman was of the opinion that for all Somalis issued with Permit F, or given leave to remain until the condition of their country changes, because they were not granted refugee asylum status, the future was very, very bleak indeed.

How bleak was very, very bleak?

'With no job prospects,' she said, 'and no chance of going to school or picking up a vocation on which to fall back when they are on their home soil, and no cohesive refugee community to organize life for them in these hard times,' and here she shook her head sadly, 'I foresee nothing but dismal prospects for them.'

I asked her to elaborate.

'I foresee suicide, I foresee delinquency,' she said, paused, then continued, 'Moreover, potential employers of refugees are cautiously not offering them jobs, given that there are many Swiss without employment.'

'Is there anything anybody can do to avert this?'

Unable to think of any redeeming qualities, Mrs von Allman reminded me that many Somalis lied in the first perfunctory interview. 'And so they spend a great deal of their time revising the small falsehoods in the early interviews, doing precious little about the important aspects of their lives.'

I presumed she was speaking about the asylum-seekers who were familiar neither with Europe nor with the Swiss penchant for detail.

'Of course there are those with plenty of money,' she said, 'who needn't bother with the charitable offerings of a few francs a month. These are accustomed to a higher standard of living, and raise such fuss when we suggest putting them up in the pensions with the not-so-well-off.'

'What becomes of them?' I asked.

'Sooner or later, the wealthy ones go to Canada, the USA,' she said, 'or go across to Holland, where there is a larger community. They are an obnoxious lot, the rich ones.'

'What of the in-betweens,' I said, 'the middle classes?'

'They show their frustration over the fact that there is no provision other than a three-month French language course,' she said, 'and with so much time to kill and nothing to do with it, and with no alternative places to go, they become prone to depression.'

There are five categories of Somalis in Switzerland.

The arrival of the first category, no more than thirty or so persons, dates back to the late 1970s. Their exodus was prompted by Siyad targeting the supporters of a militia grouping known as the Somali Salvation Democratic Front, SSDF for short. At home, in Mogadiscio, the sympathizers of the SSDF fell victim to the bullying tactics of the police state; abroad, they were hounded out of their jobs in the oil-producing Arab countries, and if they had government scholarships or were in the foreign service, their allowances were discontinued, their jobs scrapped. Rendered stateless, jobless abroad and massacred within the land, some thirty or so of them sought refuge in Switzerland.

They were all educated, chemists, bankers, professors, in no time picking themselves up, to be hired as interpreters. Because they are distantly related to one another in that they fled as a 'family', there is little of the in-fighting that dogs the lives of the recent arrivals. Their heads up, proud of their meagre achievements in spite of the limitations, they support one another, and coexist amicably with each other, meeting often to exchange visits and new rumours about a Somalia to which they are forever loyal.

The second category to be accorded 'refugee' status is a handful of recent arrivals, a special class of thirty or so men, women and children who, on the appeal and full recommendation of the UNHCR, were evacuated from refugee camps in Kenya. This group is known as 'the vulnerable cases'. I met some of them in a camp in Gersau a few days after they arrived in the country. The head of the camp told me that, as vulnerables, they and their immediate families were all given privileged status, with speedy resettlement. They were housed preferentially in tolerable conditions, and were being taught the language spoken in the canton to which they are to be allocated.

The third category with refugee status on political grounds, the status granted soon after arriving, is the smallest, no more than two prominent families. I mention this category only to underline the Swiss bias towards those who once occupied prominent positions in foreign governments.

The fourth category is composed mainly of young boys, minors sent out on their own, to scour the world, as it were, for a safe haven. Some ended up in Switzerland. I met several of them in Vevey in a centre run by the Service de la Protection de Jeunesse. These youths do not take a cantonal interview, a must for grown-ups. For them, schooling is compulsory. They receive a monthly stipend of SF 735, including clothing, and are overseen by a strict house-mistress who deducts some money if they misbehave. They live two to a room. Because they spoke no French, special tuition was organized for them when they first came.

The fifth category, more numerous than all the others put together and of which the bulk of the Somali refugee presence is made, is post-civil war arrivals. These have come from all manner of countries. Some came from countries where refugees are universally ill-treated, their meagre savings stolen, their women raped and life made so unbearable that most would have preferred to return to Mogadiscio if this were at all feasible.

Each of the five categories is issued with a permit, which indicates its current and future status. The bulk of the Somalis hold Permit F, an ambiguous status according its holder no right of asylum, no possibilities of jobs, no health facilities or insurance cover, only a minimum monthly welfare benefit as subsistence. The new arrivals are kept in camps located in villages very far from cities where they might find jobs. They are interviewed at least three times, and after a long wait, they are issued with a permit. Permit F is inaptly defined as providing 'humanitarian' status.

Permit C is accorded those who are recognized as bona fide refugees. Permit

C is coveted, second only to having a Swiss passport. With it, you may hold a job, may even aspire to taking Swiss nationality and the privilege of living where you please in the Confederation, a dream choice.

The bulk of the Somalis are resigned to their current F-fate, a loser's card, with no chance of ever making it in Switzerland. Bile Yassin Kenadid told me that there is a difference between the two types of Permit F, one given to the Somalis, the other to the Bosnians. The Bosnian one is on a par with Permit C: they are allowed to work unhindered wherever they may find a job. The Somalis with Permit F are discouraged from finding work.

Within a day of setting up in Lucerne I asked Zahra Hussen on the phone to explain the permits, the letters assigned to them, and what they mean. It transpired after a little that I had misheard, mistaking Permit 'F' for 'S'.

'S for Somalia?' I asked.

'F as in failure in English!' she said.

I was silent, taking it in.

She said, 'If French is to your liking, F as in *faux pas!*'

Chapter Fourteen

'It has been a mistake coming here!' said Abdi Moallim Mohamed. I felt he was speaking for many of the others. There were thirty or so of them, ages ranging between sixty years and a baby no older than four weeks. They were accommodated in a refugee centre with minimum facilities, established two years previously by Caritas in the village of Horow, fifteen kilometres away from Lucerne. The centre was sited in what had once served as a rooming-house for Yugoslav and Portuguese construction guestworkers. It was on lease to Caritas at a cost of around SF200,000 as basic rent, payable to Marti Bau AG, the private company owning the property. None of the seven or so Swiss staff employed by Caritas as minders lived in the camp. Two junior members of staff stayed overnight on a shift basis.

On the morning of my visit the place was boisterous with life. The female residents attended to their children's needs, the men either preparing their breakfast or in the laundry room, washing or ironing clothes. Welcomed and served tea, I sat together with those who could spare a few moments in their spacious living room, and engaged them in amicable gregariousness.

When all those volunteering to talk to me had joined us, I asked each to introduce himself or herself. They were gracious enough to go over their stories, revising them for my benefit. I was conscious of the fact that there was something a little too rehearsed about what they told, maybe because they had been interviewed several times, now perfunctorily, now in depth. Those who in peacetime Somalia were of middle-class background, of whom there were several, were prone to pointing out how 'mean' the Swiss authorities were. They couldn't stop comparing themselves to the Bosnians, of whom they were envious.

As refugees, they were getting used to having little or nothing. And despite the pervasive sorrow, one sensed a buoyant camaraderie among the residents on the one hand, and between themselves and the Swiss staff. Given a room to every family unit, they received rations once weekly, plus three francs towards personal expenses, and two and a half francs for clothing. Their housing and medical bills were covered too. Insisting on speaking English even to me, if only to prove that he was a cut above all the others, Adan Abdulqadir asked rather irritably, 'Why this meagre allowance? Are we beggars? And why are we not treated like the Bosnians, with Permit F, yes, but well looked after?'

There were a lot of spoken or unspoken frustrations, ghosts brought along from another life, some from pre-civil war Somalia. I doubt that the residents at the Horow centre opened their hearts fully to their Swiss minders, trust being one of the first things refugees part company with, before they are resigned to their condition. If I use the word 'minders' to describe the Swiss administrators of the camp, it is because the Somalis made it clear that they were in a gulag whose key was deposited not with those who ran the centre on a day-to-day basis, but with a more powerful Swiss oligarchy, whom the refugees have no chance of ever reaching.

Fingerprinted, their health screened, the asylum-seekers are interviewed a couple of days after they first come, and are taken through a most thorough interview by the relevant authorities every time they are either transferred out of one canton to another or allotted a permit. The refugees did not know what to do with their time in between. Bored out of their senses, they waited.

I asked, of no one in particular, 'Why Switzerland?'

We sat in silence. Their faces became framed with that expectant look, expressions dark as night waiting for the coming of daylight. One of them explained that they 'had arrived with a life emptied of meaning'. Did they hope, I wondered, that their lives would be filled with Alpine peace and prosperity, ever?

Then, all of a sudden, several of them started speaking at the same time, their voices clashing like rams locking horns. As a self-appointed moderator, I was able to disentangle the knotted voices from one another, then pointed at one of them to talk.

The man who spoke said his name, Musse Ibrahim. He mentioned that he had fled to Yemen, where the locals beat him up with impunity, raped his women and humiliated him, at times in broad daylight, in view of the police, who stood by, watching. One speaker after another, they spoke of how the Arabs had ill-treated them.

Once opened, the can of worms produced more of the same species of rottenness. Corroborating these, Fawzia Ahmed Mohamed Xuubay spoke of how she, pregnant, and her husband were walking down a road in the North Yemeni capital Sana'a when a police van pulled up, and they were asked to show their papers. Not satisfied with the UNHCR identification papers, the

Yemenis frisked them bodily, and while doing so, discovered the 500 Canadian dollars buried deep in Fawzia's clothing. They robbed them of their money, called them terrible names, roughed them up some more and vowed to punish them with deportation orders if they informed on them. Another story came, this time from Zahra Osman, who, arrested in Saudi Arabia, was deported, for no reason she could think of, to Ethiopia, which wasn't her country. From there she found her way into Djibouti, then was fortunate enough to make it to Switzerland, although she wouldn't tell me how.

If there was a common thread running through all their stories it was that Switzerland was not their first and at times not even their second or third choice. It appears as if, restless with worry for their personal safety, they moved on, with life's energy egging them to continue searching for a safe haven, until they turned up in Switzerland. Although they didn't have much in this land of Alpine peace and prosperity, they seemed able to catch their breath. And they were not likely to be stopped in the streets, their honour violated or abused, or dispossessed of their small savings by the police. After the humiliations in the first country of their asylum, the refugees found comfort in the thought of being housed, fed and clothed.

Was that not enough?

'We are tired, waiting,' said Adan Abdulqadir.

I asked him to describe Swiss bureaucracy to me.

'It's very much like arriving at a turnstile,' Adan Abdulqadir said, 'when you do not have the correct change, or the proper token.'

In time, the refugees informed me, their names and data would have been added to the tailback of so many undecided-upon cases, whose pending applications may extend into many more years of waiting.

Ahmed Haji Abdurahman and I met in Zurich. Too eager to speak, he started off by saying that the Swiss kindness to the Somalis was not worthy of Samaritan philanthropy. He talked at length of how all the Somalis had been unnerved first by the bureaucratic humiliations they were subjected to, not to mention the length of time they had had to wait. He went on, 'There is a wrong way and a right way of welcoming strangers. The Swiss are not being charitable to us.'

We placed our order with the waiter, and when he walked away, I asked Ahmed Haji Abdurahman to explain to me why the Swiss should be kind to the Somalis, who, by their reckoning and according to the Geneva Convention, which they invoke, do not qualify to be refugees.

'But we are refugees,' he insisted.

'Not by their definition,' I repeated.

He paid no attention to what I had just said. 'We are fleeing Mogadiscio's firebugs, otherwise known as the warlords, who enjoy the act of setting the entire country ablaze. I wouldn't be here if I weren't running away for my life and my family's.'

Remembering what Mrs von Allman had told me, I asked, 'What proof do you have, as an individual, that you will face personal danger to yourself or your property if you return to Somalia?'

Apparently he knew the argument. He was an educated man, one-time principal of a two-stream secondary school, one of the largest in Mogadiscio. He was the grandson of the most famous Somali poet, warrior, man of learning and warlord. Sayyid Mohamed Abdulle Hassan, his grandfather, died in flight, a refugee. Now I asked him if he had ever met a kind Swiss.

'I don't know any Swiss,' he said.

Did he know of any Somali who had met a kind Swiss?

'I suppose you want me to make a fool of myself,' he said.

'How?'

I repeated to him what another Somali with Permit F in effect said: that meeting a kind Swiss is as rare as encountering a he-mule with tits. He smiled for the first time since sitting down to our coffee.

'It's obvious he knew the Swiss from close quarters,' he said.

I wondered how they appeared to him from a distance.

'There is a manifest way and a hidden way in which the Swiss react to the presence of foreigners,' he said. 'The idea to invoke the Geneva Convention on first-country asylum and then to insist that every one of us must individually support with evidence that we would be persecuted are born out of the desire to keep us out. But they do it in a hidden way, quoting conventions of which they are signatory, reinterpreting the law on refugees, which they continually revise.'

'To whom do they manifest their full humanity?'

'Maybe the Bosnians, I don't know.'

'Why do you think they do that?' I asked.

'The Somalis came unbidden, and uninvited,' he said, 'and the Swiss take a grave view of those who turn up at their door and who expect to be welcomed into their homes.'

'How do they strike you,' I wondered, 'the Somalis who have come unbidden and uninvited?'

'Our trouble is, we are like beggars, whom the Swiss do not know what to make of, or do with, beggars who do not grieve in silence,' he said, putting spoonfuls of sugar into his cup, and stirring it in silence. 'Do they stop treating us as beggars, or stop helping us? Meanwhile we sell our lament in exchange for a soup of Swiss charity. In short, the Swiss are alien to our predicament.'

'How do they react to the presence of all the uninvited Somalis?' I asked.

Ahmed Haji Abdurahman replied, 'Warts have been growing on their countenance since our arrival, and more warts grow daily, they grow every time they look at us.'

I closed my notebook, put away my pens, and was ready to say my goodbyes, when he wondered if I would help him write a letter, in English, to Queen Elizabeth II, or to the British Prime Minister, in an effort to make the UK pay an overdue reparation for the colonial havoc visited on Sayyid Mohamed Abdulle Hassan, the man they had nicknamed The Mad Mullah, his own grandfather. I pointed out that the rapport between Africa and the colonial powers, and whether reparations should be paid to the continent to whose peoples were due apologies and economic remuneration, was a topic not yet broached.

'You mean we must wait?' he said.

I nodded my head.

'Wait for what?' he asked.

'Wait for the right time when Africa broaches the subject of reparations as a continent,' I said. 'Slavery, colonialism, the apology due to the peoples of the continents, these are topics that must be discussed. There is no point in each individual or family going it alone.'

'All this waiting is killing me,' he said.

Ali Samater left with his family in 1991, first for Kenya, then with the help of an Italian friend to Milan, and from there to Lucerne, where he worked in a factory as a labourer. By his accounts he was a wealthy man in Mogadiscio, with a booming business, importing photocopying and other machines direct from Germany.

'How did you come into Switzerland?' I asked.

'I came on a Milan–Zurich train, first class,' he said. 'I didn't expect much, and my family and I are resigned to our condition. You see, we can't make demands, we receive what we are given. What can we do?'

'You are not bothered by the Permit F, which you have been allotted, or the fact that your residence and work permits are up for extension on a yearly basis?' I asked.

His children went to village school, where they were happy. 'Our oldest son Mahad is in his teens, he has friends, with whom he goes on school tours. As a family, we have made acquaintances with some of the people in our village. It's not that we visit one another, no, no, but we're civil to one another. You can't expect much, we are satisfied with what we have. No sweat, we can wait, until we are ready to return to Mogadiscio.'

'How do you see yourself, as an asylum-seeker?'

'It's an ugly state to be in.'

His relationship with his family?

'We've gotten to know each other better here, and are on excellent terms after a rough start,' he said. 'And with my children too, whom I hope to continue sending to a German-language school even after we return to Mogadiscio, if there is such a possibility.'

He returned quite frequently to the fact that he had had it good in Mogadiscio, his big house in close proximity to Siyad's Villa Somalia; in fact he could hear small and big guns going from his bedroom. He had villas, and three cars, oh yes, he had had it good. And then he became a refugee. I asked what this did to him.

'To have come here as a refugee,' he said, 'meant to welcome the tread of heavy boots on memory's graveyard. Because living, I sense there is something about me that is dead.'

Almost a year and a half after being fingerprinted and having his blood tested for HIV, Abdulqadir Warsame appeared shocked at the humiliations involved.

He came in 1992 from Italy, which country he had entered on a stowaway boat that he hid in just before it sailed from the Sudan. When, a couple of months later, he was discovered to be suffering from a gastric ulcer, he was asked to report not to a hospital but to the police station, apparently because no one knew to whom his medical bill should be sent. Fingerprinted, sick with the gastric ulcer, he would remember how shabbily he had been treated by every Swiss official he had talked to.

'It's difficult enough for a refugee's memory to be fussily going over one's past details; remembering the tyranny and sadness of it all, not to forget the inexplicable reasons why one got to be where one is,' he said. 'But when one's present is equally infested with problems reminding one of those tragedies one has lived through in the recent past and survived: one wonders for how long someone like me can go on living like this. It's so sickeningly dreadful, in fact it is the stuff of which suicide stories are made.'

In Berne, I had lunch with two Swiss immigration officials, Mr Tomasi Konrad, of the Federal Office for Refugee Affairs, Africa, and Mr Groppo, responsible for everything to do with Somali refugees.

By the time our hors-d'oeuvre were served, I put forward the idea that the Swiss political menu to refugees was smeared with the partisan blood of choice. Bosnians, being of European stock, were shown preference over Somalis, who are African and black.

To exonerate their government and people of possible blame, both men invoked the Geneva Convention's oft-quoted clause about first-country asylum and the rules governing this. 'To get to Switzerland, how many frontiers would the Somalis have crossed, how many seas?' He went on, 'As for Swiss preference to Bosnians? Well, let's be frank about it, we've known and have dealt with the Bosnians as Yugoslavs for more years than we've known Somalis. And some of them have family here, some used to work here before. Geographically closer, some of them can even fly directly to Switzerland, no oceans to cross, and not many frontiers either.'

For my part I repeated the Somali asylum-seekers' argument: that one couldn't count Yemen and Kenya, where they were raped, robbed and victimized, as first countries of asylum. The Somalis were no safer in Yemen than in Mogadiscio, to which they couldn't return in any case. And lest our arguments led us to territories marked with the vague frontiers of definitions, I wondered if a refugee ceased to be one because he has come from somewhere else, not his country of origin.

'He is a refugee all right,' Mr Konrad said, 'but not *our* refugee.'

'How do you mean?'

'We can't do anything about Yemen or Kenya,' he said.

After a silence Mr Groppo refreshed our memory that most Somalis came into Switzerland from Italy, whose government's attitude of indifference to their presence is also exemplary. 'We can't return them to Italy, nor can we repatriate them to Somalia. Therefore we have had to invent an amorphous category known as 'humanitarian asylum'. And we provide them with the rudimentaries of existence, they get by.'

'And how do you feel?'

'We feel we are meeting their basic needs as humans.'

Mr Tomasi Konrad said, 'We can forget about first-country asylums, we can also forget about each Somali being asked to supply us with proof that he or she will be persecuted if they return home. We are wasting our time. The long and short of it is that the Somalis are economic refugees.'

I reminded them of the OAU refugee charter, which takes a more humane view of their condition, in that it stipulates that a whole nation may be considered a refugee population when fleeing a war zone.

Mr Konrad said, 'When we interview them, they speak of their loyalty to one of the militia movements operating in place of a government in Somalia. We feel that each would be safe in the area controlled by their clan militia. Now why don't they return and locate themselves operationally in the areas the movements, to which they are loyal, control?'

'Because they are economic refugees,' said Mr Groppo.

'Why leave Italy, from where no one is chasing them?'

'Because they are economic refugees,' said Mr Groppo.

Towards the end of our conversation, which had touched on the Tamil refugee presence in Switzerland, Mr Konrad ventured to say, 'Somalis fit ill with the environment in Switzerland, not only in matters of culture or work ethic, but also when it comes to their expectations, their ambition. Whereas the Tamils are likely to do well or even ultimately to integrate into Swiss society, the Somalis insist on standing out. And they do, there are no two ways about it.'

I told them how many Somalis with Permit F could never resign themselves to the fact that whereas they remain unrecognized, there are other Somalis, define them how you like, who are flown in, and given refugee status right away. I was referring to the category known as 'the vulnerables'.

Mr Konrad said, 'The Swiss authorities accept exceptional cases of Somali refugees in immediate danger of loss of life, if they qualify under the Vulnerable Resettlement Scheme.'

'And that's how things are?' I said.

'That's how they are,' replied Mr Groppo.

By labelling a small select group of Somalis 'refugees' and the remainder 'asylum-seekers', the Swiss immigration authorities send a clear signal to all potential entrants to the country. Some of the Somalis think of this as duplicitous and self-serving in its meanness. And they locate their rationale in the fact that these definitions form the present-day backbone of Swiss refugee policy, which defines the uninvited arrivers out.

To illustrate. Two Somalis, with aliases Mohamed and Ali, friends whose sisters were raped. Mohamed spent all the family's savings on sending his sister away to Toronto when she became suicidal, living as they did in Utange refugee camp in Mombasa, among Somalis who are habitually unkind to rape victims, whom they treat as though they brought the evil upon themselves.

Trained as an engineer at the University of Bologna, Italy, he worked in Mogadiscio's Public Works Department before the collapse, reaching the rank of Deputy Director, Logistics. He wasn't married, but he behaved as though he were, because he looked after his young siblings. In Mogadiscio, he lived with them; in Utange refugee camp, he shared a room with the 'boys', and there were five of them. His mother shared a room with the three 'girls'. Father had died a year earlier of old age.

His younger sister, the rape victim, now that she had a foothold in Toronto where her history was not known, was doing better, but she wasn't always awake to her responsibilities. She was prone to huge depressions; otherwise she did what she could, wiring them a hundred or so dollars care of an Indian money-changer whose exploitative office had opened a branch in Toronto to capitalize on the booming business of receiving cash in Canadian currency and delivering it to Somalis in the Utange refugee camp, charging an exorbitant commission at either end.

Being by nature discreet, Mohamed slipped out of Kenya, with the help of a carrier, into Milan. The idea was that once he got into Europe, he would work so as to help the rest of the family out of the doldrums of poverty and misery.

Ali too was born poor and into an extended family. He was in fact worse off than Mohamed, for he had no one to wire him any money with which to start a dream. The two friends met often enough, if only to speak of their miserable lives. They survived on the meagre UNHCR handouts just like everybody else, seemingly as futureless as the other thousands of Somalis in the same refugee camp, who, not knowing what to do, looked as though they had no dreams left in their lives.

I caught up with Mohamed in Zurich, a sad spectacle of an asylum-seeker. He had arrived unbidden and uninvited, he was undocumented, a man who had forfeited the opportunity of ever having his refugee status recognized. He had waited for a long time to get to where he was, with Permit F, and a small monthly stipend, no health cover and very little other assistance.

I caught up with Ali in Gersau, in the canton of Schwyz, barely a week after his arrival. He had been flown out of Kenya at Swiss government expense, I was told, thanks to the 'women-at-risk' programme which the UNHCR had put in place. His younger sister, also a rape victim, was the beneficiary of the programme, which entitled her immediate family to come along as her retinue and to be resettled in Switzerland. He was defined as a bona fide refugee from the instant he touched Swiss soil.

I asked Ali if he knew what had become of his friend Mohamed. He declined to speak to me, feigning ignorance. But that did not deter me from asking the others at the Gersau refugee reception centre how they were faring in the country which had adopted them.

Chapter Fifteen

The atmosphere at the Gersau centre, where the 'vulnerables' put up to receive the rudimentaries which would help them to integrate, was quintessentially different from that at the inaptly named Horow refugee reception centre where the future Permit F holders were accommodated. Here the place was more inviting, minders were more professional in their attitude, and you sensed they were a cut above those at Horow. The minders were restrained in the manner in which they shared their confidences about the groups of Somalis preceding this current lot. (Ali, who wouldn't admit to being a friend of Mohamed, had been through here a year or so earlier.) Almost all those in this German-speaking canton would be resettled in the Canton of Geneva, the city of refuge.

Pressed, the minders talked of the ugly in-fighting, and how this had adversely affected their work. But they made this known without for a moment undermining their pride in what they had achieved. Clearly, Mr Rene Landolf, the director, and his team, among them a capable Somali woman named Hayat Abdissalam and a couple of others, took pleasure in contributing to the experiment of integration. But then Gersau, a village about thirty kilometres away from Schwyz, was everything Horow was not.

The centre was located in a three-storey building with a view of the lake. The house was first used to accommodate Vietnamese refugees evacuated out of the Philippines, who were brought to Switzerland for resettlement. More recently, it was redesigned, to make it possible for those in wheelchairs or on crutches to move about it with relative ease. At one time ten out of sixty-five occupants required special facilities for the severely handicapped. On the afternoon of my visit, everyone, dressed in their best clothes, came out to welcome me. I even met a woman who had known my family, when in Mombasa refugee camp, after whom she asked.

I asked if the residents of Gersau resented the presence of the 'vulnerables' in their village. Rene Landolf replied that the people here were friendlier than those in Oberiberg, another village in the same canton and not far away, where a house accommodating refugees had caught fire twice, with arson suspected. 'However,' Mr Landolf added, 'there is a singularly provocative man, a Herr Strebel, the former head of the Patriotic Front, an extreme right-wing party with a meagre following nationwide, who drives by quite often on his way to and back from visiting his wife, a resident of Gersau.'

'How does he display his resentment?' I asked.

'He slows down as he drives past the building,' replied Mr Landolf, 'and hurls insults at the Somalis, shouting "Negroes out!" Only once did he get out of his vehicle, and he exchanged verbal abuse with the refugees.'

'What did he say to them?'

'He made an "up-yours" gesture, his two fingers extended.'

'And then what happened?'

'When one of the Somalis moved towards him, as if intending to hit him,' said Mr Landolf, 'Herr Strebel drove off speedily to the police, to whom he gave a highly exaggerated account of what had happened. He made himself out to be the aggrieved party.'

I wondered why the local authorities had done nothing about him. Landolf replied, 'The Gersau people are losing patience with him, because although he is giving their village a bad name, the man is not registered as one of its residents, and there is little they can do to punish him. He is known to be a nuisance, suing any newspaper in which an article unfavourable to him appears.'

'So what advice do you give to the Somalis?' I asked.

Landolf said, 'I advise them not to get into a slanging match with him, because that is what he likes. Anyway, what's the point?'

But what manner of refugees are 'the vulnerables'?

They were a handful of Somali refugees air-lifted by the UNHCR and the Swiss government out of the miseries of being a refugee in Mombasa, Yemen or Syria. Either they themselves qualified for the category, because they were wounded in the civil war, raped or physically victimized one way or another, or they were in a dependent relationship with someone who was thus defined.

Unsettled by a flood of unbidden memories, each spoke as though giving tongue to ghosts so far undealt with, terror demons going berserk with the vocative re-enactment of death itself.

Ali Ahmed Sugulle put it, 'Somali culture has failed in combating and beating the evil idea of death, because to date we have proven ourselves capable of killing one another along clan lines.'

It was as though they were mourning in silence, a man and a woman who let go of arrears of tears. They then took turns lamenting their and the nation's misfortunes.

Theirs was a two-year-long lament ending in an instant of rejoicing, when they arrived safely in Switzerland. And in the silence which came after, the inarticulable tensions within each family unit and within each individual made the atmosphere full of foreboding. When he realized that new untapped sources of stories he hadn't known existed were pouring out, Landolf told me in an aside, at a moment when the Somalis were busy arguing among themselves whether to tell the truth to me: 'Refugees are interviewed perfunctorily and then in depth time and again by different bureaucrats. A stickler for detail, the Swiss bureaucrat probes. Careless and laid back, the Somalis talk and talk. The upshot of it is that subsequent interviews expose differences in the versions of the stories, which do not tally. Then the Swiss raise moral questions about truth, about credibility.'

Apparently my presence brought something to a head.

There was a silence qualified in ominous ways. And I vowed to translate for Landolf's benefit whatever the refugees said in Somali. On three occasions they asked me not to translate 'faithfully'. I obliged, reminding myself that I too was privy to a few secrets of Landolf's, secrets which I had no intention of sharing with them. I intuited that soon enough, someone was bound to let go, and someone did. Landolf sussed out what was afoot, and he promised that no one would be made to suffer adverse consequences for speaking 'the truth'.

It was then that A.A. Sugulle told how, wounded, his little girl killed, his father too, he fled Mogadiscio in pain. He was not attended to by a doctor until it was much too late. His leg was amputated. He met up with his wife, who had in the meantime married another man whose child she bore. 'Now,' he said, 'touché to those of us who survived, even if we are short of a limb, or with a damaged soul.' And then with an abruptness that surprised even him, he added, 'I lied when I came to Gersau with a woman, who in truth is my wife, but whom we presented to the Swiss authorities as if she were my sister. Because of this, she is in a separate room from me, but I would like us to be reunited as man and wife.'

We shifted in our chairs, in silence.

Then S.A. Abdulle talked as if exorcizing a past no less harrowing than her future. More than any of the other speakers, she made me feel as if I had unexpectedly walked in on a blood-curdling quarrel between a man and his wife. Maybe because I was no longer inured to the tragedies that had befallen the previous speaker, I felt a sense of shock at being informed that the man described as her brother, and who was putting up in a room separate from her, was actually her spouse. 'What do you do,' she said, 'if you did not want other people in Mombasa's refugee camp to know that you gave birth to a child out of wedlock and the man who was your man but who was known not to be the girl's father registered you as his sister, because he wanted you to go with him to Switzerland?'

Next, S.A. Abdi told us that when her parents and brother were killed right in front of her, she fled, and so did seven other members of her family, in different directions. She had no idea if they were living, or where. She was taken prisoner by a man from one of the militia, who did what he pleased with her.

'Since the day that I witnessed my parents' and brother's death,' she concluded, 'I have been unable to distinguish between death and life, between truth and falsehood. My moods swing between such contrasting highs and lows that at times I wonder if I am sane, if I am dead or living.'

I asked how they looked upon their present condition. I did not put the question to anyone in particular, I just let go of it. I added a rider, 'What do you think of the Swiss who have saved you by bringing you here?'

Y. X. Xubay, a customs officer in the failed state of Somalia, who was wounded and evacuated out of a Mogadiscio hospital, courtesy of an International Committee of the Red Cross plane flying to Nairobi, revealed another secret: that he had shared a room, since coming to Gersau, with a woman who was not legally his wife, but his sister-in-law.

He went on, 'The Swiss have lit a lantern in the darkling that had been our lives. Now we can see where the darkness was and where the illumined spots are.'

The words cast a spell of eeriness on us all and we sat in an intact and ominous silence. A. Bile Gulaid said, 'Since coming here, I have come round to the idea that one can at one and the same time be very happy and in mourning too.'

As they dispersed, maybe to prepare themselves for another afternoon of French lessons, or maybe to analyse what had been revealed, I wondered what might have become of them if they had not been brought out to Switzerland as 'vulnerables', already qualified for refugee status, Swiss nationality on the cards.

I went in search of some of the first to arrive unbidden, and who waited for many patient years before being recognized as refugees, and given Permit C.

Zainab Islan was a tall woman of dignified bearing, mid-forties in age. Bespectacled, and dressed in the Middle Eastern style of a devout Muslim woman (long skirt, long blouse, head and neck covered), she met my wife and me at Lausanne railway station with Zahra, her cosmopolitan niece.

Zainab told us that she first left Somalia as long ago as 1967, initially going to Egypt and Iraq to further her education. When the 1977 war with Ethiopia broke out, Zainab stayed on in the United Arab Emirates to work, leaving her daughter with her sister. Subsequent years saw political changes obliging her to remain out of Somalia and in exile. She held jobs in Abu Dhabi, sending for her daughter and bearing a second. Sometime after the birth of her second daughter, Zainab's husband died. From then on, she continued dedicating herself to raising and educating her two young daughters.

She was not entirely safe from the Siyad regime in the United Arab Emirates, and experienced harassment and intimidation. In 1979, the seizure of her passport led her to register with the UNHCR as a prelude to seeking asylum. She eventually managed to secure another Somali passport, and immediately withdrew her application for asylum, preferring to remain a Somali. But the story did not end there. In what became an international scandal, the collusion between Siyad's regime and the United Arab Emirates security services was eventually to lead to Zainab losing her job, and, with it, her rights of residence in that country. In 1986, she travelled to Switzerland with her two daughters, planning to find work and remain there.

Her plans to find work in Switzerland were thwarted by a disability in her finger-joints. Running low on resources, and with a visa due to expire, she registered for asylum in Switzerland. Interviewed, she was asked to submit a curriculum vitae, and was told that in view of her history of persecution, there should not be any difficulty. She might even be granted asylum within six months. The Swiss being unfamiliar with the Somali situation at that time, Amnesty International, which was contacted, corroborated her story and supported her application. This promising start was soon to give way to a protracted struggle, during which Zainab was to experience unanticipated humiliations, insults and anxiety so severe that she developed stomach ulcers. It was to take five years for the Swiss to accept her application and finally award her Permit C. Throughout this period no explanations were given for the delay, nor did her constant phone calls and letters yield any immediate result. Time and time again she received the abrupt reply, 'There are many files.' Finally, despondency led her to push the case to the back of her mind and to focus on the immediacies of her situation.

Looking back at that period, Zainab, in the absence of any guidance or advice, had unwittingly breached the Swiss procedures on several counts. She did so by renting a flat with her niece, without first obtaining permission from the Swiss authorities. But she had no idea she was expected to live in a refugee centre with other refugees. She committed a second 'error' by persisting in looking for work in Geneva at a time when her application for asylum was with the Lausanne office. Again, she had no idea about this. All this led the Swiss bureaucrats to view her with suspicion.

Her worst humiliation, however, came from a young Colombian employed as her boss in a mini-supermarket where she worked. This young woman spoke no English or any of the other four languages Zainab is fluent in. Worse still, this woman was filled with antipathy towards Muslims, an animosity whipped up at the time by the publicity surrounding the Ayatollah Khomeini's 'Islamic revolution' in Iran. On more than one occasion the woman told Zainab, who was by this time rapidly learning French, 'If you were somebody at home, you are nothing here, nothing at all.'

On other occasions she was harassed with unpleasant innuendoes about her clothing. And when she complained to the superior, she was subjected to further insulting interrogations, and told that she would never be accepted in Swiss society if she continued to dress in the way that she did, that for Swiss people her head cover had the same effect as a punk's dress style, signalling her refusal to integrate.

Constantly being treated with suspicion, and with her requests for work disbelieved, her welfare assistant, aiming to prove her point, found Zainab a demeaning job, cleaning the kitchens of the local Migro supermarket cafeteria. The manager was reluctant to take her, feeling that the work was too dirty and too heavy. By now desperate for any straw of hope, Zainab begged him for the job and was assigned the somewhat lighter duty of serving in the cafeteria for twenty-five hours a week.

Elated, Zainab recalled how much this meant to her at the time. 'Until then I had felt really bad,' she said. 'I was used to helping myself and my children. I had my honour and I existed as a person. Then I became a beggar. For four months they gave us a little money. I did not know what this money was, I mean I had no idea what my relation to this money was, nor what its source was. That it was not coming from somebody related to me by blood or marriage, from my father, my brothers or sisters: this bothered me, making me wonder if I was any different from street beggars into whose cans you tossed coins. You see, when we arrived here we came with our own clothes and a few possessions. But to go to that office in order to collect this votive offering, I had to change my dress to show my degraded status. You cannot imagine the humiliations I suffered. The only thing I kept was my headscarf, a symbol of my self-honour.'

Perhaps the most upsetting aspect of becoming a refugee family was the blow it dealt to her daughters' education. Zainab describes how they had both been doing extremely well in private schools in Abu Dhabi, only to find their whole future changed on arriving in Switzerland, where they were automatically consigned to the class for failures, children deemed unlikely to continue their studies after the ninth grade, and who would perforce be directed towards vocational training rather than higher education. Her daughters did not like attending school any more; they did not like Switzerland either. It was this above all else that made Zainab want to leave the country. She became ill because she did not know how to leave or where to go.

Six months after she obtained the job at the Migro cafeteria the tide turned when Zainab was offered a job with an Arab bank in Geneva. She spoke of this breakthrough, 'This means a great deal to my self-pride,' she said. 'After all I have come back to myself, am no longer a beggar with an empty tin stretched out for alms coins to be dropped into it. This is the sort of work I was used to doing, so I am my own person again, a human being with dignity and treated with respect. There were times when I had wondered if I would ever again be useful to myself, my daughters and the larger community. I had known that in Europe after you reach a certain age there is a problem getting work on account of insurance coverage and so on.'

Since being given her asylum papers, Zainab has been free to travel and own property in her own name. She is optimistic about the future, an optimism she attributes to her faith in Allah. Of course, she would like to be in her own country, but cannot at present see her way home. She said, 'I will continue my life in Lausanne until such time as I can once again return to Somalia and *be* a human, a Somali.'

Zahra Hussein, in her mid-thirties, had lived in Lausanne since she first arrived in Switzerland in February 1979, nearly fifteen years previously. A slightly built woman, she, in contrast to her aunt, dressed in Western European styles and smoked in public. She had originally left Somalia to study in the United Arab Emirates and from there made her way to Europe. Intelligent and ambitious, she intended to study medicine. The world in which she grew up was one in which, as she put it, 'You had to look for and find everything in Europe.'

Her ambitions to study were never fulfilled. She spent the first year learning French, and then found it necessary to earn her living. When visa problems developed, she applied for asylum on the basis that there were severe political problems in Somalia and that she faced persecution. At that time it was easy enough to obtain the blue card which would allow her to remain in the country and to find work. That meant there was no chance for her to pursue her medical studies as she had hoped, since she was not Swiss, and had no refugee status which would have facilitated things. But in 1983 she was issued with the appropriate papers, and was able to enrol as a student the same year. Not lucky, she failed her exams at the end of the year, a failure she attributed to the difficulty of the system and the language. Then the charitable sources dried up.

Soon after this she took a job at the local McDonald's, still hoping to find a way of studying medicine. For a while she worked as a hospital auxiliary, and in 1986 approached another charity. She was offered an opportunity to study, but the offer depended on her agreeing that at the end of her course she would not work in Switzerland, but return to work somewhere in Africa or anywhere in the Third World. Failure to do so would mean paying the full cost of her course. Zahra was subsequently offered a chance to study not medicine but midwifery, and not in Switzerland. She would have to go to a college in Guinea, a country she had no knowledge of or contact with. When she insisted that it was medicine that she wished to study, the offer of assistance was withdrawn. Once again she began to work in McDonald's, eventually taking up a course as a medical secretary. Finally she was awarded a medical scholarship, but once again she failed her exams at the end of the year, and so lost her funding.

When we met, Zahra was working as a translator for Somalis in Lausanne, at the Centre d'Enregistrement, paid on a hourly basis. Because of her up-to-date knowledge about asylum, I asked her to repeat it for our benefit. She explained that first interviews on arrival are for no more than thirty minutes, but the second, after which the asylum-seekers are sent to the cantons for their interview, can last from one to six solid hours. All files are kept in the Berne Office of Refugees until cases are decided.

'The Swiss', Zahra said, 'are "always correct". One gets the impression that one is not liked.' In answer to the question 'Are they racist?' she unhesitatingly answered yes, and proceeded to give examples.

'When I first came to Switzerland I wanted to work because I had no money,' she said. 'I had learnt some French and phoned about a job in a bar, and was asked to come, but when I arrived there the bar owner said he was sorry, he wouldn't offer me the job because if he did he was bound to lose many of his customers, who would not like to be served by a black person.'

On another occasion she accompanied her aunt to apply for an extension of her visa, and while they were waiting, a Swiss woman came into the office and barged in front of them. On being challenged, the woman responded that they were foreigners so they would have to wait. They went to the desk together, confronting the officer whom they were waiting to see, who told them to keep him out of their dispute, because he could only see one person at a time. Zahra accused the woman of racism, and when she flounced out of the office, the official was so angry that he refused to attend to her.

But she had many Swiss friends and colleagues, and felt she had an easier time than most Somalis because she spoke the language well and had a moderately paid job, and because she 'respects the system'. For what it's worth, she considered herself quite well integrated into Swiss society. She would not, however, consider having a Swiss boyfriend or marrying: 'Because I am a Somali woman and a Muslim.' Later, on the way to the station, and out of the hearing of her aunt, she confided in us that although she was quite happy with her life, she and the other Somali women who came to Europe in their youth had missed out on one thing: none of them have been able to marry and raise families of their own. She spoke of a great many friends in cities all over Europe who were in the same situation. She regretted that after fifteen years of being in Europe she had not achieved much in the way of qualifications. She blamed the failure on the difficulties peculiar to a woman of her state of mind and condition. But she was cheerful and charmingly persistent if nothing else, for she had recently enrolled for a part-time course at the Institute of Development Studies, where she would be pursuing a degree in social sciences. Meanwhile, she had also applied for Swiss citizenship. This meant she would remain in the Canton of Lausanne for at least five years until her application was granted.

She admitted to having changed a great deal since coming to Switzerland, for initially the thought of giving up her Somali passport filled her with horror. A refugee is 'someone who is no one', she argued.

In her opinion, women, as refugees, fared much better than the men. 'It is because by the time they arrive here in Europe, the men will have lost their dignity and all the privileges attached to being males. They are no longer the kings of the household. Here they find themselves in a nuclear couple, with the women their equal. Since neither men nor women are likely to be given a job commensurate with their status, you find both doing the same kind of low job. Women are more used to that, probably because they used to do it at home! It has brought about the absurd situation in which women are the breadwinners and men the dependants. And then, the men refuse to help at home. How very ludicrous!'

'What of infibulation?' I said.

'Infibulation has decreased,' she replied, 'because the law forbids it in Switzerland and women are told it is an evil deed to subject their daughters to. Many mothers have had time to think about this and are no longer having it performed on their daughters.'

'Anything else the Somalis do and the Swiss don't like?'

'The Swiss hate seeing Somalis hanging about the station,' she said, 'a loathsome behaviour, which is in contrast to the Swiss work ethic. There are no community centres for Somalis, whereas the Tamils have a very cohesive one, with politics as its basis. All efforts to set up a community centre for Somalis have been thwarted by divisions within their rank and file. All in vain. And such acrimony!'

Bile Yassin Kenadid was one of the first of the 1980s group of Somalis to apply for refugee status and, having been issued with Permit C, now works for a contact lens manufacturer based in Zurich. He said, 'Suspecting that we had no sufficient grounds on which to file an application for refugee status, the Swiss insisted that we supplied them with watertight proof that our lives were in danger if we returned to Somalia. Meanwhile they stalled, not deciding on our cases until after four years in which we were interviewed in Berne, then in Zurich, the canton with whose police my family and I first registered. The police suggested we went to St Gallen refugee camp, then full of Poles, and where there were several persons to a room. Because we found the centre to be terribly congested, we appealed to the social welfare people to find us a three-room apartment near the place where I work. Our papers came through in 1984, and in 1986 we moved to a suburb in Zurich, into a Portuguese neighbourhood.'

Any problems? 'None whatsoever,' he replied, 'because we hardly socialize with one another. Even so, the Portuguese neighbours never fail to point out how bright-eyed and handsome our kids are.'

But why did it take so long for their papers to come through?

'Because', he said, 'the Swiss are cautious when it comes to creating a legal precedent. They investigate the private lives of asylum seekers, whom they interview several times. Have you seen the film *The Swiss Makers*? Funny but true to type. Anyway, here in Switzerland, whether you are accepted or not depends to a large degree on the bureaucrat interviewing you.'

And how did he find the presence of recent arrivals?

Taking refuge in a Somali proverb, he replied that the guests of the same household are bound to dislike one another. For my part I understood that he was referring generally to the influx of refugees into Switzerland, not specifically to Somalis, for he alluded immediately to refugees suspected of being drug-peddlers, and I knew this to be an accusation often levelled against those who hail from Kosovo.

Ultimately though, one must thank the little mercies of life, for Bile Yassin and his wife Maryam run a happy home together, with bright-eyed children who I believe are destined to enjoy a better life.

Jobless for a couple of years and now homeless, Yusuf Abdi Haji, nicknamed

Qandalo, arrived in the country in 1978. He had known Switzerland a little, for he used to come and work in the summers during his student years in Hungary. It was a pity his degree in industrial psychology was negatively assessed, because 'this means I am qualified to do only manual jobs'. Even though a carrier of Permit C, which entitles him to work and to social welfare benefit, Qandalo had no employment, on account of the current recession. 'What there is goes preferentially to younger men and women,' he said. According to a new decree, his 'unemployed' status would entitle him to draw 70 per cent of his last salary, and this for no more than two calendar years, after which it would be discontinued.

'The jobless are the first to become homeless,' Qandalo said. Then, as if paranoid, he explained that someone was intending to blacklist him. 'Otherwise, how can I explain the unsubstantiated claim that I owe the Swiss government some SF 2,500 in unpaid taxes, when I do not? You see, in this country once you are accused of tax evasion and are blacklisted you are doomed. Not entitled to a loan from the bank; not able to rent a flat in your name; not able to apply for Swiss nationality. You are zero!'

Flying out of Zurich on British Airways flight BA711 proved to be just as embarrassingly difficult as coming into Switzerland in the first instance. This time the problem originated not with the Swiss authorities, who probably would have been pleased to be rid of me, but with BA's ground staff at the airport.

I hold a visitor's visa to Britain, renewable every so often. It just so happened that my visa for Britain, issued in New York, had expired a week before the date I had planned to return to London, to be with my wife, who was expecting our first baby daughter. As my luck had it, I was able to renew the visa in Geneva, no hassle.

Nor was there any problem checking in at the airline counter, a task performed with warmth. It was when we were called to board the aircraft, and we queued, that a rather punctilious British Airways official picked me out as soon as he saw that I was travelling on a Somali passport. He told me to please step aside. Well, I am not one to stand without a fuss. And so I created a fracas. I wanted all the passengers to know what was being done to me.

It took a few minutes for the problem to be sorted out. Perhaps a phone call to the consulate, asking if they had issued it, or maybe he had the relevant pages photocopied, in an effort to prove me wrong if I tore up my passport and claimed to be a stateless person once at Heathrow. In all probability he gave a photocopy of the photocopy to the cabin crew, just to be on the safe side.

Anyway, when I finally boarded the aircraft, I was aware that everyone was avoiding my eye, as the British have the habit of doing. Except an elderly man with a heavy German accent, maybe a Jew. He indulged me with his interest, telling me that he was only too familiar with the expression 'Step aside,' being the only family member who had survived the Nazi Holocaust. I doubted if he thought that the comparison ended there.

PART VI

Swedes regard foreigners with a calmer, quieter disapproval. They simply treat foreignness as some sort of congenital indiscretion — as a kind of psychic social disease that by rights should embarrass anyone afflicted with it into lying low until the symptoms have disappeared.

Jane Kramer, *Unsettling Europe*

Chapter Sixteen

I flew into Arlanda Airport early one July morning in 1980 to meet up with the then First Secretary of the Somali Embassy in Stockholm. I wanted to have a new passport issued, not because it had expired, but because travelling as often as I did I had run out of visa pages. I lived in the Bavarian city of Bayreuth at the time, and I held the ambiguous position of guest professor.

Anyway, the Stockholm-based Somali diplomat and I had made arrangements as precise as a knitter's. If we had agreed to meet up in secret, it was because I had fallen foul of Siyad's regime nearly a decade earlier and had been aware of the attendant risks of doing so. Moreover, I kept insisting I would never exchange my Somali passport for a refugee travel document. This meant I could not travel on the dictates of a passing whim, as I had to organize a visa well in advance before crossing a border. On occasion I had to make costly detours.

I arrived at Arlanda as a transit passenger, scheduled to leave for Oslo later that very day. When I identified myself to the airline people and learnt that no message had been left for me, and nothing to collect, I rang the consular section of the embassy, only to be told that my friend Omar Abdurahman Hersi, nicknamed Ilay, because he has one eye, had travelled to Oslo on some urgent business. Giving my code name, I said where I was at the airport, and I wondered if Omar-Ilay had left 'something' for me to pick up. When the man told me he had 'a sealed envelope', I asked if the envelope was thick or thin. It was my idea to find out from the description if we were talking about a passport or simply a note saying that the Ambassador had declined my request for a passport. But the man would not oblige my request, saying, 'You come and find it yourself by collecting it. I am here, waiting.'

Growing increasingly alarmed, I pleaded with him. I explained my difficulty, that I had no visa to enter Stockholm. Perhaps, being a diplomat, he could come into the Arlanda transit lounge, where I had nine to ten hours' waiting.

My flight to Oslo was scheduled for late afternoon. No, he was manning the embassy for the day, and he couldn't assist me. I offered to pay for the services of a courier, adding that the SAS ground staff could page me. 'There's no way round it,' he said, 'you have to sign for it. Why not try your luck with the Swedes?'

I presented myself to 'passport control' and explained that I needed 'a special leave' to enter Stockholm. I was taken into a cubicle, where a more senior officer put embarrassing questions to me. In my attempt to elaborate, I discovered that the more I tried to absolve myself from ill-motivated suspicions, the less credible I sounded. In the end I was left with no choice but to plead. Whereupon the officer pressed buttons on his intercom, and we were joined by a plain-clothes officer, who lapsed into Swedish with my interrogator. The man in plain clothes said, 'We'll issue you with the application for refugee status, which is what you are asking for. Here, fill in these forms and please do not waste our time.'

As I declined to take the forms, two thoughts entered my mind all at once. The first touched on 'mistrust', something to do with Albert Schweitzer, who advised his fellow whites never to 'believe' what blacks tell them; the second made me wonder if the word 'Africans' had of late become interchangeable with 'refugees'.

Cutting my losses, I said no to the offer. I declined to be turned into a refugee when that wasn't what I wanted. Some hours later, I left for Oslo without my new passport.

Eleven years later, in the summer of 1991, I broke my journey in London, where I meant to spend a fortnight before doing a term's teaching at an Ivy League university in the States. The phone rang one morning, and the Swede at the other end, Gabi Gleichman, the President of PEN International, offered me a 'fellowship' worth a lot of money for literary exiles. I hadn't heard of the award, so before accepting it I asked about the conditions attached, what functions I would have to perform in Sweden. 'No commitments,' he said. 'Come, and pursue the vocation of a novelist.' We talked some more and agreed on a possible date when I could receive the prize in Stockholm. I would be giving a memorial lecture at Oxford on refugees in November, I told him. Perhaps I could combine the two, then return to the USA, where I would be teaching at Brown University? A fortnight later I received a letter, agreeing to my date, and stating when they expected me to be in Sweden to receive the award. We then worked out when I would return to Sweden for a longer stay, preferably in the summer of 1992.

At the Swedish Consulate in New York, I filled in the visa application form.

I stated clearly in the space allotted in the form that I required no more than two days in Stockholm, and gave the reason. I drew a blank: the man was looking at me, but not seeing me; he was listening to me, but not hearing me. I proffered the letter from my hosts, a letter which gave the same dates, the same reasons and the name of a hotel. The gentleman behind the glass cage produced an identical copy of PEN's missive. But there was a problem. It would take a month, if not more, for me, a Somali, to be issued with a two-day visitor's visa to Stockholm. I lost my calm; in fact, anyone could have heard the thunder of anger gathering in my chest. I got to a telephone booth and rang Sweden. The President of PEN rang me that evening with the news that someone high up in the Ministry of Foreign Affairs had intervened. Could I return to the consulate the following morning and have a 'three-day' visa stamped in my passport?

I wanted to say I didn't want to go to Sweden any more and to hell with the lot of you. At times I wish I had done just that. But then it would have been foolish not to go. After all, Sweden was not the property of the gentleman behind the glass cage or of a coterie of immigration officials and right-wing politicians who could do with the country what they pleased.

My third attempt to enter Sweden proved to be pleasantly rewarding. I was residing in Addis Ababa at the time, and my wife and I made a courtesy call on the Swedish Ambassador to Ethiopia, who was a friend of a friend. It took no longer than five minutes to have the three-month visa endorsed in my passport, while the Ambassador talked to us. And it came to pass that, although we arrived while Sweden's most notorious killer of Blacks (nicknamed Laserman, in reference to the gun he used) was active, my wife and I spent the most pleasant summer in Stockholm.

The Laserman was the uninvited guest of our conversations. He was the talk of Stockholm, a topic at the parties held in celebration of a summer's night, a subject raised whenever there was a row between a person with radical leanings and another from the Conservatives.

Murder imposes a different logic on people's lives in ways hard to fathom. Raymond Chandler suggested that when you can't make a story pick up an elegant pace, it is time to bring in a man with a gun. He is bound to help the tale move along handsomely. But you had better know the gunman's motives; you had better probe into the killer's psychosis; in short, you had better discover what compelled the man to commit murder.

To tell the story of the African refugees in Sweden, I bring on three men, one wielding a .357 Magnum, a second brandishing a laser gun, a third a knife.

The three death-toting men will serve as prima facie proof of how much the violence they engaged in altered Sweden. Not that Swedish society was ever as peaceful and as humane as I had been led to believe. My mind was changed for me by the powerful writing of Vilhelm Moberg, whose novels of Swedish emigration far outstrip any other work in the field, novels which attack class-based tyranny and oppression, and which articulate the voice of the illiterate classes, while condemning the horrible system which made country people's lives imponderable.

Just about the time of Vilhelm Moberg's birth, in 1920, Sweden underwent a political awakening that was to change the course of its history, and influence its place in the entire world. The gradual changes, which were radical in scope, would not mature into a 'social democratic' political platform until a decade later. It was then that the ideological differences between the Liberal and the Conservative parties were defined. A series of forward-looking bills were passed, resulting in the notion of *folkhemmet*, in which society was seen as the common 'home' for every citizen, with people's needs attended to in cases of unemployment, old age or other forms of indisposition.

All this was put into question on 28 February 1986 when the Prime Minister, Olof Palme, was assassinated. This threw the nation into a crisis, an act of catharsis it had not known for close to two centuries, leaving everyone astounded, shocked. The horror of Palme's violent death so profoundly disturbed the people of Sweden that they did not recognize themselves as Swedes any more. Less than two and a half decades earlier, jurors convened twice a month to hear minor cases of 'loitering' or 'public nuisance'. Peaceful Sweden: a land boasting a long history of explosives manufacture! Question: can the makers of lethal weapons live forever in peace, cocooned from death?

The man who assassinated Olof Palme did so at about 11.15 in the evening on Sveavegan, one of Stockholm's main thoroughfares. With his Magnum, he murdered the very statesman who, according to University of Umea social scientist Gunnel Gustafsson, 'gave [Swedes] peace in the world, a conscience about poverty and confidence in the social democratic way', indubitably Sweden's most respected politician. The killer then vanished into the darkness of a tunnel, leaving behind no trace, only 15,000 leads followed by a legion of police officers, whose work has so far not borne fruit.

The second man to arrive, and to alter our view about Sweden and subsequently the perspective of our tale, is a man with a laser gun. A Swede and not-a-Swede, depending on your vantage point, he killed a dozen or so blacks, and managed to evade capture for almost two years. When at last he was apprehended, and he talked about his murderous motives, Swedish society distanced itself from him: he wasn't, after all, a 'pure' Swede. As if this would have mattered! In their distance-taking, the Swedes pointed to his alien blood, most likely German, and that he had had connections with the racist regime in apartheid South Africa.

The third to appear before us were drunken Swedes, chasing a seventeen-year-old youth. Fleeing his molesters, he ran into a supermarket, and was cornered in the butcher's section. He took hold of a knife, because it was there, and in self-defence killed one of his pursuers, wounding a second. The youth was a Somali, who had fled the abattoir of a nation engaged in self-savagery. Might one assume that the presence of black refugees in Sweden drew out an inherent violence in Swedish society, whose raw nerves of late have lain exposed to the economic and political changes taking place within it, long before Olof Palme was assassinated?

We do not know the motive of Palme's assassin, even though, because of who he was, one assumes that he was murdered for a political reason. The Laserman committed racial murders, of the kind that made three drunken men trap a refugee youth in a supermarket. What do all these amount to? Do these negative reactions mark a Swedish turn against Palme's commitment to liberalism: Palme, who campaigned to offer asylum to young Americans, but who did not go far enough, in so far as he did not acknowledge them as 'refugees', arguing that they could not qualify for the status, coming as they did from a democracy?

A controversial man, Palme was 'more or less a foreigner in his own land,' said Arne Ruth, a Swedish friend, 'because he had opinions that were alien to Swedish society.' My friend wondered if Palme had become, in the eyes of many, a traitor, the classical *other*. The investigation into his death has been so bungled, one wonders if every Swede is being made partly culpable and is being subjected to a thorough self-questioning. It is as if Palme was murdered not by a homicidal lunatic, but by *all* Swedes, all having a hand in his death.

The murder has not been solved. Palme's assassin may actually have been a non-Swede, so that a spotlight of suspicion is made to fall on *the other*, foreigners the fulcrum turning the lever of Swedish politics. No wonder Stockholm was founded on the site of a fortress, the Old Town Gamla Stan serving as a lock, and standing guard against unwelcome visitors. It fell to Olof Palme to take Sweden to great heights internationally; and, following his death, it fell to him to help them perform an act of catharsis.

Dodging gunmen: that brought the Somalis to Sweden. They fled from bullets. It wasn't because they chose to leave their homes, or to land on the shores of Sweden's mercy, not knowing a lot about the country.

It was especially telling to listen to the dramatic story of an elderly Somali in Malmö, who had come as the head of a family of refugees. They took buses and trains, they travelled through the Middle East, they found big enough cracks in the Berlin Wall to squeeze through into West Germany, and from there to Sweden, where they waited for two and a half years before being granted the right to stay as 'humanitarian refugees'.

On their arrival in Malmö, Hassan Ali Awaleh and his travel-weary contingent were received with warmth, then interviewed, housed, fed, clothed and made to wait. 'Such an endless waiting — that was the bad part,' he stressed. And for a man accustomed to managing his and other people's lives well, it was humiliating for him to live on the votive offerings of Swedes. 'But there you are,' he said, 'it is all very, very embarrassing and difficult to contemplate. Because it is hostile to one's honour, destroys one's soul. But there you are. I would rather they had told me to go back!'

Sighing, half-chuckling, he remembered how he was sitting on his balcony, where he had the habit of spending the afternoon hours listening to the news about Somalia, 'and then bang, bang, bang!' He was being shot at by a youth on a Vespa. What did he do? He sat stunned, staring with incredulous understatement. 'The futility of it all,' he said.

Born in 1936, Hassan Ali Awaleh was a businessman, a much respected pillar of his community. 'Here, in Sweden? I am a shooting target, youths on a Vespa taking a pot at me. My world has come to that,' he said, shaking his head in disapproval. Now it didn't make sense for him to flee the bullets of Mogadiscio, and then to fall victim to a stray one in Malmö. With a touch of self-derision he remembered the savage fighting in Mogadiscio before he fled, and burst into a bitter laughter, saying, 'My future is no bigger than the hole the bullet made in the upholstery of my chair. The bullet, however, has left a huge crack in my faith in Sweden. To console myself, I tell myself that maybe only a few Swedes don't want us here, what do you think?'

Did you call the police?

'The police never returned my call,' he said, 'and nothing was done.' The way he described it, he had so much on his mind at the time that the incident did not really affect him as much as it might have if he hadn't been concerned with his situation, not knowing whether he would be allowed to stay or not, and what the following day might bring.

'Was this the only violent incident you experienced?'

'No,' he said. 'When I was in Mariehome, our camp was burnt down. Some arsonists came and poured petrol around and set fire to our camp. The fire brigade was called in and it took hours to put out the fire. This happened more than once, setting us ablaze.'

And the police?

'They tightened the security. But this did not deter graffiti artists from adorning our walls with scrawled remarks of the all-blacks-go-home genre. These worries are making me feel significantly older than my years. Maybe the strain has been too much to bear.'

He was silent for a long time. 'A krone for your thoughts?'

'It all makes you feel rather unwelcome, doesn't it?' he said.

After a pause, I asked, 'Any regrets?'

'I should think it's rather too late in the day to regret.'

Sweden is a long country and the distance between it and Africa is immense. Questioned as to why the African refugees came to Sweden in the first place, some responded that they had come as students, or with their Swedish partners, yet several of the recent arrivals turned up with a vague knowledge about the country which hosted them. There is so much raw energy of life in their stories, whether they belong to the category of new arrivals, or whether they have been there for years and have Swedish citizenship and benefits. Some would rightly insist that they did not come from 'non-places', and were not 'non-persons': that in their native lands, they held high positions. Some had had dealings with their academic peers in Sweden.

Dr Mohamoud Ali Hashi came to Stockholm to attend a conference organized by the Swedish International Development Agency, SIDA for short. I asked him why he chose Sweden. He replied, 'A refugee on the run has neither contingency plans, nor the luxury of making choices. I landed on these shores not because this was where I wanted to be, but because there was no other country that would have me.'

'But you did not come directly from Mogadiscio?' I asked.

No, he had come from Yemen, which hadn't granted him political asylum. And between Yemen and coming to Sweden, he had applied for asylum status in the Arab Emirates, their response being negative. Dr Hashi had been a lecturer in history and headed the International Relations Department at the National University of Somalia.

Another Somali, Mr Mohammed Colow, a former Somali diplomat currently living in Gotland as a refugee, said that 'even if Sweden was not a "model country", the world would be a very different place if the Swedes did not exist. I suppose you would have had to invent them. But then we are lucky, aren't we, for the Swedes have invented themselves, as social democrats. That's why I came.'

I sought the opinion of an Afro-Swede, a Malawi-born academic, who had come as a student, and was one of the first Africans ever to hold a university appointment here. I told him what the two newly arrived Somali refugees Mohamoud Ali Hasah and Mohamed Colow had said, and this was how he reacted: 'If Sweden was the best country invented by man, how come then that the public and private ideals do not cohere any longer? Swedes often believe in ideal versions of themselves, and these do not. always match their contradictory realities!'

Almost to a person, and as to be expected, the Africans who arrived in Sweden between the 1950s and the early 1970s gave a different picture from the Somalis who turned up in the late 1980s and early 1990s: they were 'pointed in the direction of Sweden', said one of their number, 'a country ahead of its time, humane'. Where the first lot concurred that they were treated as welcome guests, the recently arrived ones lamented that they were marked for disdain.

Tesfai Berhae, an Eritrean, came as a refugee in 1975. It was early days for African migration to Sweden, and after spending the first night in a police station, because he had no visa, he was taken to a hostel for three weeks before being allowed to remain. Eighteen months later, he was given Swedish papers. 'In those days, there were twenty of us in Uppsala,' he said, 'mostly Gambians married to Swedish women, perhaps two Malawians, a Ugandan and a sprinkling of students, that was all.'

I garnered from the way Somalis approached the subject of refugees that for them the key notions 'guests' and 'hosts' were of importance, notions that I did not deem either adequate, or even appropriate, when one reflected on the relationship between the Swedes and the Somalis. Because the Somalis and the Swedes did not meet in the proverbial set-up of guests and hosts. And there is something else: pity is a major ingredient of the relationship between them, with empathy replaced by resentment *after* Sweden's well of charity ran dry. The refugee were comparable to a goldfish in a fish tank with no water in it. A more appropriate image, considering that, being of a different complexion, culture and religion, the Somalis stand out, is of an elephant with a toe in a pond that has no more water.

Sigrid Segerstedt-Wiberg, a most formidable Swede in her eighties, in reference to the notion of African guests and Swedish hosts, said, 'It's very difficult for a foreigner to be accepted in Swedish society. We don't invite people into our homes. If I had behaved as a proper Swede,' she went on, 'I would not have invited you to my home, but to an office or a restaurant.'

I remarked that people whose past has become a puzzle, as in the case of the Somalis, make one feel ill at ease. Was this what was happening to the Swedes, they were ill at ease, because they didn't know what to do?

She replied, 'Sweden had not known people coming from faraway places.

Years ago, if you saw a black person, you stopped and looked again — have I really seen him or am I drunk? I remember fifties London, when you first encountered Africans there, I thought they were so beautiful. I would close my eyes for fear of staring at them so!'

She was fearless in her determination to speak her mind, and one could not help remembering how often fascists threatened her with death for her humane views. It was perhaps in an unstated reference to the violence which claimed Olof Palme's life, and because of listening to tape-recordings of death messages from fascists, that I asked, 'Are you not worried?' She remarked, 'Sweden is a calm country; it's not so dangerous. And please don't think I am a hero, I am not!' I still recall the message so clearly recorded on her answering machine, static and all.

She had worked with refugees since her student days, and recalled the 'cruel 1940s war, during which the Jews were treated unkindly. There was not much bureaucracy in those days, no files being pushed from one department to another, you didn't have two years to get accepted as a refugee. Either you were given or not given leave to remain. Even the refugees from the concentration camps would sometimes have their applications turned down, and some would threaten suicide. Some, however, were luckier, and were reunited with their families.'

'Why this three-year wait,' I said, 'this long tailback, of refugees waiting for their asylum cases to be heard and then decided, approved or disapproved?'

She said, 'It is always governments that are afraid to tell the truth, which they hide by recruiting far too many bureaucrats, to make everyone's life impossible. But I assure you, ordinary people have a better understanding. Often they welcome refugees into their lives, at times they give them jobs, even if the authorities won't issue the refugees with the proper documents, or the local council with the proper authority.'

Thandika Mkandawire, however, was of the opinion that 'Because it was politically and morally correct, the welfare state has often assumed that the Swedish public would follow its policy of adopting a humanitarian stance. It is as if they failed to comprehend that the complex, multilayered design of the welfare regime had been premised on a stable homogeneous Swedish nation, not one in the midst of a social and economic crisis, with a laserman ensconced in its midst. Naturally, the foreigners arriving later, and in large numbers, were ill-treated, because the migrants before them had not been absorbed into Swedish society.'

Mkawandire assumed that, by the late 1970s, 'the Swedes had already developed an embryonic distaste for their relationship with Africa, a distaste which caused them to distance themselves from their former, innocent selves.'

To illustrate, Mkandawire depicted African–Swedish relations as having undergone profound changes when leisure pursuits took Swedes of all ages and classes to The Gambia, where they sampled the pleasures of the tropics, where they basked on sun-baked beaches, frolicking with local fishing communities. 'The impact of the encounter between the Gambians and the Swedes on each other's soil, and the way each subsequently treated the other in their respective countries, deserves a fat sociological treatise of the cultural conflict kind.'

On coming away from Africa, many Swedes, who had enjoyed their holiday romances with the sun, casually issued invitations to their Gambian hosts, invitations which produced 'misunderstandings' when they were accepted. 'There's the story of a Gambian beach boy, one-time lover of a Swede, arriving at Arlanda and taking a taxi to a small Swedish town and knocking at the door of the woman, with several thousand kroner taxi fare to pay. Another tells of a Swedish family driving their Gambian "guest" to the centre of Stockholm and making a getaway, abandoning him there, helpless and moneyless too.'

As Mkandawire put it, 'From then on, no one was innocent. The Swedes were not; nor were the Africans, who soon became stigmatized *en masse*, increasingly excluded from clubs and pubs, and treated with suspicion and distrust. It wasn't long before the authorities began to police the African "ghetto". And you heard of deportations of Gambians overstaying their welcome in Sweden.'

Thandika Mkandawire went on, explaining that in the 1960s and 1970s in Sweden there was little experience of racism in the form of direct insults, although when it came to jobs in the academies, only Swedes would be employed on a full-time basis, not Africans. He concluded by saying, 'I am not sure if I would describe this as "racist", perhaps "exclusivist" or maybe a peculiar kind of Swedish nepotism. Because I doubt they would ever hire a Greek as a professor of Greek here either.'

There was positive racism, too, in that a girl would like an African *because* he was black, the assumption being that blacks were always adorable. Because there was no differentiation, all blacks were nice, adorable. In the 1960s, there was no hostility towards blacks as such.

For her part, Sigrid Segerstedt-Wiberg spoke of how it was suggested to a government committee in the 1970s that refugees be given preference over guestworkers. 'The argument was, we could not hope to solve all the problems of the poor countries, but we could at least deal humanely with the refugees, to whom Sweden could give a place of refuge and work. This, however, was not adhered to, because more non-refugee migrant labourers were employed.'

Then Swedish lawyers were detailed to work out the clauses, the *quid pro quos*, the commas and semicolons of the laws governing immigration and asylum-seekers. The lawyers had their brief from the government, but the sentiment which went into creating the system must have been the will of the Swedish people. The legal document drawn up by the arbiters of Sweden's civic society has remained humane in spirit and in the letter of the law too. She added with a smirk, 'But then the terms "guest" and "host" are moral, not legal, terms, yes?'

Chapter Seventeen

In Sweden, the Somalis are the largest single community of Africans. To beguile the boredom of a day in Stockholm I went to the Central Station, one late afternoon, to engage my inactive mind and watch them from close quarters. I had an appointment with one of their number, a man with an alias, Mohamed Ali Mohamoud.

Somalis have the habit of appointing a 'watering-hole' around which they congregate, where they stand in groups of all ages, many of them well dressed, and boasting the aspects of a recently fed youth. You rarely find women among these groups of men. Maybe this atavistic idea has its origins in the psyche of the Somali nomads, who took their cattle to a well, where, after months of being cut off from everyone else, the camel herdsman met others of his kind, with whom he exchanged news. This way, the nomads learnt where the grass was aplenty, or were given news about clan warfare. They might even pick up a newly composed poem, or might be told that the woman they had intended to take as a wife had married.

Baffled by the behaviour of the Somalis milling about in the Central Station, the Swedes thought it downright insensitive, maybe thinking, 'Why don't these refugees straighten out their lives?' Some saw it as a mark of ingratitude that the Somalis would be standing around in the middle of the afternoon, doing 'nothing', while subsisting on social welfare benefits, levied on the sweat of Swedes working.

Mohamed Ali Mohamoud, once I made his acquaintance, pointed out to me that not all Somalis were preternaturally prone to coming to the station, Stockholm's notorious haunt of vice and underworld activities. But he agreed that the practice had proven to be quite a sore in the eyes of the Swedish authorities, whose total contempt resulted in the police raiding the station every now and then. But what could they do? He was of the view that perhaps the sight of a number of Somalis loitering in the station, neither engaged in a fruitful vocation nor participating in the activities of the world of pimps and prostitutes, warranted an attack on the Somali community centre situated nearby. Some time later in the year, while those injured in that attack were in the hospital recovering, another Somali, this time a seventeen-year-old, became the victim of yet another attack.

In his opinion, the Somalis and the Swedes occupy the extreme ends of a generalization: the one rule-abiding, hard-working, less gregarious; the other seldom working, often surviving on the votive offerings of a working Swede. I asked him why they rendezvous in the station grounds.

'Not because they love to loiter,' he said, 'but because they live in very cramped rooms, ill-lit places in subhuman conditions. Add to this the fact that they are chased out of the cafes because they haven't the money to pay for coffee or tea: and that, when they meet, they share news about Somalia, their love and hate.'

But how come you see them at all hours?

'Many of the youths you see loitering in the station', he replied, 'have never done an honest day's work, because in Somalia the extended family indulged them with limitless pampering. Here in Sweden they are mendicants at the secular temples of the welfare state. We Somalis have a penchant for attracting negative publicity, and act as though we were a nobility in exile. Mark you, many wish to earn their livelihood, but they have no personal numbers.' He paused to explain that, in Sweden, to prove that you exist you must have your own personal number.

And after yet another pause, 'Somalis are as clumsy as a hippo emerging out of the waters of all time, who, arriving on Swedish soil, looks this and that way, suspicious, untrusting, fearful, and before anyone knows it, they are ready to leave for the shores of the USA or Canada. With suitcases forever packed, they return to Somalia at the whim of a mood. Tell the Swedes that we do not stay anywhere forever.'

But what was it that agitated them so today? It took Mohamed Ali Mohamoud and me a good two and a half hours to piece together the result of my eavesdropping. There were two incidents about which the loiterers were now agitated: one had to do with a sex scandal involving a Somali and a Swede, another had in it the sort of intrigue and underhand politics that you might find among émigrés anywhere.

Elaborated, the first story was about a Somali man caught in the act of giving a blow-job to a Swede in one of the lavatories of the station. Those sharing the cramped space with him were said to have sworn that they would ask the authorities to transfer him somewhere else.

Mohamed Ali Mohamoud gone, I sat for almost an hour and gathered from the vantage point of an eavesdropper that the group of older Somali men were discussing the matter of the Swedish documents of a fifteen-year-old Somali, who had sneaked into Canada on someone else's travel permit. I didn't wait to find out if they meant to find a youth to make use of the documents.

As I left to take the Metro, I remembered the apt remarks attributed to Gertrude Stein: that 'to be a genius, you had to sit around, doing nothing'. But then I doubted if the Somalis at the station were geniuses, or if they were doing nothing. Rather, they were busy, taming their sense of alienation, entombing their despair and engaging in occasional fits of inward-looking activities.

I asked, how did they get to be where they were, in cramped living conditions, joblessly loitering at the station? How long did it take them to get where they were, with humanitarian asylum papers, a monthly stipend and a place to live? I remembered Mohamed Ali Mohamoud saying, 'Camps!', as if the word was, in and of itself, a key to all the mysteries surrounding the Somali refugees' presence in Sweden.

I repeated after him, 'Camps!'

He nodded his head. 'That's right. Camps.'

Every single one of those who had been through the camps remembered the harsh existence and, with great understatement, referred to the year spent at them as 'a difficult one', where inhumane conditions were almost impossible to take. The camps are often tucked away in the middle of nowhere, claustrophobic, far from urban centres, with a community made up of people from different countries, classes, creeds and backgrounds, a community of disparate individuals thrown together for convenience' sake. The inmates were obliged to live six to a two-bedroom apartment, with no communal space in which to relax, read or watch television.

To outwit their ennui, the residents entertained themselves. And there was the added frustration of being without one's sexual partner in the camps. Such were the insurmountable obstacles, one had to arrange with one's flat-mates when one had a date. Out of courtesy, the flat-mates made themselves scarce while one *did* it. 'We used to say that it was better to be in a Swedish prison than an inmate of a refugee camp,' said Shadrack Gutto, a Kenyan human rights activist, now a refugee in Sweden. 'Because if you were in a Swedish prison, you had a room to yourself, and had spousal rights, and some privacy. Not so at any of the refugee camps.'

The accommodation was arranged on ethnic lines, on the premise that if you put Africans together, they would get on well. At times one was in the same cramped space as others from a rival movement from back home. The refugees lacked the luxury of privacy, without which they couldn't mentally engage in matters of importance.

Dr Mohamoud Abdi Hashi, a Somali living in Uppsala, was taken to a boat docked in central Stockholm when he first declared himself a refugee. He and other refugees were crammed four into each dark and damp sleeping cabin. He remembered the food as heinous, the noise levels quite unbearable, fire alarms sounding regularly, and the inmates forced to line up in the freezing cold while the Swedish security personnel checked the boat for fires. After two months in this subhuman condition, he was interviewed once again, and sent to a camp at Louvestbruck, where he spent a further two months. There he was fed three times a day at a cafeteria, and given a fortnightly stipend of 400 Swedish kroner. He was moved again, this time to Osterbybruck camp, where the conditions proved to be equally terrible. Once again he had to learn to live with noisy, smoking, heavy-drinking youths.

He remembered how no complaints produced any results. 'You might have been speaking to the escritoire separating you from the chair of authority in which the chief of the camp slouched,' he said. 'It was not possible in those conditions to think, let alone do research. Our situation was horrendous.'

'Who manned the camps?' I asked him.

The camps were staffed by an all-Swedish cadre not trained to deal with the diversity and range of the residents, who were subjected to an infantilizing regime. The wardens operated in accordance with the lowest common denominator by following the rigorous simplicity of prison officers, albeit with the most benevolent of intentions. 'The wardens confused language problems with lack of intelligence,' explained Gutto, the Kenyan, 'and the loss of worldly possessions with poverty.' When questioned about treating refugees far more educated than they as if they, the refugees, were imbecilic inmates of a home for the mentally retarded, the staff either quoted the chapter and verse of regulations laid down in Swedish law or chose to fall back on a pseudo-democratic rationale, arguing that they had to treat all refugees equally. Now and then, some of the residents were so highly incensed that violence broke out.

At one point things grew so tense that Gutto approached the camp authorities, and offered to facilitate exchanges between the staff and the 'inmates'. His idea was to sensitize the inmates and the minders to the nuances of the complex sociology of the camp, in the hope that a meeting might help them to handle these matters less clumsily. One meeting took place at which something of a therapeutic process began, but there was no follow-up. Shortly afterwards, a Somali resident assaulted the director of the camp.

The inmates of the camps were expected to learn to speak Swedish. Unfortunately, though, it was very difficult for them to put their mind to acquiring the tongue, because not only were they uncertain if or when their application might be approved, but the instructors had no training in teaching the language to foreigners. Such were the ugly conditions in the camp, the nights were as noisy as the days, and you didn't sleep regularly. The reckless youths stayed up playing loud music until the small hours. And so how could you study?

Dr Hashi argued that, apart from the inhumane conditions of the camps, the reason why he couldn't learn Swedish was that he was 'rather too tired to learn yet another tongue at my age. After all, I am already fluent and literate in Somali, Arabic, Russian, Italian as well as English.' He didn't think, at any rate, that mastering Swedish would improve his chance of recruitment as an academic.

Coping with the camp conditions was nerve-racking. Dr Mohamoud Abdi Hashi felt that he had to cope with the resultant stress at the camp. For this reason he marshalled all he had in the way of self-discipline. He exercised regularly, and when the warden finally gave him permission, purchased a bus pass and took himself off to the Uppsala University library.

As the slow cogs of Swedish asylum-related bureaucracy turned and as he waited, he reflected that though he had evaded detention in Africa, he found himself in a different kind of confinement, a Swedish one this time. This feeling of moving from one 'prison' to another, with only the frontiers of his incarceration changing, was to persist beyond his many months in the camp. The feeling would pervade his life as a political refugee in the wider Swedish society.

Dr Mohamoud Abdi Hashi was at long last granted leave to remain in Sweden in November 1991, and was finally in the privileged position of bringing his Russian wife and daughters out of the Soviet Union, where the flames of ethnic nationalism had erupted into fires of auto-destruction.

He knew how lucky he was, given that only a small percentage of the refugees are given Swedish leave to stay, after being there for several years, waiting in humiliating conditions in camps, and in suspense. Many Somalis have had their own passports stamped with a Swedish *permit de séjour*, valid for a limited number of years. 'Many are waiting for the day when they can go home,' he said.

Doomed to wander in the universe of their imagination, several of the asylum-seekers explained that to attenuate the immensity of their despair, they travel out of their bodies into other worlds, out of which they construct a country of hope. They sounded uniformly grateful, their nights full of naive optimism, their days of self-confidence, when they first got there, avowedly humbled by the avuncular patronage with a 'humane face'. In other words, the first flush of Swedish generosity alleviated a great deal of their suffering, but that wasn't enough.

But the memory of life at the camps, together with those long years of waiting, kept haunting them. The lives of the asylum-seekers are organized around faith and hope: faith in the host country, hope in a future at best shaky, at worst abysmal, dismal. One of the Somali women refugees quoted Saint Teresa, who said that 'she prayed better when she was comfortable'.

I asked Sigrid Segerstedt-Wiberg what she thought about the camps, and she replied, 'Because of a general lack of experience on the part of the Swedes who do not know how to deal with foreigners, there are problems.'

'What kind of problems?'

'Things became complicated,' she responded. 'There was the time when there were no camps, and little bureaucracy. The refugee came and he or she was put up in decent accommodation, and then given papers. But not now, there are so many of them. The camps were set up and bureaucracy became self-serving. Moreover, and this is very important, the Swedes living in the vicinity of the camps are not prepared for the arrival of the foreigners. Imagine waking up one morning in your small land and finding so many of them. It's entirely the fault of the immigration authorities.'

'And what in your opinion must be done?' I asked.

'They must prepare the Swedish hosts for them to receive the foreign guests, there is no way around it. Remember, even I, a Swede, was not accepted by my fellow villagers where I have my country cottage, not right away. I understand why it is more difficult for foreigners.'

Sucdi Ali Yusuf arrived before the camps were set up.

She is in her mid-thirties, an energetic and extrovert Somali woman, the mother of two. She left Somalia in 1975, when she was nineteen, and came to Europe to pursue her career and studies, at a time when women of her age had few options because of the upheavals at home. Sucdi had been tragically widowed when her husband died a few years before, leaving her to run a business in Dubai and support a string of economic dependants. Her cheerful demeanour belied the fact that she had been obliged to send her young ones away to live in Canada with her mother and sister, when it became too hard for the old woman to look after the children in an apartment in the Stockholm suburb of Tensta. She withstood the loss of her young husband with admirable stoicism.

Sucdi recalled that long-past journey to Sweden. She had her sights on the USA. Like many other young Somali women, she wanted to go abroad to study. Her family opposed her going. Among other things, her father had two wives and ten children, his being a household that needed all hands on deck.

She spoke of a happy childhood, of walking in the beautiful boulevards, ice cream in Italian cafes and, wonder of wonders, cinema houses! But later, when she grew older and decided that women were as intelligent as, if not more intelligent than, men, her mother questioned her wisdom. It used to irk her no end to be 'escorted' wherever she went by junior brothers as young as five. It was a world in which women were minors all their lives, and boys were glorified as men from a young age. She was determined to be done with that world, to go as far from it as possible.

She left Nairobi for Italy. When she failed to obtain a US visa in Rome, she came on a visit to see a cousin in Sweden, and then reapplied. When, after her ninety-day tourist visa ended and she still had no American one, in her desperation she applied for asylum. Nine months later, she was given her papers. She got herself a job as a nursing assistant in the local hospital, and began to study Swedish, realizing that she was destined not to get to the USA.

Once established, Sucdi helped her mother and all four of her full siblings to come to Sweden. This was in 1978. A year later, Sucdi finally achieved her ambition: she went to the University of Uppsala to read maths and physics, but ended up taking a course with a more definite application, a degree in business economics.

'Where did you meet your husband?'

She met and married her husband in Sweden in 1981. He had no wish to be in Sweden, he found it unbearably cold and isolating, Somalia being where he wanted to be. He stayed in a halfway house in the Arab countries, since he couldn't return to Mogadiscio for political reasons. They established themselves in Dubai, and lived there until the illness of her first child led Sucdi to return to Sweden, alone and pregnant with her second child. She recalled 1986 as a bad year, for no sooner had she arrived in Sweden than her husband was hospitalized with a heart condition, diagnosed as terminal. She persuaded him to come to Sweden, where he spent three months in various hospitals until his death. She buried him in Skogas.

She lives in Dubai and comes to Sweden periodically.

She expressed heartfelt concern for the thousands of Somalis arriving in Sweden. Her face saddened as she explained how different their situation is from that of Somalis of her generation.

She spoke of a woman who made it to Sweden, but had to leave her two young sisters in Ethiopia, where they were now destitute. 'When we came in the mid-seventies,' Suedi remarked, 'our families were safe, in a family home, and the problems were not as global as they are now, because of the civil war. The emotional toll of fleeing into exile affects the sexes in different ways. The men meet on the streets and at the central station. The women, because they do not take to the streets, an option not to their liking, find themselves alone, often with more children than they can cope with single-handedly, yet deprived of any support, and struggling to find ways of feeding them on extremely limited budgets.'

'So what happens?'

'Marital breakdowns', she said, 'result from the stress of the women's entrapment. Few of the women are educated enough to find any jobs other than menial employment, and those of either sex who are trained do not obtain jobs compatible with the qualifications. A great many women are sinking into intractable depression and psychological confusion.'

Determined not to be defeated, a small nucleus of women set up self-help projects, to enable those with more experience of Sweden to help the confused and shell-shocked new arrivals. 'It's very, very difficult,' she said.

'Difficult for both men and women?'

'Being more practical by nature,' she said, 'women are having some economic success.' She paused, and then, 'It is impossible to understand what the men want, they seem confused. When you suggest that they should study something useful to help rebuild Somalia, they are not interested. It is as if they do not see any future.'

'And the women?' I asked.

'The women see a future,' she replied, 'they see peace!'

Ibrahim Hassan, now living in Malmö, came in 1987. When he arrived, he had better luck than those who had to spend a year at a camp, and then wait for a long while to have their status processed.

A one-time lieutenant-colonel in the Somali army, he came to Sweden via Djibouti, Cairo and Copenhagen, and when he landed in Malmö presented himself to the authorities. He was warmly received as a guest, and it took him under two months to be given his 'humanitarian asylum' permit. A year later, in 1987, he was joined by his wife and five children – thanks to a kindly intervention on the part of the Swedish government, which sought the assistance of the Red Cross in matters regarding first locating the family and then helping them to fly to Sweden, all expenses paid. He and his family held Swedish aliens' passports, documents that enabled them to travel within Scandinavia with no need for visas.

His oldest son was at a secondary school. His family would wait out the war. In his late forties, Ibrahim didn't expect to start a new career in Sweden, even if he learnt enough Swedish. But how did he see himself?

'I was commanding a battalion of three thousand,' he said. 'Now I am a labourer, and the Swedes, what's more, think of me as a parasite.'

What did it feel like being a labourer?

'I find working in the factory extremely difficult,' he said, 'particularly when it comes to dealing with uneducated working-class Swedes. It is only because of my children that I stay there, otherwise I wouldn't be here even for one day!'

What about his wife?

His wife was attending secondary school, something she would not have done in Somalia. Then he laughed uproariously as he considered how domestic relations had changed since they had to come to Sweden, where they have no servants, where they both come home in the evening to share the chores.

'At home a wife was a wife and a man was a man,' he said.

He admitted to enjoying spending more time with his wife, and to sharing all the little decisions about money, buying clothes, sending money home and generally managing life in exile. His wife had also changed. He said, 'We have to understand our situation and work together.'

Omar Mohamed Aden described himself as an immigrant and not a refugee. He said he had gone to England as a student, having left Hargeisa in 1970. He completed his teacher's training in England, where he met his Swedish wife, who was studying at a nearby language school.

He had never planned to settle in Sweden: England was the land that he heard many stories about, through the ancient routes taken by Somali seamen working between the East London docks and the Somali-speaking ports. Both his uncles were seamen, who came and went, each time bringing new tales of a distant land.

Once he met, fell in love with and then married his wife, the couple came to Sweden to raise their family. Omar had no difficulty in obtaining a visitor's visa, nor was it difficult for him to obtain his residency. This was in 1974, long before the days of refugees. But despite being a fully qualified teacher, with proficiency in Swedish, Omar was only able to find work on the docks. Although he didn't want to be a docker, he was resigned to the idea, preferring it to being unemployed, and wanting to save his four children from the stigma of having a jobless, black father.

Ironically, it was the disaster in Somalia that brought Omar Mohamed Aden a chance to resume his vocation as a teacher, to instruct the young Somali refugees. Asked what he taught, he replied, 'I teach them Somali, to preserve their heritage and to continue their education in their tongue.'

Did his children speak Somali?

'My four children don't,' he replied, 'because they grew up in Sweden at a time when there were few Somalis around, and no community as such.'

'So who are they, your children?'

'They are more Swedish than they are Somali,' he said, adding, 'and our daughters have not been infibulated, even though, had they been raised in Somalia, then they might have been, because of the social pressure.'

The tone of his remarks suggested a man who had integrated quite peaceably into Swedish life, and only recently been confronted with the acculturation of his own children, a confrontation provoked by the arrival of so many of his countryfolk and the sudden development of a community of Somalis in and around Malmö.

He was no refugee, all right. He was a divided man!

My wife and I, while in Gotland in August 1992, met a young Somali who first claimed to be from the Ogaden in Ethiopia, then changed his story, to say that he was from Mogadiscio. In order to support his last claim, that he was a Somali citizen, he presented a Somali passport issued in Mogadiscio, which was discovered to be a forgery. When this was brought to his notice, he stuck to the version that he was a citizen of the Republic, this time presenting a Somali passport issued in Stockholm after the collapse. The Swedish authorities attached no value to such a passport.

But he told us his story anyway. A month earlier, two Swedish immigration officials flew with him in chains to London, where they meant to board a flight bound for Ethiopia. When they presented themselves with him on tow, the clerks at the airline listened to the Swedes' version, insisting that the young man was an Ethiopian being returned home, and to the youth himself, who was arguing that he was being taken to Addis against his will, because he was a Somali. Ethiopian Airlines wouldn't have him or the two Swedes on board its flight to Addis.

Almost a year later, in July 1993, the Swedish government decided that, because he had not been able to prove that he was Somali, he was not entitled to protection as an asylum-seeker, and there were no humanitarian reasons to grant him a residence permit.

The refugees' situation is as fluid as the decisions being taken by the Swedish government regarding them. More and more of the asylum-seekers were receiving renewable residence permits, the renewability being contingent upon the area of the world the refugee came from. In other words, refugee status, which eventually led to Swedish citizenship, was no longer on offer globally.

Almost all the Somalis I spoke to implied there was an element of racism in the Swedes denying them the right to the country's citizenship. I repeated this to Ingrid Segerstedt-Wiberg on an early afternoon in Gothenburg when, attending a book fair in that city, we both volunteered to talk to the Somali refugees in that town.

Sigrid Segerstedt-Wiberg recalled that 'all the nationals from the Baltic states used to be issued with identity papers ending with the number 9, so they could be easily identified. Only after these people protested, arguing that the Russians would identify them too easily, was the system abolished. What I mean is, it is not racism. It's just we like to be sure who is a Swede and who is not.'

What would she do about the newly arrived refugees?

'Maybe the best way is to give them leave to remain until the wars in their countries are over,' she said. 'Meanwhile, we should train them in vocations that would give them a livelihood when they return home.'

Epilogue

At some time in early July 1998 I went to Abuja to get my British entry visa renewed, and on the following day to Lagos, in order to have a year-long Schengen visa stamped in my Somali passport. I embarked on these trips well aware that I had an overwhelming number of journeys, from the third week of August until the end of November. These trips would take me from Nigeria to Britain, France, Italy and back to Nigeria; and after a change of wardrobe, I would leave, together with my wife, for Canada, then for Norman, Oklahoma. We had it all planned so that my wife could return to Kaduna within ten days to be with our children, while I embarked on yet another marathon trip in the USA, a city-a-day book promotion tour. However, the situation obtaining at the time in Nigeria made me ask myself if I would be able to travel at all.

I arrived in Abuja a day earlier, on a Sunday, with the intention of presenting myself at the British High Commission first thing on the morrow. I was through by nine o'clock, ready to have lunch with friends before being taken to the airport for my flight. In Lagos, I was picked up and taken to Susan and David Peery's home in Ikoyi, where I would be staying for the night. We were discussing the evening's arrangement, my friends and I, when the phone rang. It was then that we learnt of the death, in detention, of Chief Moshood Abiola, the civilian widely believed to have won the June 1993 presidential elections in Nigeria.

Earlier that day I had reason to think about how deaths alter one's perspective on things. I was not thinking about Abiola's death, of which I hadn't known then, but about General Sani Abacha's, whose passing away coincided with a period when Nigeria 'needed a break'. Now, if death was heavy on my mind it was because someone sitting close by, as we flew from Abuja to Lagos, had pointed Chukwuemeka Ojukwu out to me. That I was flying in the same plane as the head of the breakaway state of Biafra during the Nigerian civil war was sufficient to return my mind to internecine wars. And I thought how deaths resulting from a savage exercise of communal blood-letting cost thousands their lives, with many joining the displaced, or becoming refugees. I fell into a heavy depression, my thinking focusing on my own homeland, a country currently awash with the mad blood of civil anarchy. Would Nigeria, as a result of this suspicious death of Abiola's, go the way Somalia had gone, disintegrate?

I felt otherworldly the instant I heard about Abiola's death. I retreated into myself for a few moments, concentrating my mind on what I might do in these inauspicious times, wondering to myself if my visit to Lagos would remain memorable chiefly for its bad timing. I also asked myself if it was safe to venture out of the house on a night like this, or wise to join my friends' American friend, with whom I was meant to watch the France versus Brazil football game. What was one to do on the evening when Nigeria mourned Abiola's death? I felt ambushed by the hugeness of what had occurred: the death, within a month, of Ken Saro-Wiwa's murderer, the evil dictator the likes of whom the world had seldom known; and the man with the mandate to become Nigeria's elected president.

It was my friends' view that no earth-shattering event would take place until after daybreak. It was as I showered and prepared to go out to watch a game of football that I started to think about myself in ways I did not like, convinced that, in the soberness of the morrow, I would not approve of the figure I cut. In a passing moment, I entertained a mean thought: that, by dying today, Abiola had sabotaged my purposeful journey to Lagos. I was being mean to assume that the poor man could wilfully postpone his death until after I had left the city, after my Schengen visa had been issued. As if he were telepathic, David assured me that life in Ikoyi, where these embassies were located, would remain normal, and that the embassies were very likely to open for business.

I remember my utter distress, and, waiting for the driver to return for me, I revisited a mean thought. Later it would disturb me that at that moment, when the fate of Nigeria and its hundred million people hung in the balance, I worried about my visa. I can only ascribe my momentary self-centredness to the fact that I was thinking as exiles do, their minds forever centred on their lives. I was placing myself, as an exile, at the centre of a narrative about Nigeria at the very instant when the country was on the brink of catastrophe, and along with it the life I had built there. The world was a cul-de-sac, and I, already an exile, maybe soon to become a refugee, was at the dead end.

The Lord knows Nigeria was a difficult choice. Never mind how the choice was made, or why I consented to the conditions attached to my being granted a stay permit. I would be the first to admit that it would not be enough to say that my wife is Nigerian. Nor is it good enough to explain that we moved out of Addis Ababa to set up a home in Kaduna in order to give our children the possibility of growing up in close physical and cultural proximity to their grandparents. When journalists asked why I suffered Abacha's dictatorship in silence, my tailor-made response was that I couldn't have written or said anything more incisive than what Nigerians of the calibre of Soyinka or Achebe were capable of writing or saying. However, the truth, in part, may be sought and found in the complicated nature of one's relationship with one's in-laws.

The way things were in Nigeria: I was harassed constantly by immigration officials, when leaving or re-entering the country, officials who were adept at inventing pretexts by which to extract corruption money. My passport would vanish and I would be made to wait; I was almost always the last in the queue. But then the Nigerians were treated equally badly too. On top of that, we had the Dutch and their sniffing dogs waiting for us on disembarking from the aircraft at Schipol, where African passports and the darkness of one's skin were fair game. Africans now require a transit visa into Holland even when we are on Dutch soil for no longer than half an hour, in which to disembark from KLM and continue on an onward journey to London, for which final destination we have valid visas.

Silence as self-reprimand: I put my thoughts about my predicament on hold as I got into the vehicle that would take me to the apartment where I would watch France play Brazil. The night, as I was driven, whispered secrets to me, its dark, eerie silence stirring in self-apprehension. We did not meet a single soul until we parked in the lot of the apartment block, several kilometres away, but still within Ikoyi. I thought that nights are not an ideal time for rioters to express their pent-up frustrations, since rioters, as instant deliverers of pain, delight in the idea of being seen. Mobs, for that matter, relish the idea of seeing their victims' expressions marked with the telltale signs of their misery.

There were riots several kilometres away, in the populated parts of mainland Lagos. My Schengen visa issued, I returned to the house, where my hosts assured me of a bed for as long as the siege lasted. A day later, I was able to get back to Kaduna. I brought forward my visit to France by a fortnight, and left on the first available flight to Europe. We all knew that things in Nigeria were never going to be the same again.

Luckily, I had the wisdom to anticipate a problem or two in the territories of the European Union. On the Eurostar train between Paris and London I had met no immigration officer to stamp my passport, so I knew that at the point of departure from the territories I would be asked to explain how I entered France without having my passport stamped. To this end I kept the Eurostar train ticket and saved my Paris hotel voucher, in preparation for the day when I would have to prove that I was no illegal alien travelling in the territories of the EU.

It was at the Alitalia check-in counter in Verona that I was asked, '*Come diavolo* did you manage to enter France and Italy without having your passport stamped?' I suppressed a wince, content in the knowledge that I could have shown her the train tickets, my receipts from restaurants in Paris, in Nice, letters of invitation from my publishers, another from my translator, proof that I was no illegal alien. At some point, however, I got irritated, maybe because her English was atrocious, and I spoke to her in Italian: my mistake. Thereupon she assumed that I wasn't who I was claiming to be, that I was a Somali residing in Italy and intending to travel to Britain on a forged document. She rang and an immigration officer came pronto. He saw, he examined the documents and, unmoved, he shrugged his shoulders, informing the woman and her superiors that they were making fools of themselves. His verdict: 'These are genuine papers, no forgery.' I was given permission to board my flight, but no one apologized for the inconvenience caused to me.

A week later, this time in London, the consular officers at the US Embassy were inordinately rude to me, making me wait for several days as they processed a single entry visa to enable me to collect one of America's most prestigious literature prizes, the Neustadt. Even though they had the itinerary of my book tour, I was asked, at the interview, to prove that I would leave the USA. I asked what kind of proof, and the woman said that the onus of proof was on me. She then made me wait for several more days; and when the single visa was granted, the permit, a loose sheet with my picture on it, was put inside a sealed envelope. I was advised not to break the seal under any circumstances. Carrying my visa in a sealed envelope, I felt as though I were a minor travelling away from home, a minor with his name and destination written in block letters on cardboard tied round his neck. Only no steward was kind to me, as they are to youngsters on their own with labels round their necks.

But who is to blame?

Is the self ever to blame?

If not, then who?

You see, almost everyone who has recently had anything to do with Somalis has himself become a 'blamocrat'! Somalis blame Siyad Barre or the warlords for the mess to which we have all contributed our fair share. The Ali Mahdists blame the Aideedists, who in turn blame the USA, the USA blames the starving Somalis, whom they fed, and who, according to them, picked up the gun and shot at them, the ingrates! Surely it was Aideed's men, not the starving ones, who engaged the marines in the battles in and around Mogadiscio? At any rate, when an individual blames the community, and the community blames a leader, and the leader in turn blames his followers; or when a well-meaning American blames the Somalis and not the Americans for what occurred in Mogadiscio: then it is clear that everyone is shying away from being responsible for his or her actions. Passing the buck, everyone cites circumstantial generalizations about the culpability of the other. This is a testament to our collective failure.

Being blamocrats par excellence, Somalis do not place themselves, as individuals, in the geography of the collective collapse, but outside of it. It is as if they did not inhabit the territory in which the disaster occurred, many ascribing the collapse to Siyad's dictatorship, or more recently to the warlords and their politics. The collapse in and of itself, some of them explain, was a consequence of an inherent failure of the nature of the post-colonial state, to which the idea of democracy was anathema. But the generality of them attribute the failure to the workings of a clan structure. In short, the self is not to blame.

The foreigners who have had dealings with Somalis as refugees indulge in blamocracy too. In Switzerland, Sweden, Britain, Kenya, the men and women who look after the Somalis key in to a catch-phrase, 'the clan as a malady!' That Somalis keep alluding obsessively to families is beside the point. What is true is that, at a deeper level, they are doing something else: they are avoiding referring to themselves as individuals. The generic references to their clan identities serving as mere markers, many of the self-identifiers are intent on subsuming their individual identities in the larger unit, thereby not sharing in the censure. Implicit in the idea is that the self is not to blame, but that civil society is!

When Somalis rummage through their recent history, many become dysfunctional. They are prone to sudden outbursts, susceptible to depressive moods. I recall meeting a man and a woman, who, to get out of a refugee camp, had claimed to be husband and wife. Why did they admit to being brother and sister in an outburst of high intensity when no one had prompted them to do so? Another couple confessed to having lied about their relationship. A Swiss official later confided to me that he matured in a worldly way after getting to know the Somalis a little. I asked if he was going to give them up to the authorities. 'Most certainly not,' he responded. But he tied himself into knots of self-censure, continuing, 'We think of Somalis as a liability to the idea of being Swiss. Not that I care, considering that there is no unitary Swiss any more, just as there is no unitary refugee, Somali, Sri Lankan or Bosnian.'

During my visit to Sweden in 1994, Sigrid Segerstedt-Wiberg, a formidable human rights campaigner, employed the same word, 'liability', to describe the Somali refugees in her country. I was in Gothenburg, attending the book fair, and she happened to be visiting that city too. Sigrid phoned the welfare officer charged with the task of looking after the Somalis, who rang back with the details about an informal encounter with the Somali community in Gothenburg.

We must have cut tragic figures, Sigrid and I, as we spoke to a room filled to capacity with Somalis interested not so much in what either of us had to say as they were in my interpretation of what was happening in Somalia. One of them explained that the longer he stayed in Sweden, to which country he had first come as a refugee and of which he was now a naturalized citizen, the more he realized who he was, a Somali. Another said he carried the fact of his being a Somali in the manner a cat carries a broken leg, not knowing what to do about it. I realized that we were in the presence of blamocrats!

I did the best I could to steer clear of where they were taking us. I spoke Somali so they would follow my arguments fully and then English so that Sigrid and the other Swedes in the hall could understand what I was saying. I reiterated at some point that they owed it to those who hadn't survived the strife, or those whom they had left behind, to make a commitment to Sweden too. To my admonition, one of them retorted that he was the proverbial man who has choked on water. He wondered if drinking milk might help. He continued, 'We all feel unfulfilled here in Sweden. Of course, we're more than aware that Somalia is out of the question. It is for this that we pray daily in hope that something might unlock things and soon. As it is, our Adam's apples have been stationary for so long they are sore.'

Before I could translate what the last speaker had said, Sigrid wondered aloud, 'How can I, a well-meaning Swede, facilitate your return to Somalia? What vocational training would you like to take? There is no point sitting around, doing nothing, there is no dignity. Otherwise, you will become a liability, to us and to yourselves too.' One of the Somalis up front addressed himself directly to me, requesting that I translate the remarks about the cat with the broken leg for the benefit of the Swedes present, in expectation of making them understand where the Somalis were at. By then everyone appeared eager to speak, some raising their hands, many more talking to one another without paying much attention to who had the floor. (One of them wondered what on earth made the venerable septuagenarian lady talk of their return to Somalia, which they had no intention of doing. As though in response, another retorted that they would return when they chose, not at someone else's behest!) Even though I do not recall if I translated the remarks about the cat with a broken leg, I realized that there was a gigantic miscommunication. As I prepared to make amends, Sigrid Segerstedt-Wiberg was throwing up her arms in despair, describing the Somalis as 'a liability!' For their part, the Somalis were all speaking, telling one another why they were unhappy. Before leaving the hall, however, some of them came up to me, either to have a picture taken with me, or to ask more questions. A very tall man with a prominent stoop stayed on the periphery of the circle which formed around me, and waited for a quiet moment in which he might make a statement. I regret that I did not take his name. For, apropos my own admonition, he asked if I realized that 'we were not Somalis when we were in Somalia'.

'How do you mean?' I asked.

'Because did not we tend to divide ourselves into smaller units, each of us locating our identities in one or another of the clan families? I was a member of this family, you were probably a member of another, and so on!'

'And in Sweden?'

'Here, we are refugees first, black Africans second and Somalis last.'

'Who will you become if you return to Somalia?' I asked.

'Perhaps then we'll accept a hyphenated identity, Somali-Swedish or some such thing, if only to distinguish ourselves from the other Somalis in the diaspora who've found their way to Denmark, Holland, the USA, Canada. We'll pay homage to our being Swedes, albeit of a different kind. This is why I've come up to you, to request that you kindly assure the venerable, elderly lady and the other Swedes that maybe all is not lost. Please remind her that we are refugees and therefore a people with damaged memories.'

Another circle formed, and the man left without telling me who he was.

In October 1998, in Canada: I revisited the very same scene for the benefit of a Somali-Swede, who, together with a couple of Somali-Canadians, took me to dinner after an evening spent profitably with a select hundred or so from Toronto's large Somali community. I had met Abdurazak Sheikh Hussein in Sweden years earlier, and derived pleasure from comparing notes with him about the Somali refugee presence in Britain, Canada and Sweden, countries with large Somali communities with whose condition he is familiar. A man of immense resources, he is a fine scholar engaged in the publication and dissemination of things Somali. He was in Toronto to spend a month or so with his wife and children, who were naturalized Canadians. Would he agree with the contention that the Somalis in the diaspora were no better off than the internally displaced?

He responded that a high percentage of the Somali refugees were made up of 'the Siyad generation', men, women and youths 'raised' during the period when the country had lost its sense of direction; that they grew up in an era during which Somalis behave as orphans do, unloved and uncared for. I agreed with him that for years, Siyad Barre claimed for himself the status of being a supreme father to the nation and that his failure as a father manifested itself following the Ogaden debacle, after which Somalia became wholly reliant on foreign food aid. We also agreed that many of the refugees were raised in a period associated with failure, the failure of the Somali people to unite against a humiliating dictatorship. He went on, 'You see, it is to this end that I am interested in making my publications available, believing that only after knowing their own culture will they appreciate other cultures, the Swedish, the Canadian, the Italian and so on. Hence my efforts to make them conscious of their heritage.'

Could he describe the Somalis in Britain, Canada and Sweden?

Abdurazak Sheikh Hussein replied that when they got out, the Somalis were in a state of loss, a state of lack, and that it was impossible for them to behave in opposition to their usual selves, or in aberration to their normal way of being. He believed that they needed special care, many having been unemployed for the best part of their lives, or else dependent on the extended family's fund of generosity. And because a large number of them are unaccustomed to the impersonal attitude of the bureaucrat, many felt unwanted, became dejected, and behaved as though they were unwelcome. 'I think that their attitude is the self-justification of the doomed,' he said. 'Hence a special recovery package of self-esteem, a self-regeneration that had better concentrate on those who were too young when they left the home country, whose memory was not directly affected by what took place there. We're working on that, and are optimistic that we'll get there.'

I shall end on a personal note.

I am writing the concluding chapter of a book begun years ago in Sweden, sitting in South Africa at a time when the country is run effectively by men and women who were formerly refugees or who were forcibly exiled from their home communities and into political detention centres. I am happy and sad at one and the same time: happy to be living in a country invigorated with a new hope and run by men and women with direct knowledge of what it is like to be a refugee, what it is like to be in exile. But I am sad too that the policy-makers of this country of hope have not had the time or opportunity to turn their attention to this most burning of issues in Africa, a continent which produces more refugees than healthy babies.

Years ago, whenever I was asked what country I came from and I responded, 'Somalia', most of my interlocutors would then rejoin rather dryly,

'Oh, Siyad Barre!', a linkage which irritated me no end. I used to harangue anyone who made the metonymy, anyone who mistook the part for the whole. Nowadays, with pity on their faces, my interlocutors first recite a string of the warlords' names, then talk about the Somali refugee communities in their respective countries. So that is how Somalia is seen: refugees on the run, starving babies with drones of flies gathered around their eyes, and gun-toting gangsters on a technico-battlewagon creating havoc. Somalia has become synonymous with strife.

Our country is also in a dialogue with a tomorrow that is ensconced in a yesterday. Refugees or not, most Somalis are 'other' to themselves, a people incapable of reconciling themselves to their new 'other', victims of internal strife, a people putting running feet ahead of other running feet, a people taking off into flight, because of fright. As refugees, they take revenge on their memory of where they began, blamocrats who betray their country through a series of failures without ever for once squaring the circle.

At long last, I've flown into the empty centre of the very vortex into which most Somalis have been swept. Relaxed and no longer on my usual guard, precisely because of my unbending faith in Africa, I hadn't realized when I came to Cape Town in January 1999 that I might be sucked into the masses of the contradictory 'movements' within the South African body politic. Several months after getting here, I began to wonder if I too would be swept straight into a vortex, head first!

A setback to report. The Somali Embassy in Rome, which often issues or renews our passports, is under threat: the Italian government is determined to close it down as part of a protocol-related rationalization, Italian style. The reasoning is that, the last Siyad-appointed ambassador to Rome having died, the Italians no longer recognize the presence on their soil of an accredited mission from Somalia. Meanwhile, Rome will wait until a central government, established in Mogadiscio, appoints another emissary to replace the former envoy, and God knows when this will be, given that there is no government in Somalia at present. Myself, I see the closure of the Embassy, if the Italians go ahead with the threat, as a warning notice served on those of us who travel on Somali passports. Mine has a little under a year to go, and if the Embassy is forbidden to remain functioning, then the choices open to me are pretty limited, if I am to pursue my career as a professional novelist able to travel.

But I am not a refugee. Not yet. And I doubt that I will ever become one. My feet are firmly, defiantly and solidly placed on the soil that's Africa: and I derive a sense of solace from this! Moreover, I am no 'other' to myself, as refugees are, maybe because I've grown accustomed to 'domesticating' the deep depressions of an exile by making these feed the neurosis upon which my creativity flourishes. I am aware that this is no mean feat.

Besides, it's enough of a consolation that I live in Cape Town, a city of uncommon attractiveness and sorrow, surrounded, as I am, by my loving family, so much natural beauty, so much sadness. In South Africa, there is an ocean of stories to listen to, and a mountain of ambitions to conquer. So when I feel low, I remind myself how lucky I am in living in a city with unusual prettiness and in having a loving family and very dear friends, on whom I, as an exile, have relied. I cheer up, and keep my chin up long enough until a truant smile starts to spread downwards, in the direction of the stubble of a morning's growth.

And then ...!

Index

Glossary

Alalax	young armed thug, gang member
Bililiqo	looted goods
burcad	bandit/robber
ciyaal-dambiilay	street boy, urchin
Dayday	young armed thug, gang member
despedida	send-off
domestica/o (fem. plural *domestiche*)	domestic servant/maid (in Italy)
Faqash	corrupt military officers (term used by Northern opposition groups to refer to Siyad-Barre loyalists, especially members of armed forces and officials of regime)
Ikhwaan	brotherhood, especially of Muslim fundamentalists
Jabhadda	armed faction/front
Jirri	gangs/looters (often young and armed)
kutiri-kuteen	rumour/hearsay
maraq bilaash	vegetable sauce, usually with tomatoes
Muuryaan (or *Mooryaan*)	armed gang, often of young men
OAU	Organization of African Unity
qaat	twigs of plant grown in Kenya, Ethiopia and Yemen, chewed as mild stimulant
safar-salaamo	farewell/safe journey/good-bye
shifta	bandit/robber
soggiorno	residence permit
SPM	Somali Patriotic Movement
tagsi	1. taxi; 2. slang word referring to Somali maids in Italy
tolka	clansmen
UNHCR	United Nations High Commission for Refugees
USC	United Somali Congress
waaq	an ancient word used to refer to God
wadani	Patriot Nationalist
xambaar	slang word often used for smuggling people illegally into the West